STRESSLESS
SELLING

The Sales Professional's Bill of Rights

1. I have the right to refuse a request from a customer or supervisor without feeling guilty.
2. I have the right to feel and reasonably express anger.
3. I have the right to feel and express healthy competitiveness.
4. I have the right to use my judgment on which needs are most important to me when a conflict arises between my work and personal life.
5. I have the right to have my feelings given respect and consideration by customer and company alike.
6. I have the right to make mistakes without feeling guilty.
7. I have the right to ask for counsel and concern, and to make requests of others.
8. I have the right to be treated as a capable, human adult and not to be patronized.
9. I have the right to change my mind.
10. I have the right to say "I don't know" or "I don't understand."
11. I have the right to question those in authority.
12. I have the right to open, honest relationships.
13. I have the right to courtesy and respect as a human being.
14. I have the right to choose when to assert myself and when not to.
15. I have the right not to be perfect.

STRESSLESS SELLING

Revised Edition

FRANCES MERITT STERN

AND

RON ZEMKE

amacom

AMERICAN MANAGEMENT ASSOCIATION

Library of Congress Cataloging-in-Publication Data

Stern, Frances Meritt, 1938–
    Stressless selling / Frances Meritt Stern and Ron Zemke.—Rev.
ed., 1st AMACOM ed.
    p.   cm.
Includes bibliographical references.
ISBN 0-8144-7730-5
1. Sales personnel.   2. Job stress.   I. Zemke, Ron.   II. Title.
HF5439.5.S73   1990   89-46214
658.8'5—dc20   CIP

Printing number

10 9 8 7 6 5 4 3 2 1

This book is dedicated to
Arthur E. Lashinsky,
master of the very soft sell.

CONTENTS

ONE
Sorting Out the Stress Mess: What's Fact, What's Fiction

TWO
Four Exercises to Develop Your Personal Stress Profile and Your Personal Stress-Management Prescription

THREE
Stress-Management Strategies That Work

Appendix

PREFACE TO THE REVISED EDITION

I T'S HARD TO BELIEVE it has been ten years since we wrote the first edition of *Stressless Selling*. We have worked with many sales professionals during that decade and have learned a great deal from them. Much has changed and much has not; some ideas about the nature of stress have been revised, while other theories have become solidified. In these ten years the effects of stress have been recognized as ever more important, and "stress awareness" has come into the mainstream. We can now avail ourselves of "stress-formula" vitamins to counter the effects of stress on our bodies or use anti-stress face creams to avoid the lines and wrinkles that prolonged tension brings. A day off from work is now a "stress break," and insurance companies routinely provide compensation to "burnt-out" employees. Stress is more of an issue than ever; for some it has even become an ill-conceived red badge of courage: "My job is *so* important that I'm stressed to the point of breaking!"

Despite the hype, it's gratifying to find that people's consciousness has been raised regarding the potential effects of stress, both good and bad. Helping people has become easier because of this increased awareness, making many more people open to learning stress-management strategies and also stimulating further research. The research completed in this last decade has caused us to rethink earlier conclusions about Type A behavior; to underscore and expand our understanding of the crucial interaction between stress, our minds, and our bodies in maintaining health; and to focus on personality traits and personal beliefs as factors in successfully handling stress.

The current state of the art supports this book's original premise: the mind and body are connected; they affect one another in a powerful, though not completely understood, fashion. Our concern for the B-T-A of stress—how the body copes and gives feedback, how our thoughts and feelings influence our distress "susceptibility," and how our actions result from and feed additional stress—is as on target today as it was a decade ago—indeed, more so. The M-O-S concept that helps people identify where their stress is coming from and then determine what to do about it has withstood the test of time. It has helped people drop extraneous stress "baggage" and reduce their feelings of chronic perceived helplessness and lack of control. The M-O-S method has helped many sales pros put themselves back in control of what is controllable and let go of what isn't controllable—both on and off the job.

However, in light of what has been learned in the last ten years or so, we needed to revise the book. Great strides have been made in clarifying the important links between our minds and our immune systems. From the devastation caused by immune-system diseases such as AIDS and cancer to the chronic debilitation of rheumatoid arthritis, we have come to the possible conclusion that stress reactions may influence whether our immune system protects us or fails us. Research has indicated that stress releases an array of chemicals that provide quick energy, but these same chemicals are potent inhibitors of the immune system. This revised edition of *Stressless Selling* explains what this connection means and how you can protect yourself. In addition, researchers are now beginning to understand some of the precise mechanisms in our thinking that produce lowered productivity—in our bodies as well as our sales efforts. This information has been presented here so that you can know what has been discovered, and thus, both sell better and live better.

In addition, we have identified the buffers that protect some people (the hardy ones) and not others from the negative effects of stress. This book offers an explanation of the hardy personality and how you can apply it to your own sales efforts. The powerful parts played by your expectations and emotions are also highlighted, added to the T (Thought) part of the B-T-A equation. For instance, new evidence points to the conclusion that expectations exert a major impact on body chemistry, strongly influence the meaning we give to things, determine what we do, and ultimately decide how successful our actions are.

In this revised edition we have also included an important postscript to why some Type A people have such a hard time of it. We explain how the debilitating effects of "Type A-ness" may have more to do with a chronic emotional state, which we've labeled the bitchiness factor, than with how hard-driven you are.

The last major change in the book covers a new class of potential stressors that have emerged from the multiple-role conflict. We feel these stresses when we are called upon to be super-salespro, super-mom, super-cook, and super-calm person—all at the same time. Men and women today are faced with role conflicts that didn't exist in our grandparents' day. These conflicts are becoming increasingly numerous, complex, and more difficult to handle. The result is an array of stressors that tax one's coping skills. In this edition we devote a chapter to this issue and suggest a number of ways to manage the situation and reduce the resulting tension.

We believe that this revised edition will be useful in the closing decade of the twentieth century. It represents the work we have done with salespeople like you, and it reflects the most successful techniques and research findings available to help you turn stress into both a business and a personal asset.

PREFACE

FACT: All of us experience stress as part of our existence. It can be *constructive* stress such as the positive, mobilizing, energizing stress experienced by, say, a speaker before speaking or an athlete before competing. Or we may encounter *negative*, immobilizing stress—an unexpected, nasty retort from a prospect or a sudden skid on a patch of ice—that can cause us to panic and momentarily freeze up. Sometimes the stress we encounter leads us to experience strain or tension that is short-lived and mild. And that's fine, because it adds excitement and pleasure to what we do. An event, the anticipation of an event, even the mental re-living of a past event can trigger a temporary anxious or nervous reaction, a tension or disquiet. At other times, we experience severe, debilitating stress that seems to build slowly and go on forever. It can disrupt our ability to concentrate, create, problem solve, eat, sleep, laugh, love, and generally enjoy life in its whole and most robust and rewarding forms. And it happens to the best of us.

There are economic consequences of stress—large ones. The corporate cost of job stress comes in many forms: lowered productivity, absenteeism, and increased medical costs. Exact figures are difficult to come by, but according to an article in the April 18, 1988, issue of *Business Week*, the cost of unmanaged job stress on the U.S. economy is suggested to be as high as $150 billion—almost as high as the trade deficit.

As Alvin Toffler, author of *Future Shock*, and others suggest, the ever-increasing rate of change in civilization, technology, and life-style have taxed our innate abilities to cope, to change with change and to go on about the business of becoming who and how we want to be, accomplishing what we want to accomplish. It's unquestionably true today that many people find their innate coping skills heavily taxed. It's equally true that many people have succeeded at bringing order and joy back into their lives by using the techniques, ideas, skills, philosophies, and tips you'll find in this book.

Some of these tools are as old as the hills—but as good as gold. Others are disarmingly simple. Some are a touch esoteric and a few, quite frankly, are experimental. All of them have successful track records when used in the right situation, at the right time, in the right way. It's our goal to help you find the right way to manage and minimize, to orchestrate and control the stress in your life so you can get on with the real business of life—becoming who you want to become.

HOW TO USE THIS BOOK

THIS BOOK IS A combination of things. In part, it is a book you can sit and read. In part, it is a set of ideas and research findings to test yourself. It is also a catalog of carefully constructed stress-management exercises, techniques, and strategies you will learn and use.

The book is divided into three parts.

Part One has twelve chapters. After an initial look at the history of stress, this part zeros in on the stress issues that face the sales professional. The content comes from our separate consulting practices and our joint and separate research efforts. There are nine self-tests in these chapters. Use them to measure the degree to which stress affects you personally. But these self-tests are more than diversions and curiosity satisfiers. They are carefully constructed and tested inventories that will show you how to diagnose your personal stress problems.

In Part Two, you combine the results of the Part One self-tests with the results of three more stress inventories. We show you how to use these results to build your Personal Stress Profile and develop one or more Stress Management Prescriptions for managing your stress.

Part Three focuses on stress treatment and stress-management strategies. The strategies in this part are step-by-step "How-To" routines, designed to address the unique stress-management needs you pinpointed in Part Two. You will probably not read all of them; no one would ever need *all* the techniques, but from them you'll be able to select the strategies to solve your stress problems.

During the developmental testing of this book, a few readers questioned the logic of holding the "solutions" until Part Three. We understand, but our decision was not an arbitrary one. Stress is not a simple problem with easy solutions. It is a many-sided issue, and to effectively manage stress, you need to understand the "nature of the beast." In fact, we feel that developing this awareness is an important part of stress-management efforts. It is also important that you see your entire stress profile and that you take an active part in developing the diagnosis and building the treatment plan. It's your life, and taking a proactive approach to solving your life problems is an important part of stress management. So, the structure of this book is, basically:

Part One	Information
Part Two	Diagnosis
Part Three	Treatment

One more note. Our work with professional salespeople has taught us a lot. We are impressed with the creative, intelligent manner in which they approach their work and with the sophisticated coping skills many have developed on their own for managing the stresses involved in selling for a living. We have also found that even the sales pros with good stress-management skills are eager to add skills to their repertoires. We believe that the awareness and new skills you will gain from reading this book and working through the exercises will add valuable skills to your repertoire. But, in addition, we believe that these skills will help you free up extra energy—energy you can use for selling, energy you can use for living better and more fully, energy you can use for achieving your true success potential.

ACKNOWLEDGMENTS

THIS BOOK IS A distillation of fifteen years' experience with the stress issues faced by professional salespeople. We have worked with and learned from both neophytes and highly successful, seasoned veterans. We thank them all.

We are particularly indebted to the following special sales professionals for their specific contributions: the very analytical Sid Isler, who spent long hours nitpicking the manuscript; Norman W. Kamerow, CLU, a cerebral, effective sales professional who provided his special insights; and Frank Ward, who provided the perspective of a gifted salesman/sales manager. In addition, we thank Jane M. Shiff, CLU, who willingly shared her expertise in working with women in sales; Chester R. Jones, CLU, who helped us with the tone and feel of the manuscript; and Susan Jones, who brought her special word-smithing skills to our aid. We are also indebted to Dorothea R. Johnson, M.D., for her feedback and professional input.

Finally, we'd like to thank our respective staffs for their aid and forbearance. Among them, special thanks are due Muriel Klinger, for her seminal contributions to the project concepts; Karen Friedman, who made absolutely certain that the manuscript was in good order; and Audrey Kupers, for her dedication to excellence.

INTRODUCTION AND OVERVIEW

STRESS IS ONE OF THOSE "you-know-it-when-you-have-it-but-it's-hard-to-explain-it-to-someone-else" concepts similar to fear, fatigue, or love. A definition will be tackled shortly, since it's important that we agree on what we're talking about, but for now let's look at the forest and save the individual trees for later.

Have you ever been so worried about something that you paced about, thinking and rethinking a situation until every other aspect of your life seemed secondary and unimportant? How did all that worrying affect you? Your life? The people around you? Did you develop the shakes? Sweaty palms? Catch yourself biting your nails? Were you constantly tired and weary but unable to sleep? Did you lose your appetite? Drink a bit too much? Kick the cat and holler at the kids? Trample on the sensitivities of kith, kin, and colleagues, like the proverbial bull in a china shop?

And finally, when you think back, did any of that preoccupation, sweating, nail-biting, hollering, and hiding *solve the problem*? No, of course not. You wasted a lot of energy on unproductive activities that got in the way of everything you wanted to do. The problem, when it was solved, was resolved by—what else?—*solving the problem*. Some may argue that the stress energized you to solve the problem. That *can* and does happen. But most of us lack the skills necessary to manage and use *severe* stress in a positive fashion. Mostly, we move directly from motivated to "tilt," and only take hold of the problem *after* the stress has subsided—after precious time and energy have burned away in dysfunctional worry and anguish.

Interrupting that cycle of worry, tension, frustration, and dysfunction—gaining some "psychological space," regaining control of what's happening around you, and getting away from just surviving and into problem solving—is what *stress management* is all about. And that's all it's about. Some writers and "experts" sell stress management as the best thing since sliced bread and make it a life-style effort. That's absurd. As Abraham Maslow so candidly observed, "When you give a kid a hammer, everything suddenly needs hammering." So many stress-management experts see debilitating stress under every bush and insist that a total change in life-style is the only "solution." It's a prescription that turns many people off, including us.

Stress management is nothing more than a toolbox of fairly simple techniques to minimize both the pressure of life's traumas and the escalating annoyances of everyday "drip" stress. Stress-management tools and techniques are not mysterious or esoteric. They are things you can do to keep the daily pressure of living and selling from putting you off your feed and keeping you off your feet. They are things that can help maximize your chances of being in clearheaded, proactive, problem-solving, decision-making control of your life and work. And that's the name of the game.

Let's take the case of thirty-four-year-old Jerry Mapes, a hotshot New Orleans real estate salesman. At age 24, Jerry forsook junior high basketball coaching and teaching and, with his uncle's encouragement, went into real estate. At 26, Jerry was licensed, certified, and selling up a storm. In the next three years, Jerry moved up from "moving" small bungalows to "showing" Garden District properties. He was beginning to sell small commercial properties and medium-size multi-unit dwellings as well. His income tracked a handsome parallel with the rest of his career.

But at age 34, when Ron Zemke met him, Jerry was seriously considering running away to the farthest bayou, growing a scraggly beard, and becoming a hermit. He was willing—almost eager—to toss away a life-style most people would envy—he wasn't sure for what. And that's why he ended up buttonholing

Ron in the spring of 1978, after a presentation to a real estate group. Eventually, Jerry joined a three-day workshop where he identified the issues—both on and off the job—that made him want to opt out. He saw that the money-seeking treadmill he was on—with its uneven income flow and the long hours and weekends devoted to showings—was getting him nowhere. He was divorced but found little time for dating. When he had free time, he slept. Jerry was in an "existential crisis": all stressed up and nowhere to go. He was tired of fighting and ready to flee.

Jerry made decisions during the workshop about how much money he really wanted to earn. He learned how to worry *productively*, in ways that lead to more sales in less time (by cutting worry time to a minimum). He also learned to become less upset by, and more accepting of, the "givens" in his business: the necessity of evening and night work, and the position of constantly being "in the middle" between buyer and seller. He was able, for the first time, to look at the cost-benefit ratio of weekend work (what he gained vs. what he lost socially and personally), so that he could decide on a plan of action. He learned that his life and stress were largely products of the decisions he and others had made about this life. He resolved to take his decision making more seriously.

Jerry was then able to reevaluate and refocus former goals, plus add new goals. The high stress and tension he'd been feeling had acted as a major barrier to constructive thinking, not to mention appropriate action. Jerry established new priorities. He decided that by moving into selling commercial property he could free up weekend time for a social life. He felt the anticipated rewards of the work would outweigh the detractions of an uneven income flow.

You'll note that nothing was done *to* or *for* Jerry. He did it himself. Decreasing the stress in his life—as with everything else in selling, from prospecting to closing—was something Jerry did for himself. We simply shared some ideas with him that he found useful; Jerry drove the car, but we provided the roadmap.

Jerry's story is important, not only as case study, but as an example of what a highly stressed individual can accomplish with knowledge, training, guidance, and the right stress-management techniques. Jerry's story is also important because it typifies, in a slightly exaggerated way, the everyday pressures salespeople confront.

Selling is a high-tension occupation. Of all the fields a person might pursue, it is one of the most "naked." Salespeople succeed or fail, eat or starve, based entirely on the results they achieve in the marketplace, on the sales they make. There's no good excuse for a "no sale." There's no hiding, no glossing over, no rationalizing away your failure. The salesperson stands naked before the stark light of sink-or-swim criteria.

What are the pressures and events that often precipitate a stress reaction? For the novice or would-be salesperson, there's the anticipation or fear of failure. Selling, in many ways, is a performing art. Just as the novice actor never really knows what will happen—how he or she will respond when the curtain goes up—the beginning salesperson is never completely sure of the results—that he or she won't freeze when the door is closed and the client says, "You've gotten past my secretary and you've gotten past my assistant. What's so important that you need to see me personally?" Even an old pro feels that tension from time to time. The stress can motivate or it can debilitate. Either way, there is a price to pay.

Salespeople are also faced with the possibility of psychological rejection, those "little murders" that occur during the sales process day after day. One expert in the insurance field has calculated that for every yes an insurance salesperson hears, he or she also hears over fifty no's. Another expert has calculated that each sale a life-insurance agent makes is the result of five presentations. Each presentation is the outcome of ten initial interviews. Each initial interview is the result of ten cold calls.

Small wonder, then, that when *Training Magazine* conducted a national survey, it found sales managers complained that their salespeople are reluctant to make cold calls, call on existing accounts too frequently, hesitate to ask for the order, and spend too much time in the office.[1] Just as young children quickly learn to avoid hot stoves, salespeople learn to avoid life's punishing events.

Add to this the terror of being at the mercy of someone's

goodwill for your livelihood, and the fact that salespeople can never show ill temper, have bad days, avoid people they don't like, or talk back to the rude and crude of the world, and it's easy to picture the day-to-day stress of a salesperson. The number 1 reason salespeople leave the business is, "I can't take it—the rejection—anymore."

Another source of stress comes about, paradoxically, from efforts to improve and become a better salesperson. Every salesperson is painfully aware of the intangible difference between a sale almost made and a sale almost lost. That same difference is the margin of success upon which a sales career rests. Consequently, salespeople continually attend seminars or lectures and read about selling. They're always looking for an edge. But the hoped-for results often fall short of expectations, and when they go back to whatever it was they were doing that was effective in the first place, they don't know what it was.

Most of us are like that. We're not really conscious of the things we do that make us good. When we're good, there's no one better. When we're bad, well . . . . The trouble, of course, lies in not knowing which things produce the good results. John Wanamaker, the great Philadelphia retailer, reportedly shouted out in exasperation, "Half of my advertising is no damn good! The hell of it is I don't know *which* half." So it is with each of us, and so it is with most successful salespeople. When we're tap dancing well, we're too busy reading the audience to watch our footwork.

Too much travel, too many nights on the road, and too much weekend work—all the things profiled in Sam Susser's *The Truth About Selling*—take their toll on family life. But even more troublesome is stressful communications. A long day of being nice, glib, and verbally careful with customers is often paid for later at home. After a day of, "Yes, Mr. Objection, I can certainly understand how you might see it that way. Perhaps I can . . ." it should come as no surprise that your thirteen-year-old's "Dad, how come *I* gotta take out the trash all the time? Why doesn't Suzy do it?" often gets a short, angry response. And, of course, that doesn't play well with anyone. The sales pro ends up feeling just as bad as the spouse, the kid, or the kicked cat.

We sincerely believe that, by becoming aware of the role stress plays in the selling process, and by learning to anticipate and recognize destructive forms of stress, sales professionals can successfully deal with the fears, rejections, and pressures to perform. We believe that stress which threatens to debilitate and diminish performance, if recognized early and properly managed, can instead become part of your competitive edge.

Stressless Selling is an approach, a set of techniques, to help you deal with the tensions engendered in the day-to-day business of making a living through sales. This book doesn't present a new way to establish trust or give you twenty tricks to better closings. *Stressless Selling* won't replace Napoleon Hill's *Think and Grow Rich* as the best-selling sales book of all time. It won't supersede either Dale Carnegie's *How to Win Friends and Influence People* or Norman Vincent Peale's *Power of Positive Thinking* as the favorite inspirational readers for salespeople. It will, however, show you specific proven techniques for finding and using the energy you need to reach the goals to which you aspire, to gain control of your life, and to learn to live—not just for the bottom line but also for the life line.

CHARLEY: . . . *Willy was a salesman. And for a salesman, there is no rock bottom to the life. He don't put a bolt to a nut, he don't tell you the law or give you medicine. He's a man way out there in the blue, riding on a smile and a shoeshine. And when they start not smiling back—that's an earthquake. And then you get yourself a couple of spots on your hat, and you're finished. Nobody dast blame this man. A salesman is got to dream, boy. It comes with the territory.*

—Requiem from *Death of a Salesman*
Arthur Miller, 1949

ONE

Sorting Out the Stress Mess: What's Fact, What's Fiction

1

THE "MISTAKEN IDENTITY" PROBLEM: THE DOLLARS AND SENSE OF SELF-ACCEPTANCE

W E all strive to like and accept ourselves—to be happy, satisfied with, and proud of who we are. Not just in a professional sense, but as persons, individuals—"the worthwhile, worthy human being" sense. Sometimes we are painfully aware of the effort; other times we aren't. But in either case, this drive plays an important role in determining what we do with our energy.

In the abstract, self-acceptance is a balanced attitude of satisfaction with our qualities, our aptitudes, our achievements, and a recognition of our limitations. In practice, the having and doing of living—what we *do* for a living and for fun, what we *have* in the material sense—are intertwined with the sense of "being a person" and the reasoned sense of worth and acceptance of self stripped of cars, houses, clubs, and job. The specifics of dependence upon doing and having for defining self-worth and self-acceptance differ by occupation. For instance, clergy, medical practitioners, or laborers each have unique sets of doing and having standards they use to judge their self-worth.

A uniqueness we see in salespeople—a value or belief that sets them apart from those who don't sell for a living—is the role of money in their evaluation of themselves and in the development of their identity. Of all the occupations we have studied, only the professional salesperson's self-image, self-acceptance, and general sense of psychic well-being are directly tied to the bottom line: actual bean-counting, dollars-and-cents outcomes.

In a broad sense, most people are involved in some form of selling. The clergy "sells" faith, the doctor sells health or cures, and even the worker "sells" labor. But the direct relationship between results and rewards is critical; it's the fine line that separates the sales professional from the occasional marketer or amateur. Of all the professions, only real sales pros stand or fall—and are judged and rewarded—exclusively on the basis of the dollars and cents they go out to hustle up and bring back. Regardless of the number of people who support the sales rep, back at the head office the question, "Did you make your numbers or not?" is the yardstick sales professionals are measured by. There's no acceptable excuse and no payoff for a "no sale" report. You eat if and when they buy, and you tighten the belt when they don't. Few companies pay commissions for sales *almost* made, and they pay the same for different kinds of sales— the tough ones and the "tip-ins" alike.

No one asks the cleric to account for numbers of souls saved, nor is the worker usually paid by the number of ditches dug or nails pounded. Even the physician is accountable for trying only—anyone whose son or daughter has dealt with a dermatologist knows that results are never guaranteed.

This occupational reality has a lot to do with how salespeople judge their own "OK-ness." Many evaluate themselves— their worth as human beings—in terms of their professional success. When sales are good, they are worthy, good, important, and generally OK. When sales are down, they are bad, slothful, ineffectual, and generally not OK.

Some fields, like medicine, have built-in ethics and values that help professionals cope with the pressures of the job and give support to their self-evaluation. No such cultural or normative structure exists in selling. For most salespeople, the situation is akin to what happens in school. A student who gets a D in spelling or math often comes to be referred to and thought of as a D student: the grade gets confused with the person. In selling, if the salesperson doesn't meet quota, he or she is branded a low producer, a poor salesperson, instead of a sales rep with a poor record.

This "inner" linguistic game wouldn't matter much except for one tragic fact: salespeople who are tagged low producers often come to accept and embrace that view of themselves as failures in selling, and in life. They frequently regard themselves as less human than others, as in George Orwell's *Animal Farm*,

> *All animals are equal but some animals are more equal than others.*

The fallout from this attitude is that every tension, pressure, and strain salespeople experience threatens not only their professional achievement but their image and value of themselves.

Too Little and Too Much:
The Problem of Under- and Overidentification

In our work with sales professionals, we have developed a particular appreciation of the self-worth issue. Both personal and professonal experiences have confirmed the importance of avoiding overdependence on professional success as a measure of self-worth. But determining self-worth can be quite a tightrope act. To some extent work *does* provide people with an anchor or reference point for deciding who they are and who they want to be. The trick is to accept and value your professional role while not allowing that aspect to become the complete picture of yourself.

Negative stress is generated most often when a person's personal identification is at the extreme; for example, a person can identify too much or too little with the sales role. In too little identification, salespeople know their role and can quote you chapter and verse of win-win selling, but they exploit their customers and prospects. They see themselves as people quite different from professional salespeople. We seldom encounter these people on a long-term basis. They are amateurs who must occasionally sell themselves to a limited client list. They are also people who turn over after five or six months of selling.

People with too much identification with their professional role use superhumans like Superman, Donald Duck, Perry Mason, Brenda Starr, or Prince Valiant as their role models. Literary figures, movie stars, and comic-strip characters are not whole people. They are one- and two-dimensional figures an author or artist creates to illustrate a facet of life or a dimension of human nature. The same is true in work. Job descriptions, résumés, and sales records are but single facets of who you really are. Professional athletes often fall victim to overidentification with their role. Some stay in uniform long past their prime, while others take sportscasting and coaching jobs just to stay on the periphery of the spotlight. Still others open sports-motif restaurants and trade on the memories of yesterday.

The Case of Meredith

Meredith is an almost classic example of a salesperson over-identifying with her professional role. Here is Dr. Stern's account of the problems Meredith faced:

MEREDITH is a woman in her early thirties. She is a commercial-loan officer with a major national bank. She had been in banking eight years when she first contacted me. Three of those years were spent in operations, two on the personal loan platform, and three years ago she joined the commercial division's sales department.

Her reason for contacting me was simple. In her five years of selling, she had never—until now—experienced a prolonged sales slump. Her loan portfolio of small and medium companies was filled with high growth potential customers. She was a "star." But she hadn't added a new loan to her collection in seven months. She came to my office disgusted with herself, ready to quit the world and the business.

It quickly became apparent that Meredith had come to equate who she was as a person with her professional role and image: a role and image labeled hard-charging, successful, highly assertive financial counselor to the bright aggressive entrepreneurs of her community!

As we talked, I learned that Meredith was well aware that chaotic conditions in the money market had driven loan seekers to secondary money sources. Despite this knowledge, she blamed herself completely for the slump. Her tolerance for failure was almost nonexistent and her self-contempt for being in a dry spell bordered on vicious. Her intolerance was based on an irrational belief in what we refer to as the Isler maxim:

A real salesperson can sell a product or service to a prospect who doesn't want it, has no use for it, knows it's overpriced, and knows the salesperson has neither title to nor possession of.

Meredith truly believed that she "should" be able to sell buggy whips to Chevy owners by perseverance and sheer force of personality!

Meredith also expected quite a lot from herself. When she found out that the institution had set lower sales goals for women, she demanded her goals be set higher than anyone else in the department, male or female. These sky-high goals were an additional pressure to prove herself in the marketplace.

As we continued to talk, it also became obvious that she was depressed and, without knowing it, very angry with herself, her boss, and her industry. The past months had convinced her that she was a total failure devoid of even the necessary skills for going out to dinner with a friend. She was drowning and no one had even tried to throw her a life preserver.

Meredith was caught in an identity web of her own making. She had defined in her mind the role of "Super Salespro Making It in a Tough Market" as a model of who she should be *and* she had become it. The Achilles' heel of her strategy was that once the slump hit—a slump she as an individual was *totally* helpless to prevent—she had no "choice" but to brand herself a failure. The logic that *she* was solely responsible for her previous successes demanded that she consider herself solely responsible for her failure. Her "I am what I sell" mentality, her dependence on her selling role as the one source of her personal identity, also "logically" demanded that she brand herself and her life a total failure.

This twisted logic and unidimensional identity structure turned a once-eager, hard-charging, competent saleswomen into the sad, nervous, highly stressed person I encountered seven months after the onset of the slump.

This is the part where we are supposed to show you how the good doctor gives Meredith a magic word or a booster shot of Positive Mental Attitude, and where we brag about Meredith's instant "cure." Well no such laying on of hands took place, nor did a miracle occur. Dr. Stern and Meredith worked together for many months before Meredith began to get the picture in focus enough to begin making changes in her view of herself, her sales, and what constitutes success and failure. It would be professionally unsound to purport that a case of mistaken identity as severe as Meredith's could be instantly cured through stress-reduction techniques. Though Meredith did learn a number of these, they only allowed her to lower her tension to the point where she and Dr. Stern could deal with the basic problem. That's all we could expect of stress-reduction techniques in this case.

Meredith did eventually learn to view herself in a more realistic way. She was able to do an honest strength and weakness assessment, and she learned to separate her identity as a person from her identity as a sales professional. She began to distinguish between the things she could and could not control, and she learned to take responsibility only for the former; no more being psyched out by the money market. Meredith even learned to handle sales slumps by using some of the techniques described in Part Three. Dr. Stern ends her description of Meredith's work with her in this way:

MEREDITH will always have to deal with the issue of role identification and self-worth. We all have to from time to time. That's the way life is. Meredith was an extreme example.

It took a great deal of time, effort, and money for Meredith to get to this level of awareness and healthy functioning. In my experience such severe cases of identity problem always do. This is probably the most severe psychological problem a salesperson faces. It impacts every facet of the person's professional and personal life.

Meredith's story is presented here because it is such a clear case of how the "mistaken identity" phenomenon can precipitate debilitating stress and tension. As you will see, most stress problems are not as global in impact nor as difficult and time-consuming to solve. We bring up this knotty problem first because it is the toughest one professional salespeople face and because it is the one least "curable" using the tools and techniques that follow in this book.

Personal and professional identity is a life-and-growth issue. As we strive, grow, and change, we continuously redefine ourselves. In *Pulling Your Own Strings*, Dr. Wayne Dyer defines losers as rigid, opinionated, negative people. He terms winners those who are open, versatile, and risk-taking.[1] In our view, winners are also people on the grow, people who periodically answer the question, "OK, who am I *now?*" Welcome to the winner's circle.

Assess Your View of Your Own Self-Worth

The following inventory is designed to help you assess the degree of overlap between your personal and professional images of yourself. The more extreme the overlap, or *lack* of overlap in the two images, the more stressful selling tends to be for you. Also, the greater the overlap, the more dependent you tend to be on success in selling for your feelings of self-worth. Exercise 1, the ROLE VALUES INVENTORY, helps you to assess the overlap of images.

Since you've been reading about the self-worth issue, it will be tempting to give Sunday School answers to these questions. But be as honest with yourself as you can. If you're worried about somebody's seeing your answers, use disappearing ink. Scoring instructions and interpretations are at the end of the inventory.

In Part Two, you will be drawing together all the scores and findings from the self-inventories in Part One. These will form your PERSONAL STRESS PROFILE and will be used to help you develop an appropriate and individualized set of STRESS MANAGEMENT PRESCRIPTIONS. Some interim suggestions and thoughts follow directly after the scoring and interpretation section.

EXERCISE 1. The Role-Values Inventory

Part 1. People who sell for a living are . . .

a. Below is a list of sixty words people often use to describe other people. Read through the list twice. The first time through, put an X next to any word you believe accurately describes people who sell for a living.

The second time through, circle the X of the ten words you would feel comfortable using to describe generally competent salespeople to a nonsalesperson. In other words, pick the ten descriptors that best answer the question, "What are salespeople really like?"

People Who Sell for a Living Are:

☐ Warm	☐ Indifferent	☐ Boring
☐ Disrespectful	☐ Trusting	☐ Inadequate
☐ Generous	☐ Selfish	☐ Anxious
☐ Caring	☐ Courteous	☐ Secure
☐ Impatient	☐ Undemonstrative	☐ Happy
☐ Accepting	☐ Good	☐ Useless
☐ Unsympathetic	☐ Fair	☐ Dull
☐ Honest	☐ Worthless	☐ Assertive
☐ Thoughtless	☐ Awful	☐ Misunderstood
☐ Open	☐ Unpleasant	☐ Lazy
☐ Disloyal	☐ Sad	☐ Respected
☐ Secretive	☐ Happy	☐ Efficient
☐ Loyal	☐ Pleasant	☐ Upbeat
☐ Considerate	☐ Nice	☐ Pushy

☐ Suspicious   ☐ Valuable   ☐ Effective
☐ Angry   ☐ Unfair   ☐ Competent
☐ Deceitful   ☐ Bad   ☐ Insecure
☐ Understanding   ☐ Confident   ☐ Unintelligent
☐ Intolerant   ☐ Successful   ☐ Inefficient
☐ Patient   ☐ Valuable   ☐ Complacent

b. Write the ten descriptions you chose on the ten numbered lines below. Now rate the positive and negative value of these ten words, using the 7-point scale next to each. Think about each word and decide if, in your opinion, it is a positive or a negative word. Then decide <u>how</u> positive or negative it is. Circle the number that best describes the degree of positiveness or negativeness you feel about each word.

My Evaluation of the Words
I Use to Describe Salespeople

Words I Use to Describe Salespeople	*Very Negative*	*Negative*	*Somewhat Negative*	*Neutral*	*Somewhat Positive*	*Positive*	*Very Positive*
1. _____	1	2	3	4	5	6	7
2. _____	1	2	3	4	5	6	7
3. _____	1	2	3	4	5	6	7
4. _____	1	2	3	4	5	6	7
5. _____	1	2	3	4	5	6	7
6. _____	1	2	3	4	5	6	7
7. _____	1	2	3	4	5	6	7
8. _____	1	2	3	4	5	6	7
9. _____	1	2	3	4	5	6	7
10. _____	1	2	3	4	5	6	7

Add up the numbers you circled and put the total in this box. ☐

Now go on to Part 2 of the ROLE-VALUES INVENTORY.

Part 2. I am . . .

a. Below is the same list of sixty words people use to describe other people. Again, read through the list <u>twice</u>. The first time through, put an X next to any word you believe accurately describes <u>you</u>.

The second time through, circle the X of the ten words that <u>best describe the way you feel about you</u> at this time. In other words, pick the ten descriptors that best answer the question "What am I <u>really</u> like?"

I am:

☐ Warm	☐ Indifferent	☐ Boring
☐ Disrespectful	☐ Trusting	☐ Inadequate
☐ Generous	☐ Selfish	☐ Anxious
☐ Caring	☐ Courteous	☐ Secure
☐ Impatient	☐ Undemonstrative	☐ Happy
☐ Accepting	☐ Good	☐ Useless
☐ Unsympathetic	☐ Fair	☐ Dull
☐ Honest	☐ Worthless	☐ Assertive
☐ Thoughtless	☐ Awful	☐ Misunderstood
☐ Open	☐ Unpleasant	☐ Lazy
☐ Disloyal	☐ Sad	☐ Respected
☐ Secretive	☐ Happy	☐ Efficient
☐ Loyal	☐ Pleasant	☐ Upbeat
☐ Considerate	☐ Nice	☐ Pushy
☐ Suspicious	☐ Valuable	☐ Effective
☐ Angry	☐ Unfair	☐ Competent
☐ Deceitful	☐ Bad	☐ Insecure
☐ Understanding	☐ Confident	☐ Unintelligent
☐ Intolerant	☐ Successful	☐ Inefficient
☐ Patient	☐ Valuable	☐ Complacent

b. Write the ten descriptions you chose on the ten numbered lines below. Now rate the positive and negative value of these ten words, using the 7-point scale next to each. Think about each word and decide if, in your opinion, it is a positive or a negative word. Then decide <u>how</u> positive or negative it is. Circle the number that best describes the degree of positiveness or negativeness you feel about each word.

My Evaluation of the Words I Use to Describe Myself

Words I Use to Describe Myself	Very Negative	Negative	Somewhat Negative	Neutral	Somewhat Positive	Positive	Very Positive
1. _____	1	2	3	4	5	6	7
2. _____	1	2	3	4	5	6	7
3. _____	1	2	3	4	5	6	7
4. _____	1	2	3	4	5	6	7
5. _____	1	2	3	4	5	6	7
6. _____	1	2	3	4	5	6	7
7. _____	1	2	3	4	5	6	7
8. _____	1	2	3	4	5	6	7
9. _____	1	2	3	4	5	6	7
10. _____	1	2	3	4	5	6	7

Add up the numbers you circled and put the total in this box. ☐

Scoring and Interpretation

1. Count the number of words common to both of the ten-word lists you created. Multiply that number by 10 and enter it in the Percentage of Overlap box.

☐%

PERCENTAGE
OF OVERLAP

2. Put the total you arrived at in Part 1 of this exercise, "My Evaluation of the Words I use to Describe Salespeople," in this box.

SALESPEOPLE

3. Put the total you arrived at in Part 2 of this exercise, "My Evaluation of Words I Use to Describe Myself," in this box.

MYSELF

• *0 to 30% Overlap.* If three or fewer of the words you chose to describe <u>yourself</u> are words you used to describe <u>salespeople in general</u>, there may be some strain between your self-concept and your concept of your professional role.

If, in addition, your evaluation of <u>salespeople in general</u> is negative (fewer than 35) and your evaluation of <u>yourself</u> is positive (fewer than 45), you can be pretty sure there is conflict between your view of yourself and your view of the professional selling role.

If, however, your evaluation of <u>yourself</u> was negative (less than 35), while your view of the <u>salespeople in general</u> was positive (greater than 45), you could be trying to use the sales role to cover up or hide a sense of low self-worth.

Stress enters the picture when your evaluation of self-worth is <u>negative</u>, your evaluation of the sales role <u>positive</u>, and the overlap between self-descriptors and sales descriptors is low.

You seem to be saying, "Salespeople are OK but I'm not." In addition, you may be saying that you haven't much in common with the competent sales professional. This can easily lead to a situation wherein you view sales success to be too far above you. Striving to overcome the distance between your view of the competent salesperson and your view of yourself can be highly stressful. It can also quickly lead to an exit from selling in general.

• *40% to 60% Overlap.* Overlap between <u>yourself</u> and <u>salespeople in general</u> of this magnitude is appropriate for the well-adjusted, striving sales professional. Your sights are up, and at the same time you aren't totally dependent on sales success or the salesperson role for your sense of self-worth. Your goal setting is probably reasonable—just enough stretch but not unrealistically high. You probably also feel pretty good about yourself and you see value in the work you do.

If your views of both <u>yourself</u> and <u>salespeople in general</u> are positive, you are in the best of all possible worlds. If one or the other of your evaluations was negative, you need to examine some assumptions. For instance, if you had a negative evaluation of the sales role, you might need to re-examine your assumptions about the contribution salespeople make to society and the value of salespeople as people.

• *70% to 100% Overlap.* Such a complete overlap in the views of <u>yourself</u> and <u>salespeople in general</u> may be a problem. You could well be dependent on the sales role for your sense of self-worth. This is most likely to be the case if you also evaluated <u>yourself</u> as negative and <u>salespeople in general</u> as positive. If you seem to be saying to yourself, "Selling is great, salespeople are nifty, but me—I'm not so hot," then you need to rethink your dependence on your professional role. If you set low or un-challenging goals for yourself, it's a sure sign that you are using the sales role as a crutch or cover-up for feelings of low self-worth.

Bring the Images Closer Together

Sometimes a wide disparity exists between your views of yourself and your professional role because you have a mistaken idea of what is expected of a professional. Doctors who believe they should be able to diagnose every disease and cure every patient, lawyers who think they ought to win every case, and salespeople who feel they must sell every potential buyer share a common potential for a low self-image. "*Shoulding,*" "*oughting,*" and "*musting*" imply that you believe a professional to be a model of perfection: no mistakes, no lost sales, no bad days, and no doubts and fears. But people are never, ever perfect. Nor are paintings, loaves of bread, or cars. One ingenious English fruit-cake company actually puts obvious flaws in its fruitcakes so people won't know they are machine made. Indians in the American Southwest put errors in the blankets they weave and Persian rug makers put mistakes in their weavings so the gods won't think they are imitating perfection.

Perfection may be a good goal for machines and saints, but it is a terrible one for people. Competence, pride, and joy from performance are more human strivings—and more achievable ones. We once heard the chair of the board of one of the three largest banks in the world say, "If half the decisions I make in a day move the corporation ahead and the other half at least don't hinder it, I've had a heck of a good day!" If you want more than that, we suggest a modified 80/20 rule:

If you do it right 80 percent of the time, no one is going to doubt your competence.

Follow that rule. For example, none of us speaks perfect English 100 percent of the time, but if we speak properly 80 percent of the time, we are invariably judged competent users of the language by our listeners. As long as our ratio of successes to failures favors success, we should judge ourselves as competent—everyone else does anyway. Why be harder on yourself than the rest of the world is?

Changing Negatives to Positives

If you view the sales role as negative, you may be listening to old tapes in your head that say salespeople are exploiters and users. If *"caveat emptor"*—"let the buyer beware"—appears beneath your mental image of a sales pro, you are about eighty years behind the time. Today's sales pro, the seller who is in the business for life, knows that, in the words of two great old sales pros:

1. "Nothing happens until somebody sells something [*Red Motley*]."
2. "People love to buy and hate to be sold [*Bill Gove*]."

If you are concerned with changing your concept of yourself or the sales role, the strategy "Six Ways to Get High on Yourself" (Part Three) will help you get started.

Summing Up Self-Worth

The concept of self-worth and the feelings the idea tries to communicate are elusive. Self-worth is really the product of many pieces that come together in a single *gestalt*, or holistic feeling. Achievement, goal setting, beliefs, comparisons of self with ideals, and comparisons of self with others all play a role in the summative feeling called self-worth. Keeping a positive, balanced sense of self and of professional role would be easy if the world were a static place. It isn't, however, and nor are you. The world changes, and you are continuously changing and growing. You wouldn't be human—or alive—if things were otherwise.

So there is no choice. The effort must be continued. If you see that as a positive part of life, you win. If you see it as a negative, you lose. The way you feel about yourself and your professional role is critical to both your long-term happiness and your selling success—not to mention your endurance in the sales field. Ideally, we all need a positive view of ourselves and a positive view of the roles we play in life, especially our roles at work.

Equally important is the distance we perceive between our *real self* and our *ideal self*. If whom we are is too distant from whom we want to be, we can feel threatened by the thought of bridging that gap and become demotivated. We quit striving when there is no distance between who we are and who we want to be. If the ideal we strive for is trivial or low-level—too close to where we already are—we tend not to strive. The best of all self-worth worlds is having a positive feeling about who we are and who we ideally want to become and, at the same time, believing that there is a realistic distance between the now and the ideal which we can travel and enjoy—when we learn how.

2

STRESS: AS COMMON AS THE COMMON COLD

S TRESS is as common as the common cold—and in some ways just as poorly understood. Contrary to what you might think, stress has been a problem for a long time. Even in ancient Greece, men of letters lamented the emotional toll of the "pace of modern civilized life." Contemporary experts have defined stress as:

- The wear and tear of life
- The inevitable cost of significant achievement
- Life events demanding an adaptive response from the organism
- The cost of being alive
- The spice of life

People see stress as both a trigger and a response; a force acting on a person (bills or clients) that is strong enough to cause an undesirable response (heartburn, emotional upset, sleeplessness). And they are accurate. But they usually leave out an important newly recognized dimension of the distress equation, one that is based on how a person *views* things.

It seems perception can affect a person's vulnerability or hardiness to the slings and arrows of outrageous fortune.

While an all-inclusive definition of stress may seem a big mouthful, here it is:

Negative stress is the phenomenon that occurs when a person believes that the demands made on him/her exceed his/her ability to cope and that seems to threaten mental or physical well-being. Positive stress is exactly the opposite. It stretches rather than exceeds tolerance levels and enhances rather than threatens well-being.

Regardless of who does the defining, there seem to be two common elements. The first is that descriptions of stress are never precise about what stress is or does. They lack the precision and technical language we've come to expect from modern medicine. But that's an honest and essential feature of stress and stress-related maladies. It doesn't fit the standard "get sick and get well" model. For instance, we need some stress in our lives: to be alive is to be stressed. Getting married is stressful. Going on vacation is stressful. Calling on a new prospect is stressful. Without stress, we wouldn't be sharp and alert. The absence of stress is death!

Even when stress goes beyond our normal tolerance and becomes distracting and destructive, it doesn't act like a disease. Stress lacks the obvious disabling signs that characterize a broken leg or a case of measles. The symptoms of stress can be tension headaches, sleep problems, heartbeat irregularities, fatigue, choking sensations, irritability, nervousness, inability to concentrate, indigestion, or diarrhea. But these symptoms could belong to any number of diseases. And so, like the protective coloration of some animals, stress is often hidden by its physiological symptoms. It often looks like something else—something that it isn't.

Stress often appears to be a simple organic disease, but the critical difference is that treating the diarrhea, insomnia, or migraine headache doesn't eliminate the stress and sometimes even fails to relieve the symptoms. In the medical argot, stress is a "functional illness," a condition that impairs and looks like an organic disease, but is not.

The second common characteristic of definitions of stress is the necessity of considering both the physiological and the psychological nature of the problem. That's not especially comfortable for modern medicine. Traditional medicine tends to treat the body as a machine, which is a good concept when dealing with a broken leg but breaks down when applied to stress. Stress is a combination of psychological and physiological responses to the ordinary and extraordinary pressures of life. Some medical people, such as Dr. Alan McLean, author of *Work Stress*, consider it a psychosomatic or mentally induced illness.[1] As we'll soon see, psychological subtleties such as a perception of events or an interpretation of situations and understanding of options are extremely important in the management and control of stress. In short, our heads play a critical role both in our becoming stressed and in managing that stress. Since stress can have psychological and physical origins and symptoms, we need to be aware of both the psychological and physical characteristics to effectively control the stress responses in our lives.

Here's how we will look at stress: Stress is our body's psychological, physical, and chemical responses to events that frighten, threaten, excite, confuse, annoy, irritate, invigorate, or endanger us. The specific events, or the accumulation of events, that trigger a *stress response*—let's call them stressors— can be good or bad, happy or sad; and are fairly individualistic. An event that may cause a friend to sweat profusely may be a yawner for you. The thought of delivering a public address may terrify a college speech student, invigorate a politician, and bore an ambassador.

As we look at various stress reactions, we'll become aware of "size" differences. Some stress reactions are quite subtle—so mild that we never notice them. Some responses are painfully obvious: trembling hands, sweaty palms, heart pounding, cracking voice. Who didn't notice Richard Nixon's shaking voice and sweaty upper lip as he spoke his words of resignation? Even the most rabid Nixon hater couldn't fail to appreciate the stress so clearly displayed in living color (ashen).

We'll also take a quick look at the physical and medical costs and causes of stress, and we'll become aware of the tangled thicket of the illness-stress relationship: the interplay between stress and disease. It's sometimes difficult to tell which piece of the puzzle you're looking at and experiencing. Being stressed can make you ill—and being ill can make you stressed.

We'll look carefully at the behavioral aspects of stress. How we act toward situations, people, and life in general says much about the origins of our individual stress. And stress has important impacts on our behavior toward ourselves and others. We'll suggest some behavior-change ideas along the way. Finally, we'll look at stress as a very individualistic problem, with individual management needs.

A Brief History Lesson

We've found that people need to understand a little about where an idea came from and how it evolved before feeling comfortable with it. A touch of background helps all of us to quickly connect the new idea with the things we already know. Using this approach has been helpful in understanding stress and stress management—and in sorting fact from fancy.

A *note of caution:* The early work on stress comes from the medical world. Until quite recently, medical and physiological research treated human beings and mice as relatively equivalent organisms, the mouse being the more cooperative of the two for research purposes. This early medical work caused some confusion because it tended to focus on the physical aspects of stress, ignoring the behavioral and mental connections.

But as we all know, the environment, the mind, and the body all work together, intertwined in the matters of stress and stress management. We deal here with three environments and the way they work together and separately to create stress: the *external physical environment* (heat, cold, air, light, sound, and the like); the *internal physical environment* (physical systems—blood, digestion, nerves, glands, muscles—and drugs, age, and condition of organs); and the *internal psychological environment* (thoughts, emotions, experiences, perceptions, knowledge).

In the Beginning

In the late 1800s, Claude Bernard, a French physiologist, theorized and demonstrated that the internal environment of human beings must remain fairly constant if the human being is to remain existent. Body temperature, blood pressure, and chemical composition of body fluids and tissues tend to remain constant regardless of changes occurring around the person. This miracle takes place despite the adverse things we do to our bodies.

Bernard's specific contribution toward understanding stress was to prove that the constancy of this internal milieu was a desirable condition. When our body's self-regulating system has a "power failure," we can experience illness, disease, even death. Stress can bring on such a power failure, knocking the self-regulating system out of wack.

Round 2: Fight/Flight

Some fifty years later, in the early 1900s, Harvard physiologist Walter B. Cannon coined the term "homeostasis" to describe the power or drive of the body to maintain its organic steadiness or equilibrium. Cannon also believed that if the body is thrown out of balance and, for some adaptive reason, must move away from homeostasis (or if it is stretched beyond its normal shape or function by an outside force), it almost immediately begins struggling to return to "normal." Illness is not just suffering; it is also a fight to bring homeostatic balance to organs and tissues, despite damage the body may have incurred.[2]

Cannon's best-known contribution to the stress picture is his discovery, around 1909, of a bodily reaction known today as the fight/flight response. Cannon and his colleague Paul Bard noticed that, when repeatedly placed in a harmful situation, an animal develops a "get-ready" response. That is, lab animals that have been experimentally shocked, restrained, or in some way harmed respond quite differently when brought into the lab than do "naive" animals. Cannon and Bard noticed that these "experienced victims" responded in an "integrated physiologic fashion"; the animal's body began preparing to run or fight.[3]

Once aware of this learned response (our term), Bard and Cannon began to see almost identical physical symptoms among their human patients. It was Cannon who documented the case of a woman whose body ceased normal digestive functions and who exhibited extremely anxious behavior when visiting in Boston. The explanation, it turned out, was that the woman's husband often used the occasion to go on a real bender, to "become uncontrollably drunk," as Cannon put it. The day after the anticipated "toot," the woman's anxiety disappeared and her digestive system resumed normal functioning. Cannon made no record of the husband's state of "day-after" functioning.[4]

Cannon and his colleagues soon began speculating that we have a built-in fight/flight response that can be triggered by situations we learn to perceive as threatening. Various theories suggest that the fight/flight response is probably one of the built-in mechanisms that helped primitive cave dwellers avoid being dinner for stronger and quicker neighbors such as the sabertoothed tiger.

Even today, when confronted with a threatening situation—say, on a dark street in a strange town at 3 A.M., facing an unfriendly stranger with a gun—we are suddenly aware of the fight/flight response. This response is characterized by coordinated increases in oxygen consumption or metabolism and increases in blood pressure, heart rate, and volume of blood pumped to the skeletal or action muscles. Evidence shows that the blood actually becomes thicker as clotting agents are secreted, and the capillaries and vessels near the skin's surface shut down, as do digestion and digestive-juice secretions.

When faced with a mugger, an imminent automobile accident, or an athletic competition, these reactions are helpful. But there also are times when reactions are dysfunctional. You can't, for instance, solve a selling problem by becoming fight/flight activated and clobbering a buyer. Running away from an irate boss doesn't solve much, either. And what sense does it make to be aroused for survival in the middle of a five o'clock traffic jam? Civilized humans have learned an alternative to fight/flight called problem solving. But how do we tell our bodies that we don't need a full-blown fight/flight response all the time? We can't, completely. So often, when we are being chewed out by a customer, a cop, a boss, or even a spouse, we find ourselves physiologically aroused and ready to reach for the jawbone of an ass—or the ass's jawbone—but we resist and exercise "civilized control." That, of course, leaves us stressed up with no place to go. The only clobbering that takes place is the beating our bodies take from the physiological stress of still having that fight/flight response and resisting it.

Thirty Years of Time Out

A critical debate raged throughout the 1920s and 1930s about the origin of emotions and their relationship to the body and its chemistry. On one side were Cannon, a number of physiologists, and the one or two early behavioral psychologists. On the other side was a group of philosopher-psychologists led by the persuasive and erudite psychologist William James and the Danish physiologist Carl Lang.

The debate centered on the relationship between emotion, perception, and the biochemistry of fight/flight. The questions debated were essentially these three:

1. Do we "feel" emotions because of changes in bodily chemistry?
2. Do we have bodily chemistry changes because of the emotions we feel?

and

3. What is the role of the mind's appraisal of the threat of a particular set of circumstances in emotion and the body's biochemical reactions?

In more basic terms, do we see the bear, run, and then become frightened? Or do we see the bear, become frightened, and then run? Or is neither of the above the correct answer?

A Little Guy With a Hole in His Stomach

During the early 1940s, researchers Stewart Wolf and Harold Wolff got one of those lucky, million-to-one breaks scientists are afraid to hope for. They "discovered" a man named Tom who was forced, through the circumstances of a freak accident, to live most of his adult life with his stomach open and connected to the surface of his body. Though Wolf and Wolff intended to concentrate on the study of the mechanical actions of Tom's stomach functions, they found that his moods, feelings, and even thoughts had a significant effect on his stomach function.

In one reported example, twenty-four hours after Tom had a particularly distasteful encounter with a pompous hospital administrator, Wolf and Wolff happened to be working with him in their lab. During preparation for the experiment, Tom began to relate his tale of woe and humiliation of the previous day. As he relived and related the incident, Tom's stomach-lining redness, volume of free stomach acid, and acid secretion increased. The researchers then made an effort to distract and divert Tom's attention from the unhappy incident. Within thirty minutes, most of the arousal characteristics had reversed themselves. Wolf and Wolff's work with Tom was important in demonstrating that mental, emotional, and behavioral events have as much of an impact on the body as do drugs, germs, alcohol, and other tangible physical events.[5]

Stress Becomes "Legit"

Despite all the work we've recounted to this point, few of us would know about stress if it weren't for a brilliant and dedicated researcher, Dr. Hans Selye (1907–1982). Current awareness of stress as a health and happiness issue is due primarily to his work. Born in Vienna, Selye trained in endocrinology and biochemistry in Prague, Paris, and Rome. He received his M.D. and a Ph.D. in philosophy and science at German University in Prague. In 1936, Selye was the first to use the term "stress" to describe the phenomenon he had been studying for almost ten years.*

From 1945 until his death, Selye served as director of the Institute of Experimental Medicine and Surgery at the University of Montreal. He wrote 32 books and more than 1,500 tech-

---

* In the 1976 revision of his classic 1956 book, *The Stress of Life*, Selye reveals that in the days when he was fighting the battle to make the term "stick" to the phenomenon he was studying and writing about, his English was less than perfect. Had he to do it over again, he suggests, he would use the word "stress" to represent the cause and "strain," the effect. That way, the engineering and medical meanings of stress would be similar. Today, of course, we are stuck with "stressor" as the cue (cause) and "stress" as the result. This lack of parallel linguistic structure between engineering and medical uses of the word "stress" sometimes leads to confusion, especially among careless pop-psych writers.

137, 240

nical medical articles. By his own count, he had the world's largest stress library, boasting 110,000 titles! Small wonder he is referred to as *the* Dean of Stress Research.

Early in Selye's medical studies, he became interested in understanding exactly what it meant to "be ill." As a student, he noticed that, regardless of the specific disease, illness, injury, or trauma the body suffers, there are a number of common responses.

Later, in his own laboratory, Selye saw that regardless of the damage he imposed on experimental animals, a peculiarly consistent, general pattern, or "syndrome," of responses accompanied the specific injury responses. Whether he exposed his lab rats to extremes of heat or cold, excessive X-ray irradiation, physical abuse, prolonged immobility, forced exercise, or traumatic surgery, the same three general responses were always present. In every case, he found: considerable enlargement of the adrenal cortex—the outer surface of the adrenal glands; intensive shrinking of the thymus, the spleen, and the lymph nodes—all of which are related to the cleansing of body fluids; and bleeding and ulceration in the stomach lining and the duodenum, the uppermost part of the intestine.[6]

Selye eventually called this response pattern the stress syndrome. Early in his career, Selye wrote about the body as a machine that responds automatically to trauma. Until the 1960s, he took only minor interest in the emotional, cognitive, and voluntary behavioral aspects of stress response. He considered psychological stressors in his work, but he looked mostly at the body costs of being stressed and ignored the psycho-emotional costs. That's not a criticism or a discount, just a fact. What Selye did, he did better, more creatively, and more thoroughly than anyone ever before. His contributions to our understanding of stress were enormous.

Further research showed Selye that the body's response to stress changes over time. That is, the longer the stress persists, the more likely it is that the body's response will change. Selye documented a three-step pattern he called the general adaptation syndrome.[7]

1. *Alarm Stage*. When the body is initially stressed, it responds with an alarm reaction; it mobilizes. This mobilization

is basically the activation of fight/flight, though Selye never used that term. This is also the stage Wolf and Wolff studied in their work with Tom. Selye referred to this stage as "the bodily expression of a general call to arms of the defensive forces of the organism."

2. *Resistance Stage.* After a persistent and prolonged exposure to the stressor or stressful situation, the body begins to resist its own alarm reaction and, in a sense, acts as if the stressor is no longer present. The body begins regenerating itself: blood returns to a normal density and chemical composition, body weight increases, and adrenaline begins to return to a normal level. The adrenals even begin to warehouse adrenaline again.

3. *Exhaustion Stage.* If the stress continues too long, or if the stress load increases substantially, the body goes on alert again and pumps adrenal-gland hormones into the system. This second arousal reaction continues until the defenses are drained and the body ceases to have any adaptive response capability—hence, Selye's emphasis that stress is a disease of adaptation: "We are just beginning to see that many common diseases are largely due to errors in our adaptive response to stress rather than to direct damage by germs, poisons or life experience. In this sense, many nervous and emotional disturbances, high blood pressure, gastric and duodenal ulcers, and certain types of sexual, allergic, cardiovascular and renal derangements appear to be essentially diseases of adaptation."[8]

If stress continues unabated, the only remaining outcome is death. In a sense, the body becomes its own worst enemy.

Selye pointed out some important cautions regarding the general adaptation syndrome. First, few people ever reach the exhaustion stage; those who do rarely experience true exhaustion long enough to significantly damage their bodies. Arctic explorers, people trapped in very hostile physical environments, excessively abused P.O.W.s, ruthlessly tortured political prisoners, and a few extreme athletes—the ones who attempt to swim around the world—do experience the deep and prolonged exhaustion that leads to irreparable physical damage and death. But in normal living, people tend to only experience exhaustion in mild forms and in small, short doses. They do, however, commonly experience the alarm and resistance stages. Second, Selye emphasized that even when people do experience the exhaustion stage, they are seldom in any immediate danger—unless, of course, they choose not to, or can't, heed the built-in warning to slow down.

As an example of how the general adaptation syndrome works, let's take a run with George:

GEORGE is a recreational distance runner, a jogger. In this scenario, he is about to take part in the "Over-the-Hill-Gang" 10 Kilometer Fun Run. First, George warms up by stretching, jogging about, or otherwise doing something to get into it. Though he isn't aware of it, warm-up activities are essentially a way to put the body on alert, to purposely induce a mild alarm reaction and signal the physical systems that increased activity is coming.

Heart beating quickly, adrenaline pumping into the system, aroused and alert, George hears the gun and sprints off with the pack. During the first mile, he probably settles down and begins to run at an even, regular pace. Eventually, he settles in rather comfortably for the run. George trots along feeling great, body working at maximum efficiency, leg muscles and cardiovascular system pumping along at an even pace. George is experiencing the resistance stage.

Eventually, though, he begins to tighten up. His running begins to be effortful and he notices himself tiring. This is the onset of the exhaustion stage. At this point, George consciously "pulls himself together." His body goes back on alert and he gets that second wind. Things feel great again—for a short time.

However, George's legs soon begin to feel heavy. Perhaps his stomach cramps. His skin may get "hot and cold," his heart may seem to be pounding irregularly, and oxygen may get tough to come by. George begins sucking wind, as the horse trainers say. He is becoming exhausted.

Let's assume George has been training by running two or three miles every other day for the last two months. Suppose also, as is quite likely, that it's at about the four-mile post of the race that the exhaustion stage sets in. George probably won't do too much damage to his body by finishing the race. In fact, it may be beneficial to his overall fitness to push himself a bit. At worst, he might experience sore legs and a stiff back for a couple days, and he might feel tired the rest of the race day. He might even have a headache the next morning, but that's about all the damage, assuming he is in normal, good health.

Suppose, though, that George is under the illusion that one must "face" and "run through" pain. He decides that if a little pain is good for you, a lot will be better. So not only does he finish the original 6.2 miles but runs another 10 miles. The chances are pretty good that George is heading for heavy-duty trouble. He could definitely overtax his body's adaptive systems and damage his vital organs or tissues.

For a less sweaty example of the general adaptation syndrome, take the case of making an important group sales presentation:

ON the way to the call, you "psych-up." You mentally rehearse your tap dance and give yourself a pep talk. You get to the call, do some relationship building, provide some scene setting, and then settle down to work. You rise to your feet and begin your presentation. You feel tingly, alert, conscious of your "upness." Translated back to Selye's terms, you're in the alarm stage.

But fifteen minutes into your presentation you relax your shoulders, your mouth stops being dry, and you feel in the groove. Of course, you are still alert, still feeling that extra bit of aliveness that always accompanies the challenge of a tough call, but you definitely feel in control. You've entered the resistance stage.

Suppose your presentation lasts another two hours. You're beginning to wear out. Now comes the famous "Any more questions?" of the meeting, and some bright guy says, "I'm convinced. Why don't we go pitch my boss!" Of course, his boss has never heard of you or your proposal and thinks that your "gatekeeper"—the joker you mistakenly thought to be the decision maker but who isn't—is a bit of an easy mark for salespeople. Net-net. You have to start all over. But you're tired and operating on only three cylinders. Mr. Boss, of course, has a "few" questions for you, beginning with, "Now, just why do you think we need *your* help in this matter, Mr. Vendor?" You dig in, find a second wind, and are off and running—right into the exhaustion stage, that is.

If a good night's sleep or a couple days' of rest bring you back up to par, you've simply experienced the stress phenomenon. And so what? But suppose the stressful situation continues unabated and you feel doomed to ever-increasing exhaustion. For example, you've done such a beautiful job with the group sales presentation, surprise and all, that your boss decides you should make all the group presentations for the office. Not only that, but he schedules one for every other day of the next month. Then you're likely to experience a level of stress that can become dysfunctional, and you're potentially headed for the physical problems so well documented by Selye's pioneering work—a lifetime of work that has brought him to conclude:

> Life is largely a process of adaptation to the circumstances in which we exist. A perennial give-and-take has been going on between one living being and another ever since the dawn of life in the prehistoric oceans. The secret of health and happiness lies in successful adjustment to the ever-changing conditions on this globe; the penalities for failure in this great process of adaptation are disease and unhappiness.[9]

3

FINDING THE MIND-BODY CONNECTION: EQUAL RIGHTS FOR THE PSYCHE

THE final piece to the stress puzzle is the mind-body link: What roles do our emotions, thoughts, and perceptions play in the way we experience and physically respond to stressful situations? We have seen that Cannon, Wolf and Wolff, Selye, and others acknowledged that the mind is an important factor in stress. But as physiologists and medical researchers, they were much more interested in the body as a machine. They tended to relegate the mind to the status of a picture window, through which impressions and sensations freely flowed much the way sensations of heat and cold flow through the skin.

To them, the role of the mind as a data processor and interpreter of events seemed to be of minor importance. This closely paralleled the attitude most medical practitioners once held toward psychosomatic, or mentally induced, physical illnesses. Certainly, common speech had long been flavored with expressions hinting at the mind-body connection. Armies "travel on their stomachs," people are able to "worry themselves sick," anger is credited with the ability to "stir the blood," and joy has the power to "make one weep." Love has been compared favorably with heart palpitations, fever, goose bumps, and pain. Obviously, everybody has an intuitive grasp of the relationship

31

between health or physical well-being and thoughts or emotions. The scientific study of this intuition has only just begun in earnest.

One of the earliest efforts to systematically study the relationship between mental stress and bodily response was conducted by a Czechoslovakian scientist. In one of the experiments, a group of young adults were placed in a room, instructed to solve a series of arithmetic problems in their heads, and report their answers to the scientist's assistants. The assistants, however, were instructed to chastise the subjects for their slowness in solving the problems and otherwise harass them about their performance.

The scientist measured the subjects' blood pressure and took blood samples immediately before and after the experiment. He found that blood pressure was significantly higher and the volume of blood circulating was significantly increased; an analysis of the pre- and post-experiment blood samples revealed much higher concentrations of adrenaline and other arousal hormones at the end of the experiment. This was solid evidence of a mind-body link. By the way, it was also pretty good evidence that job or task stress can be physically dysfunctional.

The next major event in the development of the mind-body link occurred during the Second World War. Two U.S. Army Air Force psychiatrists, Roy Grinker and John Spiegel, made careful and detailed observations of hundreds of young combat pilots. Their observations, published in 1945 in *Men Under Stress*, made a significant contribution.[1]

Key among Grinker and Spiegel's findings was the high degree of individuality they observed in stress responses and the progressive nature of the stress reaction. While previous medical stress research had focused on finding predictable patterns of physiological stress response, they found that the specific symptoms an individual manifests tend to be related to personality and early life experiences. According to their observations, a flyer who had lung trouble as a child, for instance, might be expected to develop lung trouble when under the severe prolonged stress of combat.

Whether the reason for that response has to do with a predisposing physical weakness of the lungs or is simply a learned "illness pattern" the individual is familiar with and uses to express stress is unclear but intriguing. By analogy, most child psychologists—and parents—are familiar with the missing tonsils syndrome. A youngster who has received considerable attention, sympathy, love, and chocolate ice cream before and after a tonsillectomy will occasionally develop a sore throat and need attention and more chocolate ice cream weeks or months after the tonsils are gone and the scar tissue has healed. The birth of a sibling or the looming threat of an upcoming spelling test have been known to occasion the onset of such mysterious sore throats. The point is that under stress any of us may return to an old illness to "express" or "exhibit" the distress we are feeling. But whether the illness is organic or functional, the illness is real and not imaginary.

Grinker and Spiegel's long-term, detailed personal observations of human beings living with the prolonged stress of war brought home the mix of psychological and physical stress reactions humans can experience.[2]

Their work, and subsequent work by psychologists and psychiatrists in VA hospitals, has been influential in establishing psychological disabilities as legitimate illnesses. Without this precedent, it is questionable whether topics such as stress could be discussed and dealt with as openly and honestly as they are today.

There are two more important research events to discuss, and then we will have covered what we need to know to understand the psychological effects of stress in the selling process. One of these studies concerns the effect of cognition (thinking) on stress and the other concerns behavior. Both arenas— thought and behavior—have significant impact on the origins and management of stress.

In the early 1960s, psychologists Stanley Schachter and Jerome Singer suggested that the way we respond to physiological arousal is, in large part, determined by what we think and believe about the situation and the way other people behave in the same situation.[3] One of their experiments makes the issue clear. Schachter and Singer injected a group of students with a solution the students were led to believe was a vitamin shot. The injections were, in fact, adrenaline. Some students were told the vitamin shots would cause side effects of heart palpitations and noticeable tremors, both of which are common with adrenaline. Others were told that they would experience itching and headaches, neither of which is an adrenaline side effect. A third group was told that the vitamin shots would have no side effects.

To complicate matters, the researchers asked each student to sit in a waiting room, under the pretext that he or she would shortly be given a vision test. During the wait, each student was joined in the waiting room by a "stooge," or confederate of the researchers, who acted either very angry or silly and giddy. Part of the time the stooge laughed and danced around the room, and part the culprit stalked about and finally made an angry display of tearing up a questionnaire he or she had been filling out.

When all the shots and stomping and dancing had finished, some important results were apparent. First, Schachter and Singer found that those students who had not been told to expect side effects from the shots—who had no way to explain the real physiological effects they experienced—described their own feelings in a way reflective of the behavior of the stooge. That is, students who had the shots but were given no information about side effects reported feeling angry if they were in the waiting room with an angry-acting stooge and happy if they were in the waiting room with a happy-acting stooge. In other words, the students who had no information, no set way to think about and explain what they were feeling and why they were feeling it, tended to attribute their feelings and actions to the influence of the "stooge," regardless of how the stooge behaved. Students who *were* told what to expect in the way of physiological side effects and feelings were more likely to feel what they were led to expect and not very likely to be influenced by the stooge.[4]

Schachter and Singer concluded that the emotions we feel are a product of both our physiological state and the way we learn to interpret that physiological state. When translated into the language of stress, that means that the way we respond to a stressor is dependent on more than just the changes that occur in our body. In other words, the way we perceive, interpret, and have learned to think about those changes is also very important.

The practical point here is that we can be inadvertently

"infected" by other people's stress. We are all, as Schachter and Singer demonstrated, very "suggestible." Simply observing the behavior of others can strongly influence our behavior and emotions. We can be stressed by being around stressed people. If two people are walking around the office at 9:00 A.M., wringing their hands over the news that the new sales manager is the company's answer to Simon Legree, they will have the entire office polluted with anxiety before lunch. And what shape do you suppose anyone from that office will be in for making a 2 P.M. call on a prospect?

Schachter was satisfied to suggest that first we are aroused and then, depending on what's going on in our heads or in the environment around us, we interpret the situation—and our feelings—as happy or sad, threatening or benign. Our next character in this cast, Dr. Richard Lazarus, was convinced that emotional reaction and bodily arousal follow our perception and appraisal of a situation.[5] He started with the simple observation that a person who gets cut while peeling a potato or whittling a whistle has a very different bodily response from someone on an operating table with his or her chest cut open for heart surgery. In the case of the cut finger, there's immediate body arousal. In the case of the anesthetized heart-surgery patient, there's no alarm reaction, no adaptation stage, no stress response at all.

Lazarus argued that consciousness and interpretation are critical to stress. Suppose you are walking through the zoo and a lion springs out of the bushes and pounces on a person not twenty yards from you. It doesn't take much imagination to picture yourself running away, heart pounding, limbs trembling, mouth dry, and pants wet. Now picture yourself in your living room, watching Marlin Perkins wrestle a Bengal tiger, or imagine yourself on a zoo walkway, passing a cage with a Bengal tiger. It isn't hard to guess at the contrast in your responses. A real lion, attacking someone in a real zoo in front of your eyes, would probably rate a 15 on a stress scale of 1 to 10! Watching Marlin Perkins do his deed with a 1,500-pound tiger may have a stress value of only 3 or 4; walking past the tiger cage at the zoo may be—at tops—a 2.

To test the role thoughts and interpretation play in stress,

Lazarus and Alfert, in a particularly graphic experiment, showed a film to three groups of college students, which depicted adolescent circumcision rites of a primitive tribe. The students were "wired" so their heartbeat and galvanic skin response (GSR) could be measured while they viewed the film. One group was shown the film with no sound track. A second group saw the film with a sound track explaining that the people in the film were actors and that no one was being hurt. A third group not only heard the disclaimer on the sound track but was told, before seeing the film, that the people were actors and the action bogus.

As you might expect, the third group—those who were told what they would be seeing as well as what to expect and think before viewing the film and again during the film—showed the least change in heartbeat and GSR.* All groups reacted to the first incident of circumcision on the film, but the third group recovered and quickly returned to normal. By the end of the film, this third group was quite relaxed. The other two groups continued to be shocked by the incidents. The group seeing the silent version reacted the most and was the only group that did not return to a lowered stress level by the end of the film.[6]

Emotions, argued Lazarus and colleagues, play a primary role in the length and strength of the stress experience. And emotions are very much related to an individual's interpretation of the events. This concept—that our attitudes about the events around us plays an important role in the stress we experience— is the focus of most current stress research, the research of the 1980s.

Suppose you're making a third call on a prospect. You've been sharing information and acting as counselor to the prospect in the hope that this value-added effort will make the difference you need to beat out the lower-priced competition. But Mr. Prospect has other ideas. "Sam, I can't thank you enough for all the help you've given me and my staff getting this program organized and moving in the right direction. Unfortunately, my boss is a price buyer, I know you have better quality but he could care less. I'm sorry, but that's the way it is."

---

* GSR, or galvanic skin response, is a measure of how well the skin conducts electricity. When we perspire we conduct more current. GSR is often used in lie-detection equipment.

Sam A might react this way:

INTERPRETATION: He thinks: "I'm a failure. I didn't get to the right people and I didn't make the right moves on Prospect's boss. Boy, did I screw up that one! What a dumbbell. I'm just a washout."

IMMEDIATE RESPONSE: Depressed, feels a sense of loss, a little panic, is angry at himself.

LONG-TERM RESPONSE: Sulking, withdrawn, continually tired feeling, wants to hide from everyone.

But there are alternative scenarios. Sam B might react this way:

INTERPRETATION: He thinks: "You S.O.B. I'll fix you for this. . . . What a louse you are!"

IMMEDIATE RESPONSE: Ears burn, stomach churns, shouts at Prospect. Slams doors, stalks out, throws things.

LONG-TERM RESPONSE: Writes scathing letters to nerd and to nerd's boss. Calls successful bidder and accuses him of duplicity with nerd. Ulcers, hypertension, bad relations with nerd's company.

Sam C might react still a third way:

INTERPRETATION: He thinks: "Aw nuts! Well, I did the best I could. That's the situation. Maybe I can get a referred lead out of this, anyway."

IMMEDIATE RESPONSE: Understanding of limitations of the situation. Disappointment. Conciliatory. Effort made to "keep door open."

LONG-TERM RESPONSE: Follows up later on referred lead aspect. Able to forget about incident and go on to greener pastures.

There is another important implication to this research. If our emotional response to situations is pretty much under the influence of the way we perceive, interpret, and think, we are not helpless in the face of stress. How we think, feel about, and interpret the events around us is under our control—or can be.

That means we can control our stress response. And the most recent research is beginning to show that the ability to control stress reactions through conscious, positive management of one mind-body connection can have far-reaching implications for our lives.

The Mind-Body-Health Connection

Today, the most energetic work on the mind-body-health connection is being done under the auspices of a field of study called psychoneuroimmunology (PNI). As that ungainly term, coined by Robert Adler of the University of Rochester Medical School, suggests, medical scientists are becoming increasingly convinced that the connection is real and important. In fact, researchers such as Joan Borysenko, a Harvard physician and founder of the Mind/Body Group at Boston's Deaconess Hospital, are increasingly sure that the power of the mind can be used to revitalize the body and cause it to fight back against not only stress but also such catastrophic disorders as cancer, herpes, and AIDS.[7]

In the early 1970s, two Texas clinicians, Carl and Stephanie Simonton, claimed that cancer patients they had taught mental visualization and simple relaxation techniques lived longer.[8] Today PNI researchers are increasingly convinced that the mind can be used to bolster and activate the body's immune system. Medical researchers have long known that strengthening the body's immune system produces positive effects on the body. What the PNI researchers are finding is that when ill people are coached in relaxation and positive mental imagery and when they take an optimistic, positive view of their future, over time they benefit in two ways. First, there is decreased pressure on the immune system. Many—if not most—of us respond poorly to the news of a catastrophic illness. We get mad. We get sad. We become depressed. We are stressed by the knowledge that we have a life-threatening condition. Our negative feelings about our situation put additional pressure on our immune system— on the body in general—and we become further susceptible to the ravages of the catastrophic disease. Positive thoughts and visualizations reduce our susceptibility.

The second benefit is that the body seems to make a "healing" response to a positive, optimistic mind-set. A University of Maryland research team found that the immune system of cancer patients who had regular mental-imagery sessions for a year produced more disease-fighting white blood cells and that these white blood cells accelerated the rate at which they attacked foreign bodies in the blood stream.[9] At Ohio State, senior citizens who were taught relaxation and guided-imagery techniques produced a special type of white blood cell that helps fight tumor growth.

So the latest from the research front is doubly hopeful. On the one hand, it is possible to free the body from the pressure not only of stressful reactions to both everyday situations and events but also to events as traumatic as learning that one has a life-threatening disease. And added to that is the surprising bonus of finding that the mind can very possibly play a role in strengthening and healing.

In the end, the lesson is that we can, indeed, turn the tables on our own natural reactions and learn not only to manage the stress we encounter in our day-to-day lives but to turn it to our benefit. It is, indeed, a very positive message.

The Mind-Body Connection for Fun, Profit, and Positive Performance

What Selye, Schachter, Lazarus, and the PNI researchers have been learning tells us a lot that bears on managing the stress of selling. We have built a simple three-step model, based on the foregoing research, to explain the process and dynamics of becoming stressed (see Figure 3-1). Understanding this simple model is an important part of learning to manage and control your stress.

Step 1: Something Happens

To start the "becoming stressed" process, something must act as a stress cue, or trigger. This something, this potential stressor, can be a thought or image that originates in your own mind, it can be a word or actions of others, or it can simply be a situa-

Figure 3-1. Sources of and responses to stress.

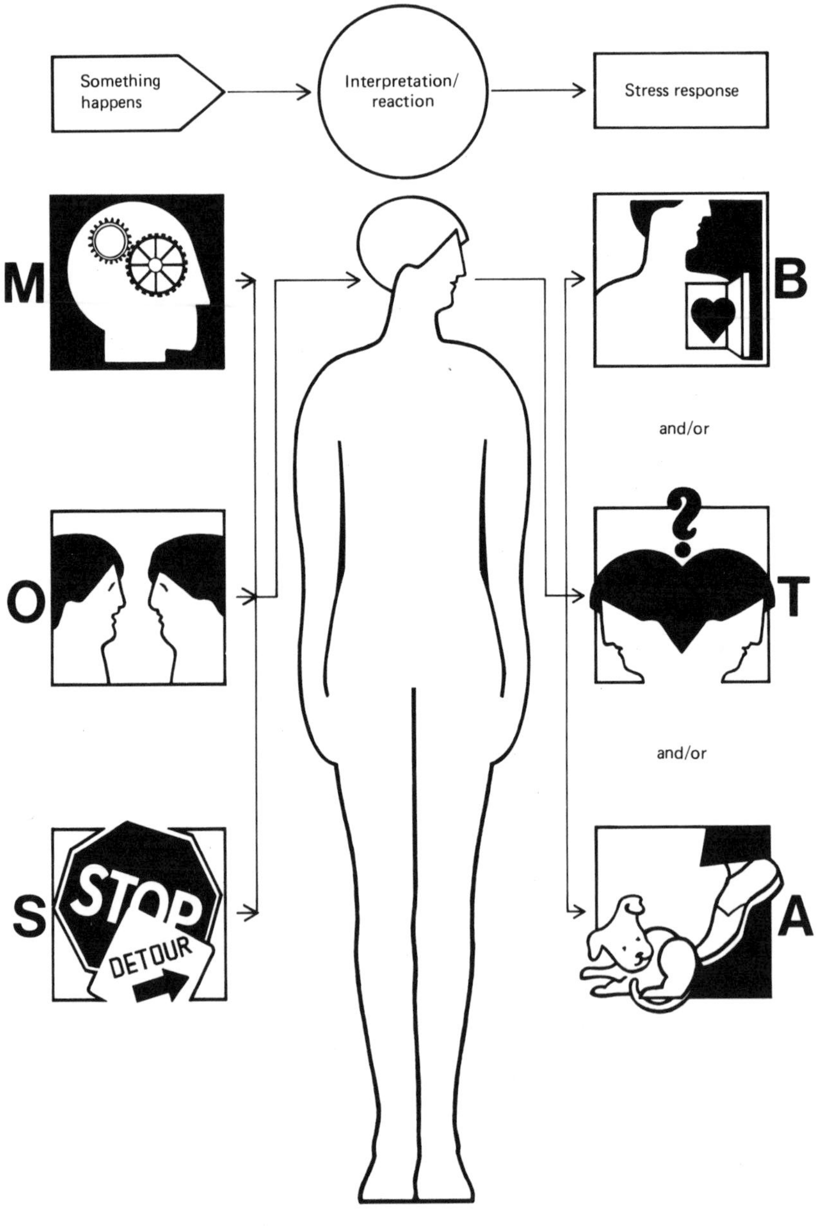

tion—something that just happens around you. We refer to these as:

M MYSELF   Your own thoughts, ideas, and images
O OTHERS   The actions, words, and emotions of other people
S SITUATION   Things that just happen around you but are somewhat impersonal to you, like a traffic jam

Let's suppose we have total access to the thoughts, actions, reactions, and emotions of one Thomas Browne, a sales rep for Amalgamated Industries:

IT'S Tuesday the 14th, the day Tom has set aside to make a Green Widget proposal to Ann Chandler, the purchasing agent for Basic Gears, Inc. His game plan is to leave the office at 9:15 A.M.; meet with Chandler from 10:00 A.M. till 10:30, as scheduled; drive back to the office; and about lunch time, start announcing to the world that he has a signed-on-the-dotted-line contract with Basic Gears, Inc., for 200,000 Amalgamated Green Widgets.

That's Tom's plan. But as with many plans, the story looks better on paper than happens in reality. Let's look at the step 1 part of the tragedy that is about to become Thomas's day.

ON the way to the office, Tom begins to think about his up-coming call on Chandler. He remembers how rude she can be with salespeople. And how she hates it when someone's late for an appointment. And how *really* tough she is to deal with when she has had a disagreement with her spouse, a peer, or the staff. That thinking is a *potential stress cue* generated solely from Tom's MYSELF (M).

Tom sidesteps the MYSELF trap, gets to the office, and zips around, collating the last copies of the proposal, to get ready for the Chandler meeting. The boss spies Tom and comes charging out of his office waving a copy of the Chandler proposal, breathing fire and bellowing, "What'd ya' think you're doing with this proposal? I told you we want to upgrade Basic Gear to yellow widgets this year. Change the proposal—*now!*" A potential stress cue originating from OTHERS (O) has just entered our hero's purview.

Let's give Tom an A+ for flexibility and suppose that he has sidestepped both the M and O stress cues and is now in his auto headed down Interstate 94 toward Basic Gears' world headquarters.

SUDDENLY a trailer truck, loaded with live turkeys on its way to the local processing plant, jackknifes thirty yards in front of Thomas's car. It's flapping wings, sliding cars, and pandemonium all over the Interstate. Tom slams on the brakes, the car swerves, he almost loses it in a skid, and comes to a stop mere feet from the overturned flatbed.

This is a definite candidate for an S, or SITUATIONAL, *potential stress cue.*

You undoubtedly noticed that we are calling these hypothetical happenings *possible* or *potential* stressors. That is because M's, O's, and S's don't automatically act as stressors. A potential stressor or stress cue only becomes a stressor as a result of step 2.

Step 2: The Mental Interpretation/Body Reaction Phase

Interpretation. How the mind evaluates events—how we perceive and interpret the threat potential of all the M's, O's, and S's we encounter day after day—determines to a large extent our stress reactions to these events. The "somethings" that happen to us—and to our friend Thomas—are potential stressors or stress cues until we think about them and interpret their meaning and personal significance.

If Thomas thinks about Ms. Chandler's nasty behavior toward salespeople and tells himself, "Yeah, she's a tough one all right, but those are the ones I *really* like to sell. That's a sale that *is* a sale. When I bag this one, I'll have really sold something. None of those 'order takers' could bag a big order from Basic. It takes a real pro like *me* to do that," he is using Chandler's potential behavior toward him as a cue for positive behavior, not a negative stress response.

If, however, Tom goes into the rest room at Basic Gears, straightens his tie, looks in the mirror, and says to himself, "Well, big fella, it's you and me against Chandler; and *personally*, I think we're gonna get clobbered," then Thomas is setting up the conditions for his thoughts, or MYSELF (M), potential *stress cues* to become stressors.

The same logic holds for the boss's bellowing and the highway accident. If Thomas interprets the jackknifed truck of turkeys as the funniest highway accident of the year, it is much less likely that a high-stress situation will ensue. Though Tom will be fight/flight aroused by the accident, the response will be much shorter than if Thomas interprets the accident as death narrowly avoided and he lets that thought run rampant through his mind for hours. A caution: Sometimes the interpretation of an M-O-S event is so fast we scarcely notice thinking about it. In truth, many interpretations are so ingrained and long-standing that basically they are conditioned reflexes.

Body Reaction. As you already know, the body's first response to threatening events, be they M's, O's, or S's, is the marshaling of the primitive fight/flight response Bernard, Cannon, Selye, and others investigated so thoroughly. Tom's thoughts about Chandler, the boss's behavior, and the brush with death on the freeway, when interpreted as threatening, fire the fight/flight response. And as we learned from the medical researchers, especially Selye, prolonged arousal—regardless of its magnitude—leads to step 3, the stress response.

Step 3: Stress Shows Up

The research suggests that people respond to continuous or intense activation in one or more of three ways:

1. Through our BODIES   B
2. With our THOUGHTS   T
3. Through our ACTIONS   A

Depending on the form they take, these reactions can, in fact, be stress reducing and can dispel the negative tension. However, they can rev you up even further and act as cues for producing additional negative stress. As Professor Lazarus showed with the students watching the circumcision-rites film, the longer some stress cues last, the more the emotional reaction and the higher the stress and tension become. But as he also showed in that experiment, the right amount and kind of information can dampen and control—and even eliminate—the stress response.

Now let's check on our friend Thomas to see how he looks, feels, and sounds now that the M's, O's, and S's have "gotten to him." Somehow, despite all the obstacles we've thrown in his path, Tom has made his way to the headquarters of Basic Gears, Inc.—just a little late—and is seated in Ms. Chandler's office, stressed to the gills. As "wired" as he is, Tom can react in any one, or all, of the three ways we discussed—B, T, or A.

One possible effect—or stress response—is that Tom's BODY will telegraph his "revved up" state. Sweaty palms, cotton mouth, jittery mannerisms are all possibilities; they are bodily responses any or all of which Thomas may manifest for the world—and Chandler—to see.

The second possible stress response—the almost invisible one—is what's taking place in Tom's mind, or THOUGHTS. He may sit there with Chandler talking and listening, but with his mind miles away. He could be ruminating over the near miss on the highway or dialoguing with himself about the boss's autocratic behavior. Regardless of which he does, he will surely miss the subtleties of Chandler's part of the discussion. He will probably be so "into his own head" that he will miss buying signals he would ordinarily pick up on in a flash.

We know a salesman who was going through a difficult divorce. He reported that even in the presence of an important customer his mind was constantly filled with "Janey, Janey, *why are you doing this to me?*" and "I'm blowing this sale, Janey, and it's all your fault. Why can't I concentrate?" At one point he even caught himself discussing his marital consternations with prospects. Though extreme, the occurrence of thoughts that are irrelevant and detrimental to the task at hand are as common as maladaptive somatic or body symptoms.

The third possible stress response is an ACTION, or behavioral outcome. An ACTION stress response could be as simple as rapid speech and telegraphic sentences or as complex as suddenly becoming accident prone, stumbling over lint on the carpet, kicking over the presentation easel, dropping handout materials in the parking lot, or spilling coffee on the client's desk. And, of course, the worst response of all is the one wherein Tom hears his customer suggest that yellow widgets cost too much and his response is to fly off the handle and give the buyer a piece of his mind.

What are the effects on the sale? When the stress is low-level and the customer's need for the product or service high, sometimes no harm is done. The buyer may have a passing thought about Tom's odd behavior, but that's all. At other times, the bumblings of a highly stressed salesperson can snatch defeat from the jaws of victory. At the extreme, an irreparable breach can develop between buyer and seller.

Step 4: The Sometimes Step

There is a possible fourth step in the becoming-stressed process. Sometimes a stress response boomerangs, acting as a cue for yet another stress response. This negative boomerang effect sets into motion a spiral, or stress chain. Each stress response becomes a *potential stress cue*, forging the next link in the stress chain. This violence-begets-violence cycle is shown in Figure 3-2.

Let's raise the curtain on the final act of our "Poor Thomas" melodrama and watch the stress cycle destroy his relationship with his customer. As the scene opens, Tom is going into the meeting with Chandler highly stressed, a little shaky, and not in complete control of his concentration skills. But let's soup it

Figure 3-2. The boomerang effect.

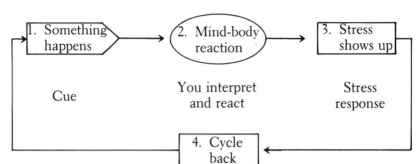

up some more. Say, Tom gets the clumsies and drops his proposal, spills his coffee, and trips on Chandler's rug. Worse yet, his mind keeps recycling thoughts about how Chandler hates salesmen, how the boss made him change the proposal from green widgets to yellow widgets at the last minute, and how Chandler is going to toss him out the door on his behind.

Chandler knows her lines and plays her part well. She doesn't go for the proposal and instead gives Thomas a lecture about being on time and the value of an asthetically pleasing proposal, and she tells him not to come back until he is ready to make a reasonable proposal for green widgets. Thomas leaves the office with his heart beating in his throat, extremely upset by both the outcome of the interview and the prospect of being chewed out again by the boss. On the way back, Thomas gets stuck in traffic. The result? Tom now has a whole new set of potential stress cues, the dressing down from Chandler, the mental image of the dressing down that the boss is surely going to deliver, and the traffic jam. The net result is more boomerang and more stress response. This little melodrama, wherein a stress response becomes a potential stress cue and leads to even more stress for Thomas, is the classic stress cycle on parade. Its not uncommon and it's not easy to avoid.

Drip, Drip, Drip vs. Crash, Boom, Bang

We discussed earlier two kinds of stress situations. One—the stress-event situation—is when something clearly happens that triggers the three-step process:

stress cue → interpretation/reaction → and stress response

That's what we just detailed using Thomas as the example. We also mentioned the slow seeping, or "drip, drip," kind of stress. The major difference between the two situations is that the drips accumulate slowly, to the point where a noticeable stress response takes place. Before there is an observable stress response, however, the potential stress cue, as well as the interpretation/reaction part of the system, is in effect.

There definitely are both psychological and physiological events occurring. They are, however, only slightly above and beyond the normal pressures and responses of living, so there is no obvious or observable stress response. After a period of continued "insult," they eventually lead to a stress response others can notice or that dramatically interferes with performance. Look at it this way. One or two or thirty or even a hundred drops of water hitting the same spot on a marble slab make no noticeable impact. But keep that dripping up till 10,000, 100,000, or 1 million drops have dripped and there is a hole in the marble. Drip stress acts the same. We can all shrug off a slightly surly waiter or waitress; weather an occasional abrasive remark by a colleague or loved one; and not get too bent out of shape from stepping in a puddle on the way to an important meeting. It is only when these insults, inconveniences, and nasty little breaks continue for a long time that they finally take their toll and kick in the process of:

full cue → interpretation/reaction → response-cycle back

The Punch Line

We promised not to tell you more about stress than you wanted or needed to know.† We suspect that we are pretty close to that threshold, so it is time to compress this information and get to the punch line. The following summary should be helpful for remembering the most essential facts about stress:

† For those who have an interest in knowing more about medical aspects of stress, Appendix A contains the answers to ten questions most frequently asked about stress and health issues.

1. *Stress is inescapable:*

- Everyone experiences stress. The total absence of stress has a technical medical term—death! Stress is a product of living and striving.
- Too little stress can be as harmful or aggravating as too much. Many of us rely on hobbies and recreation to add stress to our lives. (Sky divers, athletes, and stockbrokers may not be teched, but for sure the zest they look to add to their "you only go around once" way of life is a greater dose of stress than a glass of Bud.)

2. *Stress is personal:*

- Events that stress one person may please another.
- How a person reacts to stress depends on a number of social, hereditary, and learned factors.
- We all have different stress-tolerance levels. Some of us can handle more stress than others. Regardless of where you start, your stress tolerance can be increased by practice.

3. *Stress is circular or cyclic:*

- Once stress starts, it has a tendency to grow and carry on. It has real momentum. But it isn't a perpetual-motion machine; it just feeds on itself.
- Being stressed and tense can lead to hollering at a client or co-worker. The hollering can lead to self-deprecation and devaluation, thus act not just as an outcome but as a cue as well, adding fuel to the stress fire.

4. *Stress can dramatically influence behavior:*

- A positively stressed athlete runs faster, jumps higher, and endures longer during competition than during practice.
- A negatively stressed athlete panics, using the energy needed for performance in such nonproductive activities as worry, anger, and raging self-doubt.

- A positively stressed salesperson is alert, confident, and able to solve client problems creatively.
- The negatively stressed salesperson is touchy; he blows up at friends, family, and buyers, and gives up on tough cases; he asks wrong questions, doesn't "hear" answers, fails to read client feedback, and generally blocks the use of the sales skill and knowledge he possesses.

5. *Stress can be an asset or a liability:*

- Stress in the right amounts and when properly managed can motivate, increase good feelings about yourself, and prime you for a good performance with a prospect or client.
- Stress that's too intense, lasts too long, and goes on unmanaged can debilitate. Negative stress can precipitate bodily disorders, worry, anger, and self-doubt. As a precipitator of bodily disorders, it can lead to ulcers, hypertension, and heart disease. As a precipitator of negative thoughts and attitudes, it can shut down creativity, interfere with problem solving, and lead to a negative self-concept and, eventually, withdrawal from selling altogether.

6. *Stress can kill you or cure you:*

- Stress, especially combined with illness or disease, can be life threatening.
- Stress that adds to physical disability and the energy drain required to combat a serious illness can be more debilitating than either alone.
- Using the mind-body connection in a positive fashion can not only defuse stress but also add a positive weapon to the disease-fighting arsenal.

A construction foreman attending a stress-management workshop summarized the stress balancing act beautifully. "I get it," he observed after hearing the "stress and you" story:

It's like when we build one of them suspension bridges.

If the wires that support the bed are stretched too tight, they snap and the bridge falls down. If the wires are too loose, they don't support nothin' and it falls down. The trick is to get the tension just right. Then you got a bridge.

To get from where you are to where you want to be sometimes requires a bridge—a bridge of good performance and positive action. When the tension is just right, that bridge between you and your clients, you and your goals, you and your loved ones stands up. The traffic flows, and you reach those things you want on the other side. It's all in knowing how to string the wires.

4

IDENTIFYING THE STRESSORS IN PROFESSIONAL SELLING

W E have been preoccupied with giving you a clear and concise picture of what stress is, where it comes from, and how it effects you—in general. Awareness—knowledge—of just what the stress problem is and what you can expect when stress mounts up is an important first step in gaining control of the stress in your life. Defining the problem is almost always the hardest part of any problem-solving effort. It's time to home in on the unique problems of stress in selling.

In Chapter 3, we cite the work of a number of experts dealing with the medical and psychological aspects of stress. From here on, you are the expert. Most of the testimony in this chapter has come from your colleagues who sell for a living. It contains things sales professionals have told us about stress during workshops, on questionnaires and tests, in focus groups, and in one-on-one less formal settings. It also contains our insights gained from traveling with salespeople, making sales calls with them, and watching and listening as they went about their business.

If we have done our job, you will see your reflection in this chapter. The ideas and self-tests are feedback from you; they are about you, filtered through us. Our goal was plainly and simply to stand in your shoes, discover your needs, and hit your hot button—to do those things you have shown us are important when one person attempts to communicate with another.

Compared to Whom?

FACT: Professional selling is *not* the most stressful occupation. Health-care professionals, air-traffic controllers, accountants, big-city police, and—believe it or not—waiters and waitresses all report more on-the-job stress than do salespeople. So, although there are times when it may not feel that way to you, there are a few tougher, or at least more stressful, ways to make a living. But the stresses and stressors of selling are unique. We believe that selling, in some ways, has a more detrimental long-term effect than all but one or two of the extremely stressful occupations.

In a survey of 2,800 dentists, conducted in conjunction with *Dental Economics* magazine, for example, dentists ranked *patients experiencing pain or discomfort* as the situation most likely to make the dentists experience the emotional and physical arousal of stress. Only slightly less stress-inducing to these same dentists was having a patient in the chair who squirms, spits, and moves the tongue about (referred to as tongue play) while they try to work in the patient's mouth.[1] In other words, dentists report that they are most stressed when their patients are in pain or are behaving in a manner that is likely to cause the dentist to cause the patient avoidable pain. So, all those jokes about dentists and pain aside ("I'd never let my daughter marry one. Who wants a son-in-law who can make your mouth feel like it has a hernia!"), your dentist is as concerned about your experiencing pain as you are.

Obviously, the stressors in selling are totally different from those in dentistry. In a study of 375 Million Dollar Round Table (MDRT) insurance salespeople,* we found that the event most likely to cause these crème de la crème insurance pros to feel stressed is *losing an old and valued client.* Our MDRT sample ranked this situation as the number 1 stressor they encounter, and they did so 20 percent more frequently than the number 2 stressor we found in this study, *having no active prospects.* This

---

* The surveys were filled out by MDRT members at their 1979 national convention in Chicago. The data were subsequently published in *Round The Table* magazine.

response was selected out of a group of fifteen events or situations suggested as most stressful. One MDRT insurance agent explained to us the significance of losing an old client:

> Look, the goal in life-insurance selling is to have a lot of policies in force. That's your income base. It's like coupon clipping or drawing interest on savings. When you lose one of those people, you've lost part of your capital. It's like having your house burn down and finding out your homeowner's isn't any good. But it also means that you haven't been servicing the account. You didn't even get a chance for a counterproposal. Somebody or something unsold your sale. It's like losing a valuable family heirloom ring overboard when you're at high sea. You've lost something of both economic and emotional value. It's a credibility and an integrity issue, and that really hurts.

Different Strokes for Different Folks—Sometimes

Just as the stressors for the dentist and MDRT groups differ, there are also differences in specific stressors among different kinds of selling. People who sell intangibles and services—like life insurance—report their top ten stressors somewhat differently from those listed by photocopy-machine or liquor salespeople. Note, though, that these differences aren't the "night-and-day" dissimilarities we noted between the dental and MDRT groups. Salespeople are more alike than different, but some of the differences are revealing.

For instance, *home and family pressures* is a more significant stressor for salespeople who spend an average of three nights a week away from home than it is for those who spend less than three nights a month away from home. Both groups, however, rank *home and family pressures* among their top five stressors.

Let's identify *your* important stressors. The following exercise will start you on the road to analyzing and understanding your stressors and stress patterns.

EXERCISE 2. Identifying Your Top Ten Stressors

What are *your* stressors? You'll be making a detailed analysis of your personal stressors and your stress tendencies in Part Two, but to give you a start and to satisfy initial curiosity, here's a list of fifty events, situations, and problems that salespeople often report as stress producing. Go through the list quickly and put an X next to any item that has been related to some noticeable amount of tension for you in the past year. Then go back through the list and circle the X's next to the ten items you believe to be associated with a significant amount of stress in your life during the past *six months*. In making your selection of these ten stressors, consider both intensity and duration. If an item is low in intensity but constantly present, you may want to select it. After you have finished, compare your list of stressors with the list on pages 56–57.

_____   1. Being late for an appointment.
_____   2. A prospect who is late or stands you up.
_____   3. Making a presentation to someone you know (or suspect) is not the decision maker.
_____   4. Not feeling well.
_____   5. Not being well prepared.
_____   6. A prospect who allows many annoying interruptions during the sales call.
_____   7. Knowing your prospect (or customer) is not listening to you.
_____   8. Deliveries to your customers that are embarrassingly slow.
_____   9. Having just made an error in judgment.
_____ 10. Preparing to make a cold call.
_____ 11. Losing an important sale.
_____ 12. Being given a new sales territory.
_____ 13. A new sales manager having just been appointed.
_____ 14. A favorite product/service having just been discontinued.

_____ 15. A conflict between what you see as customer needs and company policy.

_____ 16. A sales quota having just been established.

_____ 17. Personal production that is low.

_____ 18. A buyer (customer) who requests price concessions.

_____ 19. Your performance being evaluated.

_____ 20. A customer who complains that your product/service fails to perform as promised.

_____ 21. An argument with your sales manager.

_____ 22. Knowing your production is too low to win an important sales contest.

_____ 23. Disputes with other salespersons.

_____ 24. Working more hours than are desirable.

_____ 25. Home or family pressures that affect your job performance.

_____ 26. Company policy that must be defended to a customer.

_____ 27. Having to counteract serious competition.

_____ 28. Company policy that is changed suddenly.

_____ 29. Losing an old, valued customer (buyer).

_____ 30. A new product or product line that must be introduced.

_____ 31. A need in your job for constant travel.

_____ 32. Not enough support from the sales manager.

_____ 33. Low morale in the company.

_____ 34. Insufficient sales training.

_____ 35. Unnecessary or excessive paperwork.

_____ 36. Your company offering a low rate of commission, salary, and/or bonus.

_____ 37. Others leaving you out of decision making that directly affects your sales effort.

_____ 38. Doing things you know are wrong to make a sale.

_____ 39. Not receiving enough recognition for your sales efforts (performance).

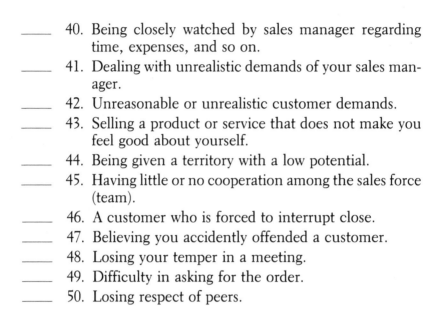

_____ 40. Being closely watched by sales manager regarding time, expenses, and so on.

_____ 41. Dealing with unrealistic demands of your sales manager.

_____ 42. Unreasonable or unrealistic customer demands.

_____ 43. Selling a product or service that does not make you feel good about yourself.

_____ 44. Being given a territory with a low potential.

_____ 45. Having little or no cooperation among the sales force (team).

_____ 46. A customer who is forced to interrupt close.

_____ 47. Believing you accidently offended a customer.

_____ 48. Losing your temper in a meeting.

_____ 49. Difficulty in asking for the order.

_____ 50. Losing respect of peers.

Complete this exercise before going on. The information will be important to you in Part Two, when you pull the self-tests in Part One and develop your Personal Stress Profile.

Commonly Identified Sales Stressors

The following list was compiled by asking 400 salespeople (a statistically sound number), in a variety of industries from real estate to computer hardware, to perform approximately the same exercise you just completed. The major difference was that we also asked them to rank the high stressors from most to least stressful. (We rank your stressors in a special exercise in Part Two.) The fourteen stressors listed here are rank ordered, from most to least stressful, for these 400 salespeople. (The MDRT group is _not_ included with this group.)

1. Low personal production
2. Cold canvasing
3. Losing an old, valued customer/client
4. Home or family pressures

  5. Losing an important sale
  6. Poorly prepared for a sales call
  7. Late for an appointment
  8. Serious misunderstanding with prospect/customer
  9. Prospect/customer not listening
 10. Your product/service performs badly
 11. Conflict between customer needs and company policy
 12. Conflict with sales manager
 13. Performance evaluation
 14. Company morale

Each of these is an important stressor. After all, they were picked from the original list of fifty possible stressors. Rank ordering simply shows the relative importance of these known high stressors.

You probably found a number of your high stressors on the composite list. It would be surprising, however, if one or two of your stress hot buttons weren't missing. If you're in insurance or real estate, you might have had *Lawyer or accountant who kills sales* someplace in your top ten list. Automobile or photocopy-machine salespeople seldom have that stressor on their lists since they almost never encounter this third-party obstacle.

But beyond the differences in specific stressors in different markets and industries, there are some substantial similarities in the nature of selling pressures that transcend product, industry, income, education, territory, geography, race, sex, and age. These lead us to suggest that there are pressure points in selling that are more subtle and, in the long run, potentially more detrimental to job performance, health, happiness, and simple human survival than the pressures of dentistry, accounting, banking, bill collecting, or any of the other occupations we've studied "up close and personal," as Mr. Cosell might say. These pressure points are the subject of the next eight chapters.

Our Research and You

We've worked with a lot of sales pros and gathered a lot of formal and informal information from them over the last twenty years.

We've surveyed them, stress-rank ordered them, and conducted one-on-one interviews nationwide; in fact, we've gathered data in every possible mode. In the 1970s, male sales pros interviewed outnumbered females approximately five to one. In the 1980s, they outnumbered females about three to one. We believe this to be reflective of the makeup of the American sales force both then and now. There is no question that women have entered the ranks of this often exciting and usually better paying field in great numbers. The jury's still hung on whether and how this will change selling in the 1990s.

There is no question that some items are high stressors for every professional salesperson. Losing an old, valued customer, low personal production with no active prospects, and home and family pressures proved stressful across time and sex differences. Yet there were some differences between the seventies and the eighties.

Using the sales stress rank order presented in this chapter, we'd discovered a number of interesting interrelationships between stressful situations by 1979.

- Sales pros told us that they got very stressed when going against personal values to make a sale or when selling a product they didn't believe in.
- Low income and the intrusion of a competitor are both independent stressors. But they work together: The more money made, the less stressed you feel by competition.
- The better prepared for a sales call, the less concern with being "trapped" and unable to answer a customer's question (a function of training and time in the foxhole).
- The more change perceived in company policies, the more concern salespeople express over losing existing valued customers.
- The more travel required, the greater the concern about competition.
- The more conflict existing between company practice and customer need, the more stress felt before asking for an order.

Those things haven't changed in the eighties. Many items

are universal and timeless factors involved in direct selling. But there have been some new twists added.

- Men and women view home and family pressure as stressful, especially if there is a lot of travel involved. However, women tend to rate home and family pressures as among their highest stressors, while men tend to rate it—on average—two or more notches lower.
- The more you see yourself as unable to control or influence the factors affecting your life, the greater the accumulated stress and the more strongly you experience each stressor related to the issue.
- The use of and need for high tech sales equipment and paraphernalia, coupled with the amount and nature of paperwork, is rapidly becoming a high stressor of the next decade.

To sum up what we've learned, it seems that many of the circumstances sales pros find stressful are universal and timeless factors. Many of these factors are directly related to selling for a living; others seem to signal a change which has begun in earnest over the last decade. Home and family pressures, cited by men and women alike, seem to hit women especially hard when the pressures relate to their efforts at trying to manage many different life and work roles. Most women have two full-time jobs, one as a sales pro and the other as a homemaker. This may account for their reporting more role conflict stress.

The perceived inability to control or influence the things that affect your work and life may produce what we call the "treadmill effect." Here, sales pros see themselves as unendingly putting one foot in front of the other, eventually "numbing out" or looking for "excitement" and "control" in unhealthy or excessive ways.

High tech and paperwork issues, which include the use and misuse of a whole new array of recording and information-accessing options, increase stress levels. Many sales pros are thrust into the age of information and easy access for which they are not prepared or trained to handle.

STRESS AND CONTROL OF THE SALE, OR WHO'S IN CHARGE HERE?

D R. Neal Miller, a professor of psychology at Rockefeller University, has found evidence that a "sense of being in control" can decrease the physiological effects of stress. In an experiment performed several years ago, Miller exposed two groups of rats to repeated, painful electrical shocks. One group, however, was taught a bar-pressing routine for controlling the number of shocks received. By the end of the experiment, rats in both groups had received the same number of shocks, though the trained rats took a little longer to get their quota of zaps. Despite the fact that both groups had received the same number and intensity of shocks, the untrained group developed five times more stomach lesions—a malady similar to ulcers—than the group with the "control-the-zap" training.[1]

Miller concluded that, even for rats, there seem to be physical benefits to turning worry into positive action. Other researchers who have followed similar courses of study agree with Dr. Miller that taking some sort of positive action can reduce the unhealthful side effects of stressful situations. Doing something—almost anything—when you're in a tight spot is apparently one of those strategies that pays off.

Why is this finding important to selling? The idea of taking control is a very important one to people who sell for a living. Each of us has a set of beliefs or a life philosophy concerning the extent to which we have personal control over the events around us and, ultimately, control of our destiny. Julian Rotter believes that for some of us, our locus of control (LOC) and life philosophy are external and some of us have an internal LOC belief system.[2]

People described as highly external believe that luck and fate are important factors in their lives. They see forces and events over which they have no control as more important to winning and losing than personal effort. "How can I be expected to meet *that* quota with *this* product? It's out-of-date, too expensive, and the factory never delivers on time. What can *I* do?" Externals see a lot of truth in the lament voiced by the Duke of Gloucester in Shakespeare's *King Lear:* "As flies to the wanton boys, are we to the gods; They kill us for their sport."

People described as highly internal see themselves as controlling and shaping their own destiny. They believe they make their own breaks and create their own luck. To be able to say "I did it my way—with hard work and PMA [positive mental attitude]" is important to them. Internals are ready to agree with Shakespeare's Cassius when, in *Julius Caesar*, he lectures Brutus: "Men at some time are masters of their fates: / The fault, dear Brutus, is not in our stars, / but in ourselves, that we are underlings."

The Internal LOC Salesperson

It has been our experience that a high proportion of salespeople are internals; people who need to feel that they are in control of the world around them, actively influencing the people and events about them. The problem, of course, is that when everything is perking, the "take charge" salesperson is living up to his or her own expectations, feels in control, and feels good about him or herself. But when things are going poorly, the extreme internal LOC salesperson can be personally brutal and unforgiving. The extreme internal, used to attacking life, to being proactive rather than reactive, begins lashing out, trying to regain control. He or she increases the call rate, becomes aggressive with clients (and everyone else), takes courses, pours through tips-and-tricks books, and literally comes to the point where the tension is so steep that he or she will try anything to get back on top. And that's exactly what happened in the case of Paul the Pilfer. As Dr. Stern explains:

PAUL, a young, aggressive securities dealer whose income ran to six figures, was sent to me by his company. It seems that Paul had embezzled a great deal of money in the previous seven months. After working with Paul for three sessions, it became evident that his pilfering could be directly related to stress factors.

When Paul had a month of low production, he would start juggling figures around. He viewed himself in charge of what happened in his life and suffered severe loss of self-esteem when his sales strategies didn't work out. Paul seemed to truly believe that no one need have a slump if he or she was a "super salesman," which he viewed himself to be. His mounting tension acted as a barrier to the effective utilization of the skill and training he possessed. Paul's reaction to the stress was to "borrow" from Peter to pay Paul. Only this time an internal audit tripped him up.

Paul's company wanted to keep this generally productive, high-powered salesman, so they were willing to invest in his coming to see me. I taught Paul how to keep his mounting stress in check when the monthly figures were below his expectations. He also began to wrestle with the erroneous belief that one "should" always be able to control things.

Eventually, Paul was able to survive a dry month without panicking and doing something foolish (and illegal). He came to accept the fact that low production months do occur—for everyone—occasionally, and that they are often followed by peak production months. Believing, and acting on this belief, put an end to the problem.

Are You an "Outtie" or an "Innie"?

A number of tests are available to measure Locus of Control orientation. You can get a feel for your external/internal orientation by using the ten-item scale that follows. This scale isn't as accurate or as rigorous as the tests and measures developed by Dr. Rotter and others, but it will give you a feel for your LOC orientation, or life philosophy.

Immediately following the survey is a discussion of how the internal and external function in the sales situation and how each type manifests and manages stress. We have met successful internal LOC salespeople and successful external LOC reps. They succeed simply by using different strengths.

EXERCISE 3. Internal-External Belief Inventory

Instructions

Taking this self-quiz is a two-step process. Below are ten pairs of statements (A through J). For each pair, *first* decide which statement of the pair you agree with; *second*, decide how strongly you agree with the statement. Indicate the strength of your agreement by circling one of the numbers under the statement you agree with.

EXAMPLE:

X	
I am master of my fate.	A great deal of what happens to me is a matter of luck.
6 5 4	3 2 1
Strongly Agree Agree Agree Somewhat	Agree Somewhat Agree Strongly Agree

In the example, the person has chosen the right-hand statement, "A great deal of what happens to me is a matter of luck." This person has also circled the 2, indicating that she *agrees somewhat* with the statement. Remember, first decide which statement in the pair you agree with and *then* circle the number

under the statement that best indicates *how much* you agree
with it.

	A	
When I'm right I can convince others.		It's silly to think that one person can change another's attitudes.
6 5 4		3 2 1

	B	
Success depends a lot on inherited abilities, the right schools, and the right family.		In our society, a person's success depends on drive, hard work, and developed skill.
1 2 3		4 5 6

	C	
People generally get the respect they deserve in this world.		Often an individual's worth passes unrecognized, no matter how hard the person tries.
6 5 4		3 2 1

	D	
Capable people who fail to succeed have only themselves to blame.		Without the right breaks, hard work and genius often go unrewarded.
6 5 4		3 2 1

E	
Success in world leadership is a matter of being the right person, in the right place, at the right time.	Events and circumstances have little to do with world-class leaders rising to prominence.
1 2 3	4 5 6

F	
People who experience "bad breaks" usually bring them on through mistakes they made.	Many of the things that make a person's life unhappy have a lot to do with bad luck.
6 5 4	3 2 1

G	
High income in sales is due in large part to having the right product and the right territory to sell it in.	Earning a top living in sales requires good skills, dedication, and a lot of hard work.
1 2 3	4 5 6

H	
You can be the nicest person in the world and there are still going to be some people who won't like you.	People who can't get others to see that they are OK haven't developed good communication skills.
1 2 3	4 5 6

	I	
You pretty much inherit your personality traits.		Life experiences and exposure to options determine people's temperaments.
1 2 3		4 5 6

	J	
In selling, you have to raise the fever and make your presence felt.		Many sales are made by "hanging in tough" and waiting for the right opening.
6 5 4		3 2 1

Scoring and Interpreting. Add and total all ten of the numbers you circled. Put the total here. ☐

If your total was 20 or less, you tend to be an *external*.

If your total was 50 or greater, you tend to be an *internal*.

If your total was between 20 and 50, you are probably an *internal* when you make the sale and an *external* when you lose it.

Internals, Externals, Selling, and Stress

The importance of the internal/external belief system lies in its relationship to your sales performance and your approach to the tensions of selling and living. According to the research, your internal/external orientation does indeed affect your sales effectiveness, your health and happiness, the way you are stressed, and how you can best manage that stress. Let's see how.

Ten Things to Know About Your
Life-Control Philosophy

A note of caution: Most of the research on the internal and external beliefs focuses on extremes: those at the limits of either the external or internal. Most of us aren't that way. People tend to be just a bit to one side or the other of center. Extremes are exaggerations of tendencies. Don't be surprised if you see a little of both viewpoints in yourself. Now, on to the ten ways an internal or external belief system relates to your stress, happiness, selling, and health.

1. *Persuasion Skills.* Internals tend to be better persuaders. They believe that they can talk almost anybody into anything. When the client says no, they turn on. They don't even have to believe what they are arguing for. The down side is that internals prefer to win the battle and not worry about the war. They won't comply with a client's view without first being convinced of it and personally accepting it.

Externals must be convinced that what they argue for is "truth." And they tend not to argue even then. But they are very supportive of their clients. They can go along with almost anything the client says and not worry about it. They can comply with the customer without accepting his or her viewpoint.

Under stress, the extreme Mr. Internal will beat the customer over the head with a proposal he planned to sell and end up losing the sale. Mr. External will promise the client the moon and deliver cream cheese.

The stress connection is straightforward. When an internal meets sales resistance, he or she puts coal on the fire and attacks. Both customer and salesperson get stressed. An external doesn't fight very well or very often, so he or she meets objections with acquiescence or caves in. Thus, the external stands caught between customer and company, looking for an open window.

2. *Reaction to Stress.* Internals react to stressful situations by attacking and making everyone miserable. The internal doesn't always "feel" that stress or read it in others. The internal can escalate the discomfort of the situation, heating the place

up very quickly. If the customer turns him or her off with a "not if your product was the only one in captivity," the internal rationalizes the situation in this fashion: "This account isn't worth my effort. I've got better prospects down the road." Unfortunately, the internal is also whipped up by confrontation. The stress result is that the internal is highly susceptible to hypertension. The extreme internal is sometimes too much in control and holds the whole incident inside, letting it burn up stomach and heart.

The external reacts to stress by giving in, promising everything. The external will hang in tough with a low-potential prospect or small-potatoes customer, hoping that something, anything, will happen. When conflict between client and company mounts, or when the customer or boss or colleagues have dumped a big load of stress on the external, he or she just runs off, curls up, and hides. Stressed externals spend a lot of time sleeping, being tired, and working in a sleepwalk.

3. *Handling Failure.* Internals brush off failure and go running after a new bright bauble. They can even forget a failure totally. That, by the way, doesn't give the internal a chance to learn from his or her own experiences. And the penchant to race from flower to flower—without really smelling any of them—just aggravates the internal's tendency toward hypertension.

Externals have an elephant's memory of failure. They remember and they brood. And where the internal blows up, cuts, and runs, the external shrugs and hangs in. But since externals can't forget, won't split, and don't have the skills to talk themselves out of taking the problem personally, they tend to carry the problem around all day, getting more and more depressed and withdrawn.

4. *Influence of Others.* Internals and externals don't differ much in their willingness to go along with the crowd. But when experimenters like Julian Rotter have placed both types in a situation where they don't agree with majority opinion, or with what the group wants to do, and asked both to "put their money where their mouths are"—that is, to bet that they are right and the group is wrong—the internals take the bet and the externals

back off. Even when the externals do wager on their convictions, they risk much less than internals do.[3]

In terms of stress, both types feel the pressure of being in opposition with the group, but in different ways. Internals are angry at being unable to control opinions. Externals, on the other hand, feel both the tension of waffling between their own opinion and the group's. Equally distressing is the feeling of being out on that limb alone. Does it sound like the external may be more susceptible to stress and affected by more types of stressors than the internal? In a sense, internals cause trouble and externals buy trouble, tension, and anxiety from others.

By the way, if internals perceive that the group is trying to pressure them into its way of thinking, a heck of a fight can ensue. The external might "go along to get along," but at the price of never trusting the people in the group again. Both the internal's explosion and the external's pocket of paranoia are stress inducing.

5. *Work Group Preferences*. Internals and externals have different preferences in work groups. To be specific, externals enjoy, and are more comfortable in, structured groups run by firm leaders. Internals prefer, and are happier with, unstructured groups and loose leadership. If the external or internal gets in the "wrong group" at a client meeting, a stress cycle can start. First, the sales rep gets uncomfortable with the group process. The external withdraws and looks too passive to the client. The internal will try to take over the group, and that doesn't win many clients, either.

As a corollary to the meeting-style preferences, internals and externals have different likes in sales training experiences. Externals do better and are happier with classroom situations. They enjoy the people, respect authority, and need lots of feedback on how they are doing. Internals prefer self-directed study and self-measurement of progress: "Just point me in the right direction and move out of the way." Internals are much more aggressive in seeking out self-development experiences and opportunities, but they don't learn as much from a self-help seminar as an external does. Of course, the external, who isn't much of a joiner, isn't likely to be there, so he or she learns zero.

6. *Behavior in Sales Interviews.* In the sales interview, both internals and externals have tendencies that can potentially irritate a prospect. Externals share a lot of personal information, counting on friendship to help with the sale. The internal, however, shares very little of the personal. That can increase client tension and raise questions of trust and integrity. Most prospects need a sense of a sales rep's "interactive integrity"—trustability—before the two can do business. Also irritating and stressful to clients is the internal's desire to take his or her best shot and run. Equally tension raising is the external's propensity to hang around and try to make friends. Too much contact with the client can be as tension producing for the buyer-seller relationship as too little.

On the plus side, the internals tend to be creative and flexible, so prospect meetings can be high energy with ideas bouncing off every wall. Equally positive is the external's tendency to spell out details and elaborate on the proposition before the buyer.

7. *Career Goals.* Internals tend to be impatient with career progress, and they get tense about a slow climb up the ladder, including "moving up" in markets. Externals fare better on the patience side since they don't get tensed over slow career development, however, they suffer the understress phenomenon, wherein the work stops being a challenge and frustration rolls in. Sorry, externals, but you are a bit more stress prone than internals.

8. *When Tension Mounts.* When tension mounts, externals and internals go off different deep ends. As you probably could have predicted, internals tend to go bonkers and be agressive toward others and others' property. They pick fights. Externals accept the blame for the world's woes and tend to be self-destructive or suicidal. Booze and drugs are common solutions to an external's tensions.

9. *Illness.* When illness sets in, externals and internals respond differently to treatment. Internals have a track record of being ex-smokers, able to give up the habit much more easily than externals can. In stop-smoking clinics, we've found that asking an internal, "What does it feel like to be controlled and

manipulated by a stinking weed?" can lead to a lot of hollering and shouting—and quitting.

Internals also tend to question their physicians, nurses, dentists, you name it—to death. They ask more questions about the nature and extent of their illnesses, acquire more lay medical knowledge, and are less likely to stick to their doctors' instructions. They believe that they can cure themselves with will power instead of pill power. Externals are ideal patients. They go to bed, take instructions well, don't ask questions, and learn less about the causes of their illness. However, they stay in hospitals longer and tend to be repeaters in old age.

10. *Recreational Activities.* When it comes to recreation, internals and externals differ again. Internals prefer somewhat more risky adventures while externals like safer activities. At gambling tables and slot machines, externals and internals show their true nature. When internals play games of chance, they raise their bets after success and lower them after failure. Internals seem always to be looking for the system or skills necessary to beat a game. When they win, they think they have it; when they lose, they think they've lost it. Internals tend to be "card counters." They try to keep a mental log of which cards have been played and which haven't.

When externals play games of chance, they tend to increase the size of their bets after they lose and decrease their bets after they win. It seems many externals judge gaming situations to be just dumb luck. However, they seem to act as if the "gambler's fallacy" is true—that the probability of winning and losing changes, depending on whether they have just won or lost. They act as if they are "due" after a loss.

Once an internal, always an internal? Not quite. Chances are, you can change, move away from the extremes, if you are an extreme internal or external. That movement, of course, is part of the stress-management regime for both belief systems. For internals, rethinking can work well. Externals often respond well to assertive communication. We'll work with both of these strategies in Part Three.

For the moment, let's suggest that the best strategy for the extreme—external or internal—is one of mental moderation. It's fun for the internal to imagine standing on the observation deck of the Empire State Building, shouting, "Look out world, here I come." Or for the external to match his or her day to horoscope and biorhythms. But it's ridiculous for either to put on the hair shirt for stumbling over a curbstone—or agonizing over a blown sale.

To paraphrase an old sales maxim:

Three out of every ten prospects wouldn't buy water from you if you had the only faucet in the Sahara. At the other extreme, there are three prospects out of every ten who would buy the sand if you asked them to. Between these two extremes are the 40 percent who need help buying. Selling successfully to that group is the differ-ence between a sales pro and an order taker.

This balancing act between external and internal extremes is best characterized by Reinhold Neibuhr in the Serenity Prayer:

God, give us strength to accept with serenity the things that cannot be changed, courage to change the things that should be changed, and the wisdom to distinguish the one from the other.

Translated to selling, the message is awareness: Don't get bent out of shape over hard heads who eat little children for lunch; don't become euphoric over those crazy "tip-ins" who won't let go of your leg until you take an order; *do* feel good and successful and professional when you show one of the doubters that you and your product can meet their needs and you close the sale; above all, make it a practice to take the time to learn to tell one from the other.

6

TYPE A BEHAVIOR: THE STRESS-PRONE SALES REP

ACCORDING to cardiologists Dr. Meyer Friedman and Dr. Roy H. Rosenman,* certain people—those who exhibit what they have dubbed Type A behavior—are three times more likely to experience heart attacks than Type B behavior people.[1] Friedman and Rosenman's conviction comes from a ten-year study they conducted of 3,500 healthy San Francisco businessmen between the ages of 30 and 60. The two doctors studied a wide variety of life-styles, personalities, and physical factors among these executives and found that none of the commonly correlated heart disease factors—cigarette smoking, high cholesterol level, high blood pressure, and the like—were as powerful a predictor of coronary incident as the temperament or personality pattern they labeled Type A behavior. In fact, research suggests that high cholesterol level, high blood pressure, and so on may be by-products of being a Type A person. Putting a Type A in a competitive game leads directly, *and almost instantaneously*, to elevated cholesterol levels. This, without any dietary change in cholesterol.

What is Type A behavior? You've probably already guessed.

---

* We discuss Friedman and Rosenman's *Type A Behavior and Your Heart* briefly in Appendix A. We repeat a little of that discussion here, but mostly we are concerned with new information and with giving you an opportunity to assess your Type A tendencies.

The doctors describe these heart-attack prone people as highly competitive, achievement-oriented, impatient, time-pressured, fast-moving, emphatic-speaking, hair-trigger individuals who want and try to get ahead at any cost. And that, of course, is a near letter-perfect description of the American way of living, loving, managing, and selling.

A Type A person might, for example, take up jogging to relax and reduce tension and stress, but dilute the possible benefits by setting a host of "challenging" time and distance goals. The typical Type A jogger is constantly annoyed and upset when other runners overtake and pass. Type A's competitive drive won't allow a challenge to go unanswered.

The Type A is also the person who "cheats" on physical examinations to get a "good report." And equally typical of the Type A is the individual who becomes enraged and upset because he or she is standing in line at an airport behind someone who is asking detailed questions about flight schedules to Pago Pago.

Are you a Type A person? Do you have these supposedly fatal personality and behavior characteristics? The following checklist should help you decide. But first a caution. We are not—nor were Rosenman and Friedman—condemning Type A behavior. What is important is to be *aware*—there's that word "awareness" again—that some people run a higher risk of cardiopulmonary occlusion than do others. Don't panic if you decide you are Type A. Just be aware of your potential and be careful of how and when you roll the dice. The trick is being able to learn when and how to turn Type A off and be a bit more Type B. After all, if Rosenman and Friedman are at all correct, 60 percent of the adult U.S. population suffers from heart disease. Obviously, there are a lot of Type As who have learned to use and not be abused by their own behavior, who have benefited from the healthful aspects of "A-ness."

We've learned a lot in the fifteen years since Rosenman and Friedman did their landmark book on Type A personality. In the ensuing years of research, it's become clear that not all Type As develop health problems as a result of their personality style and behavior. Some work in pressure cookers, rarely let up on themselves and others, and seem always to sweat the small stuff, but do not become ill—some even thrive in these conditions. Why does one hard-driving, time-pressured, need-to-win workaholic fall apart while another similarly disposed individual does not?

The "Bitchiness" Factor

One promising answer, according to Redford Williams, lies in the emotional side of the typical Type A. All of us get angry sometimes and we can become hostile, no matter what type we are. The key may be in the intensity and pervasiveness of the hostility.

Bitchiness (our label for the syndrome) of the long-standing, deeply ingrained variety may be what makes some Type A's come physically unglued. Often without realizing it, these Type A's are cynical people who emphasize the negative in life. They are the true believers in Murphy's Law, and they represent the dark side of the Type A personality.

Dr. Redford Williams, who followed young healthy medical and law-school students for twenty-five years, found those who tested very hostile were from four to six times more likely to have died early from heart disease and other causes than those who were not hostile. A 1988 follow-up study on the Type A led this researcher to feel that the impact of hostility on health is great, especially in young adults. As a result, many of them are prone to the damaging effects of hostility and may die by the time they reach middle age. His new book, *The Trusting Heart*, points to the existence of definitive biological correlates to hostility and anger and how they lead to disease. Dr. Williams broadens the story by examining the biological correlates to positive emotions that seem to be health promoting.[2]

As Daniel Goleman pointed out in a fairly recent Sunday *New York Times* Good Health supplement, there is a growing suspicion that a hostile rhythm to one's life, with an antagonistic style grounded in cynicism and mistrust, may be the most poisonous aspect of anger.[3] This style, rather than the factor of being a Type A, may increase the risk of getting a range of maladies from heart disease to cancer, and make "bitchiness"-prone people more likely to die prematurely of *all* causes.

Let's face it. You won't die if you're late for a sales call, get stuck behind the slowest human on a two-lane highway, and become impatient. But you just might die if you spend the time pounding the steering wheel, cursing the slowpoke, or furiously blowing your horn in anger—especially if this is your usual approach.

EXERCISE 4. Type A Behavior Inventory

Below are fifteen short paragraphs, each describing some facet of Type A behavior. Read each, then decide how close that paragraph comes to describing your behavior. If the description is very much your behavior, circle number 5, "Fits me to a 'T.'" If the paragraph does not describe you at all circle 1, "Not like me at all."

After you have rated yourself on all fifteen of the characteristics, ask someone who knows you well—a spouse, co-worker, or close friend—to rate you also. After your helper has finished, discuss the exercise and come up with a rating for each characteristic that satisfies you both.

Scoring instructions and interpretations are at the end of the inventory.

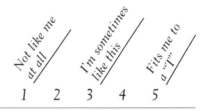

Not like me at all 1   I'm sometimes like this 3   Fits me to a "T" 5

1   2   3   4   5

1. Winning is everything.

Vince Lombardi said, "Winning isn't everything, it's the only thing." That is Type A thinking. It confuses achievement with victory over others. Such people become very unhappy if they aren't number one in business and social

Not like me at all		I'm sometimes like this		Fits me to a "T"
1	2	3	4	5

activities. Enjoyment and pride in doing the activity as well as possible does not motivate Type A's. They strive for striving's sake.   1   2   3   4   5

2. Look at *me*, World!

"Turn on the spotlight; here comes Sonny!" is a Type A feeling. Getting angry, hostile, and downright nasty when recognition for accomplishment is withheld is also typical. External recognition is more important than personal satisfaction. Wealth and possessions are used to prove achievement to others. Type A's count and compare everything. They think about themselves a lot.   1   2   3   4   5

3. Move it, Meatball!

Type A's have no patience with people they believe to be "dogging it." As managers, they even "correct" people who report to others. They interrupt and suggest "faster and better" ways, and are exasperated with anyone who they perceive not doing 130 percent. They make the same demands of themselves. They tend to lecture their prospects during sales calls.   1   2   3   4   5

	Not like me at all		I'm sometimes like this		Fits me to a "T"
	1	2	3	4	5

4. Time is money.

Everything is timed and planned to the minute, from shower to symphony. A day never seems long enough for everything the Type A "should" or "must" accomplish. Type A's are continually frustrated by the weight of what they have yet to do to meet goal. The Type A response to this self-imposed pressure is abruptness with others and hostility to interruptions or changes in plans.

1   2   3   4   5

5. This *is* relaxing!

Type A's feel guilty and are literally incapable of doing nothing. They think, talk, eat, and sleep tasks. Social life is a chore and a business necessity. Golf or tennis with a hot prospect is Type A people's idea of "off-duty." They feel uneasy and restless being someplace without a purpose or goal.

1   2   3   4   5

6. Machine-gun mind.

Type A's think and speak rapidly and expect that of others. If you're stuck for a word, they supply it—even if you're pausing for effect. They abhor silence. They interrupt and summarize the point you're making before you make it. They "talk over" others with a string of "Uhuh, uhuh, yes,

Not like me at all		I'm sometimes like this		Fits me to a "T"
1	2	3	4	5

yes, yes" comments. They often are thinking about the afternoon appointment during the morning sales call. They eat, read the paper, open the mail, listen to the radio, and watch TV all at the same time.

| 1 | 2 | 3 | 4 | 5 |

7. The juggling act.

Leading two task forces, chairing three committees, coordinating four programs, and heading the little league fund-raiser all at once is Type A. Promising four proposals for the same week; making sales calls in Toledo, Cincinnati, and Pittsburgh in the same day, and continually underestimating the time a project needs for completion is Type A. The more balls kept juggling at once, the better.

| 1 | 2 | 3 | 4 | 5 |

8. Plan your work and work your friends.

Type A's overplan. They impose unrealistic and unnecessary goals and deadlines on themselves. Sixty hours is a typical work week. Type A's believe current and future success depend on willingness to accept this grueling pace. Breakfast, lunch, dinner, weekend, and evening meetings with clients are usual. And perfection *is* the name of the Type A game.

| 1 | 2 | 3 | 4 | 5 |

Not like me at all	I'm sometimes like this	Fits me to a "T"
1	2 3	4 5

9. And I won this one for—.

The Type A personality's office walls are covered with skiing, hunting, and joining awards. Only first-place awards, naturally. Competition is great, but a constant need for comparison with others and little appreciation of self-progress is Type A. Winning isn't good enough; trouncing is barely acceptable. The enemy must not only be beaten but completely vanquished.

1   2   3   4   5

10. A fool for a boss.

Type A's ignore all aspects of life that don't have client-grooming potential. They like others to see how hard they work. They carry around pounds and pounds of rate books and new product manuals; for weekends they put half the office in a suitcase and cart it home. When Type A is self-employed, the sign reads, "Open for business 24 hours a day, every day."

1   2   3   4   5

11. The look of labor.

Type A's "look" tense. They walk fast, talk fast, sit up ramrod straight! Tense facial muscles are common, and a handshake is an arm wrestle. Slight tics and facial mannerisms are typical, as is the

	Not like me at all		I'm sometimes like this		Fits me to a "T"
	1	2	3	4	5

appearance of continuously struggling for control of self and situation. — 1 2 3 4 5

12. Move it, *Move it*!

Type A's read book condensations and book reviews to save time. They do a fast burn in slow traffic and leisurely paced restaurants. Filling out bank deposit slips, completing call reports, and paying the bills are annoying and sometimes done sloppily. If it doesn't look goal directed, "let somebody else do it" is a Type A attitude. — 1 2 3 4 5

13. Next case!

Type A's don't quite seem to be in the room with you from time to time. And it's true; their attention *is* elsewhere. Type A minds are random-access rats' nests of racing thoughts. Now the Smith project, now the car needs a tune-up, now the Ryerson account, now the dinner meeting with old Bainbridge—and so it goes, all day. The Type A thinks about the future, the past, and the bottom line but seldom focuses on the here and now for more than a few minutes. Even when Type A's appear to be listening, they are actually thinking of several other things. — 1 2 3 4 5

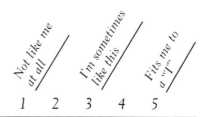

	Not like me at all		I'm sometimes like this		Fits me to a "T"
	1	2	3	4	5

14. My Type A can whip your Type A.

Type A's are not kindred spirits. Lock two Type A's in the same room and one may come out feet first. They become aggressive, play games of "can you top this," and compete for "King of the Hill" honors with each other.

1   2   3   4   5

15. Roses—what roses?

Type A's are not likely to take time to smell the flowers or feel the breeze. They screen out these frivolities. They can seldom describe the offices of their prospects or remember any interesting details of a new route taken while driving to a sales call. They will remember to the second how long the route took and how much faster or slower it was than the old route.

1   2   3   4   5

Scoring

If you are truly a Type A, you probably haven't taken the self-quiz yet. You are reading the scoring instructions and interpretation to see what score you "need to get." Take the quiz straight; it won't hurt you.

When you are satisfied that your answers reflect your behavior, add up all the numbers you circled. Place your score in this box.

• If you rated yourself *70 or higher*, you are probably a for-real Type A. All is not lost; some of our best friends are Type A, so keep reading.

• If you scored yourself between *40 and 60*, you are a sometimes Type A. That's great if you are doing that as an active choice, but not so good if you just stumble in and out of Type A. We'll confront this situation in a minute.

• If you scored yourself *40 or less*, you may be a Type B. For sure, you aren't a Type A—unless you're that son-of-a-gun who is reading ahead to see what answers you "should" give.

THE "BITCHINESS" QUOTIENT

To assess your bitchiness—the degree to which you are prone to be both Type A *and* hostile to boot—you need to add up separately your scores for items 2, 3, 12, and 14 of the inventory. Put your score for these four items in this box:

• If your score is between *12 and 16*, consider yourself in the "yellow light," or caution, zone. You aren't absolutely a hostile Type A, but are in danger of becoming so.

• If your score is between *16 and 20*, you fall in the "red light," or definite danger, zone. You are very much at potential risk. You are a hostile Type A.

Type B Behavior

If you view yourself as stressed, and pride yourself on the pressure you can "take," you probably are a Type A. Rosenman and Friedman found that Type A's are prone to exhibit both emotional and physical stress symptoms. They found, for example, that Type A's excrete certain enzymes associated with cardio-vascular problems.[4]

An assumption people sometimes make about Type A's is that they are *always* the winners. Many people believe that Type A characteristics are critical, useful, and necessary for success. *Not so!* A Type B person can be—and often is—as career serious and successful as a Type A. The difference is style and strain. The "pure" Type B is more easygoing and seldom becomes impatient. A slow client, one who stalls making a decision or asks for extraordinary proof and data, doesn't rattle a Type B. He or she just hangs in with, and hangs on to, that sort of prospect. Type A's lose—really throw away—prospects who don't meet their criteria for customer behavior. Type B's center on the sale, not the time involved or the championship image. Type B's work for a sale, not to slay some mythical dragon. The close is not the end of a competition, it's the big turn-on.

When you're starting out in sales—or any career, for that matter—Type A tendencies are probably helpful. They get you up and moving and motivated when you're green and don't really understand or have a feel for the business. But for the long haul, Type A behavior can be self-destructive and career damaging. It has been said, and with some justification, that more Type A's become stress victims than ever become company presidents. If you don't believe it, check the coronary-care unit of your local hospital.

Type C—An Alternative

Most people have both type A and type B behaviors in their repertoire. If you have an abundance of Type A behaviors, learn to modify them with Type B behaviors. Stress is *not* the inevitable price of success. Stress and tension can be managed by learning to reduce the intensity and irrationality that accompany many Type A behaviors. The techniques suggested later in this book can help.

We like to raise a third possibility, or alternative to Type A, that's the behavior style we call the Type C personality: an individual who has learned how to integrate Type A and Type B responses. He or she is a "reformed" Type A and is able to flow from Type A to Type B to cope with the demands of the situation. Thus, a Type C person uses Type A or Type B responses as *coping strategies*. Type C personalities turn on their Type A behaviors for the following reasons:

- To reach a specific goal
- For an identified length of time
- In a well-defined situation
- When Type B behaviors are perceived as not having the desired impact

These people generally are aware of what they are doing and are able to step back to evaluate the costs and/or benefits of a Type A response. Type C personalities are comfortable with both aspects of their personality. They are able to function in the Type B mode when they perceive Type A actions as unnecessary or counterproductive.

The Type C person:

- Is selectively competitive.
- May react quickly to frustrations, but the response is short-lived.
- Can reduce strivings and "do nothing" sometimes.
- Is able to see the humor and/or futility in prolonged Type A behavior.
- Allows time pressures to gain control for short periods only.
- Takes some time to enjoy leisure activities.
- Becomes angry, but anger is specific, short-lived, and reasonable.

Is it realistic to think that a bonafide Type A can become an authentic Type C?

Our experience tells us yes. And others agree. The approach they applied was Dr. Albert Ellis's highly unique Rational-Emotive Therapy (RET) system. Dr. Ellis's premise is that as we grow up we learn erroneous beliefs or rules that influence our behavior.[5]

Dr. Ellis found that wrong (erroneous) beliefs begat stress. A typical erroneous Type A belief is "I must always win." It's an incredibly bad belief for a salesperson to hold, since even the best of the best never have a 1:1 call to sales ratio.

Ellis's approach is to help the Type A person learn to replace the "I must always win" with a more realistic statement such as "It's nice to win but not essential all of the time" and "Losing can't kill me."

By combining Ellis's RET approach with innovations of our own, we have been able to help Type A's develop an integrated A-B behavior style—what we call Type C—in a relatively short time and with surprising ease. We have also found that the A-B integration process leads to lowered stress levels for the Type A and a hardier personality.

Much of the Type A research has focused on the negative— on people especially vulnerable to stress disorders. But there has *also* been some research on people who are unusually resistent to stress. These stress-resistent types have come to be referred to as hardy personalities. They tend to be people able to absorb more tension, suffer fewer ill effects from stress, and stay glued together in the face of circumstances that make others fall apart. Suzanne Kobasa defines hardy people as having a sense of commitment to their work and lives, a feeling of control over what's happening in their lives. They have the ability to see change as challenging and remain flexible.[6]

We will describe the process of becoming a bit more type B in Part Three. For now, let's look at the approach to reducing the unhealthful aspects of "A-ness" suggested recently by Meyer Friedman on the syndicated PBS television show *To Your Health*.

Friedman, a self-professed Type A with a heart attack and a coronary bypass to prove it, suggests that Type A's need to learn patience, relaxation, and "positive self-talk." They need, in his words, to "learn to acknowledge their successes and take time to smell the posies."[7] He is especially high on teaching Type A's to analyze successes and failures. When they take time to do that, Friedman suggests, they invariably find their successes are a result of hard work, good ideas, long hours, and getting along with people.

On the reverse side, Friedman asserts that Type A's invariably find their failures related to the "AIAIP" factors: *anger, irritation, aggravation, impatience,* and *pressure.* Because of their goal directedness, Friedman suggests, Type A's understand the cost-benefit of eliminating such obstacles to success. In Part Three is a routine called "The Sales Call Postmortem," which you can use to analyze successful and not-so-successful sales calls.

7

THE STRESS CARRIER: SPREADING IT AROUND

EVER meet someone who just simply made you uncomfortable? Made you feel tense and uneasy? Who seemed to brighten the whole room by leaving it? You may well have been in the presence of a stress carrier. Believe it or not, there are people—some are sellers, some are buyers, some are bosses, some are peers, and some even are spouses—who spread stress to other people as surely as Typhoid Mary spread germs to half of New York City.

TAKE Ted Johnson. Sales Manager for slightly over eighteen months, half the troops are sore at him and half are in hiding. Behind his back people say things like:

> The guy holds a twenty-minute sales meeting and burns out half the people in the room before it's over. Unbelievable! He could give a rock ulcers!

> He's aggravated most of the administrative types onto tranquilizers. Lucky we're in the pharmaceutical division. At least the breakdowns will be cheaper.

> He can't let go. The right way, the wrong way, and Ted's way—those are the options. He says he wants people to share opinions; he means *his* opinions— that's what he really means.

Listen, if I ever need a heart transplant I want his. No malice intended, but if I need a new heart I want one that's never been used before.

The only time he says "well done" is when he's ordering steak.

When Ted holds a meeting, he *holds* a meeting. He speaks in staccato bursts, his suggestions and criticisms concise and his verbal delivery machine-gun quick. He bites off the ends of his sentences—and the heads of anyone who suggests he might not be seeing the whole picture. Take Sterling, the intellectual type who smokes a pipe and says things like, "Let's look this over from both sides—there are a lot of angles to consider." He also sells up a storm, though Ted hasn't the slightest idea how.

Sterling only made the "Let's think about that idea for a minute, Ted" suggestion once. Ted, in no uncertain terms, made it clear to Sterling that thinking was Ted's job and selling was Sterling's. "These meetings are too long and mostly a waste of time. And that's the kind of question that slows them down. Now let's get on with it. If you have constructive comments, make them—otherwise, keep it to yourself." Ever since then, meetings *have* been shorter, agreement easier to come by, and Ted's ideas accepted with little critique. People sit with their hands folded or their faces buried in their note taking. Ted has managed to make stress victims of half the people around him and has zero awareness of it.

Here's another example:

MARY Brownlee represents a line of high-dollar fashion accessories. She has her sights set on being number one in the division. She can't wait for that trip to Hawaii, the president's dinner, and the You're Number 1 trophy. She has also set herself a grueling schedule to make her goal. Right now she's cooling her heels in Bill Herbert's waiting room, and has been for forty minutes. Herbert is an accessories buyer for Schlem's Department Stores, of which there are ten. Mary is restless, fidgiting and starting to fume. She has a 3:00 P.M. call all the way across town, and if Herbert doesn't see her in five minutes, she'll never come close to being on time. Mary can't tolerate lateness in anyone, thinking, "Who does this Herbert think he is to waste my time like this?" She is going to give him a piece of her mind. And on top of that, he called *her* to discuss a deal.

When Herbert finally arrives back in his office, he explains that he was having lunch with the president and the topic under discussion was the special order he wants to give Mary. But Mary is in no mood to hear good news. She turns and twists in her chair, drops her pen twice, and makes little or no eye contact with Herbert. Herbert is in an effusive mood and wants to share his elation over having his idea accepted by the boss. Mary just wants the details for the order—after all, she *hates* the idea since it wasn't hers to begin with, so how can she get heated up over it? She interrupts, keeps checking her watch, asks for specifics at every turn, and has four suggestions for improvement before Herbert has a chance to explain the big picture of his idea—or to crow about his coup. Fifteen minutes later he has cooled toward Mary considerably and "giving you an order" has changed to "asking you to submit a bid."

Just as small children and pets "smell" fear and anger in other people, Bill Herbert sensed Mary Brownlee's stress and was infected and affected. He grew uneasy and uncomfortable with her. A vendor he always had a high regard for was suddenly a questionable commodity. And how do you suppose Mary's 3 o'clock appointment felt and reacted when Mary came "dashing in" late, overheated and uptight?

Some stress carriers are aware—nay, proud of their ability to stress other people. They assume that part of their effectiveness *is* this ability to get customer and colleague "on the ball" and keep people "on their toes!" As one sales and marketing vice-president tells it, "I don't get stress. I give it!" Unfortunately, he is only half-right. You can't give away what you don't own, and his high tolerance for stress doesn't mean that stress will avoid him—eventually. The stress carrier wears stress like a badge of honor, convinced that it is a personal key to success and that stressing others is management magic.

If you've noticed obvious similarities between the Type A salesperson and the stress carrier, go to the head of the class. Type A's often *are* stress carriers. The stress carrier role is an add-on to being a Type A. If you are Type A and don't push your perfection under everyone else's nose, you're probably *not* a carrier. You're more likely a Type A by choice, maybe even close to being a Type C. To find out if you are a stress carrier, do the following exercise.

EXERCISE 5. Are You a Stress Carrier?

It's a little tough to tell whether you are actually a stress carrier or not. Part of the problem—and one of the clues—is that stress carriers tend to be insensitive to other people's stress. The following quiz may help you identify your stress-carrying tendencies. Read each question, then check the response at the right that best characterizes your answer. The choices are *yes* (I do that), *no* (I don't do that), and *?* (I'm not sure).

	Yes	*No*	*?*
1. When you hold a meeting, do you seem to do most of the talking?	___	___	___
2. When you call on a prospect, does he or she seem restless or fidgety five or ten minutes into the interview?	___	___	___
3. Do you often cut off a prospect's questions with phrases such as, "We'll be coming to that point in a minute"?	___	___	___
4. Do people seem more reluctant to offer *you* suggestions than others?	___	___	___
5. Do discussions over politics, religion, the weather, or the oil shortage often go from friendly to tense with colleagues or loved ones?	___	___	___

	Yes	*No*	*?*
6. Have you gone through more typists, secretaries, and administrative assistants than other salespeople in your office?	——	——	——
7. Do you have a tough time getting typing from the office typists? Tougher than other people?	——	——	——
8. Does your boss tend to deal with you behind closed doors and in a little more stressed fashion than with others?	——	——	——
9. Do people tend not to give you much feedback on your behavior?	——	——	——
10. Do you believe that "keeping people on their toes" is the best way to deal with people in the office?	——	——	——
Totals	☐	☐	☐

Interpretation

If you have four or five *?* responses, then you should be suspicious that you are a stress carrier. Have someone you trust go over the items with you and ask him or her to give you honest feedback. Be calm and cool about this suggestion and encourage honest help. If the person you ask is edgy and seems to be giving guarded and careful answers, you probably are a carrier. See if you can help that other person with his or her obvious discomfort. It will be good practice for what we'll be prescribing in Part Three.

If you have four or more *yes* responses, you are probably a stress carrier, *but* you are more sensitive to your problem than most. You need only think your way through your behavior—distance yourself from the melee a bit—and observe your behavior, and other people's responses to it. In Part Three you will be directed to some specific exercises and ideas that will help.

If you had three or fewer *yes* responses, you are probably

not a carrier. We all stress others from time to time. Sometimes it's a good tactic for getting the energy flowing in your office or in your prospect. As long as you do it under control and are aware of what you are doing, there's no harm done.

Stop Spreading It Around

If you are a stress carrier, you have taken a giant step toward change by acknowledging it. You probably already knew that often you are tense and stressed, but you were not aware that others noticed or were affected by your stress. Now you know. In Part Two you will pull the self-test data together and prescribe some change strategies for yourself.

The second half of the stress-carrier problem is the part we referred to in Chapter 3 as the cyclic phenomenon. Both the bona fide full-time stress carrier and the sales rep who only walks into a prospect's office "stressed up" once in a while are guilty of instigating and escalating stressful situations. We refer to this runaround as the stress cycle.

Round and Round It Goes, and Where It Stops. . . . The Stress Cycle in Selling

You need to understand the stress cycle to get an idea of how stress escalates in a face-to-face selling situation; how it is possible to inadvertently stress yourself and your prospect, and, conversely, how easy it could be for your prospect to start the cycle rolling for you.

We mentioned in Chapter 3 that there seems to be a "violence begets violence" cycle in stressful selling. Once a salesperson begins to be stressed, especially at vulnerable times such as during a client presentation, a sales interview, or in the midst of a disagreement, the stress-caused changes in thoughts, feelings, and behavior act as triggers for yet more stress. At times, the awareness of stress is a stressor itself. So, like inflation, once stress hits it tends to spiral onward and upward out of control.

Take a simple hypothetical case:

YOU'RE sitting at your desk, reading a *Wall Street Journal* article about a prospect you're going to be calling on in two hours. Your boss walks by and tosses a comment to the effect of, "Don't you have anything better to do than read the paper? You don't have *that* many laurels to rest on!" It's meant to be a joke—at worst, a mild rebuke. But you are already a little "wired," psyched-up for the call. You misinterpret what was said as a straight rebuff and snap back with, "Those who can, sell. Those who can't supervise." Before you know what's happened, you and the boss are locked in one of those lose-lose struggles referred to as the Uproar Game. And you're both probably stressed to the teeth. With luck, you'll be calm and collected enough for your appointment, but for sure you're done with your attempt to prep for the call for at least an hour.

In-office struggles and conflicts are bad enough. Worse yet is the potential for stressing the prospect and not knowing it. Consider the true case of a saleswoman we call Joan White, who, for a very brief time—forty minutes—was a client of Dr. Stern's. Joan was a stress carrier, and it almost destroyed her career in sales, thanks to the cyclic nature of stress. Here is Joan's story as Dr. Stern relates it:

JOAN White was trained as an elementary-school teacher. She also was the first woman ever hired by her company to be a sales rep. Joan left teaching with a bad feeling. She felt she had abandoned the career she was trained for and had let down the parents who had sent her to college. She was determined to make good—more than make good—to be one of the top people in her new highly competitive job.

Joan also brought a highly feminist attitude to the new job. Because she was aware of her uniqueness as the first woman in this new job, she became ultra sensitive to any slight—imagined or, all too often, real—implying that she couldn't succeed because she was female.

Joan received only minimal training for her selling job,

mostly product information and not sales skills. Her prior training had emphasized communication skills with ten-year-olds, not adults.

Because she was the first woman selling for her company, her sales manager, peers, and customers regularly found little ways to remind Joan of her uniqueness. She soon developed a chip on her shoulder that acted as a trigger for many stress-escalating incidents. She was almost at the point where a simple "Good Morning" received an "Oh yeah? What do you mean by *that*, buster?" When I met her, she was seriously considering leaving the business. But worse than that, she was suffering from insomnia and headaches, and was fairly nervous.

The trigger for her discussion with me was a talk I gave at a local chapter of a professional businesswoman's association of which she was a member. She asked me to join her for coffee—and though I drink tea, I did. She related this story. Just that morning she had blown a sales opportunity with a big potential buyer. This buyer was one of the most offensive Joan dealt with in terms of snide remarks—or so she believed. She showed up at his office determined not to let him "get away with any more of that crap." About five minutes into the interview, Joan mentioned that she had burned considerable midnight oil on this proposal and felt it was just what he was looking for. The client made an off-hand and careless remark to the effect that "women's work is never done." Fifteen minutes later, Joan stalked out of his office, her carefully developed proposal in tatters.

Joan had already done most of the work in her head. When we went for coffee together, she knew that she was a stress-cycle victim. She was already able to verbalize that she had been stressed up and out of control in the client's office and had infected him in the bargain. She also was ready to admit that the "chip" she was carrying around was stressing her and dragging other people into the cycle with her.

After fifteen minutes of dialogue about techniques for breaking the stress cycle, Joan wrote herself an action plan on one of the coffee shop napkins. Part of her plan specified learning to communicate her feelings when she was feeling them.

Another part had to do with reducing her sensitivity to client remarks, unintended and otherwise. A week later she called to inform that she was sleeping better, taking an assertive communication class, and her headaches were much less severe than before. Is Joan White still in the business? Probably, but I don't know. We haven't corresponded. But whatever she's doing, Joan is fully aware of how stress can cycle and spiral out of control, and how to break into that cycle. Joan's stress-management training was less than two hours—a forty-minute speech and forty minutes more in the coffee shop.

Breaking the Stress Cycle

The easiest way to break the stress cycle in the face-to-face interview is to keep it from starting. For example:

YOU are making a call on the purchasing agent at XYZ Corporation. The appointment is scheduled for 1:30 P.M. on a Friday afternoon. You arrive on time but the meeting starts late. Fredericks, the purchasing agent, has been at a three-drink luncheon for a departing colleague. He comes back to see you but you sense that the party is where he really wants to be. On top of that, the air-conditioning system is all messed up from attempts to meet the new government temperature standards. It's 80° in Fredericks' office and he's about to nod off. You may have a lot riding on this presentation, but that's a "so what?" issue at this point. If you press on, Fredericks will only hear a miniscule part of what you want him to, and the harder you press for his attention, the more likely it is that you are going to kick a stress cycle into action. The smart bet is that Fredericks will respond positively to the idea of a quick and easy meeting, a rescheduling of your presentation, and a fast adjournment back to the party. In short, meetings that get off track or look like pending fiascos aren't worth holding. Simple saying, "Mr. Prospect, this doesn't seem to be the best time for me to be bringing this proposal to you. Perhaps it would be better if we rescheduled it for another day," gives the prospect an out for a meeting he doesn't want or need at that point. Chances are, the client will respect you for the decision—and for letting him or her off the hook.

The tougher go, and the more normal one, is to "stop the cameras" long enough for you to get a tight rein on your stress and to temper your prospect's tensions. Rest room or coffee breaks work; so does lunch. When you just can't get on the beam and the stress is mounting, gain space and self-management time by getting the prospect to elaborate on his or her objections. When all else fails, ask the prospect to help solve the problem. The simple phrase, "Mr. Prospect, this meeting seems to be going badly for both of us. What can we do to get it back on track?" is disarming, honest, unexpected—and it works.

But the main point is that you can control the tension level of most meetings simply by controlling your own stress level. A prospect, boss, or peer may want to "dump" on you to lower his or her tension, but that doesn't mean you have to accept what is offered. You can literally let it roll off your back. Being your best stress-managed you is among the most effective ways to control the stress cycle. When you can act positively to manage your tension, you will be inoculated against the stress carried by others, and you will have nothing to spread to them. The most effective key to a cure is—as always—prevention. More tips on breaking the stress cycle are provided in Part Three.

8

STRESS AND STRAIGHT THINKING

SUCCESSFUL salespeople tend to share common characteristics. A characteristic we've become aware of—one that others also have commented on—is a sense of being in tune with yourself. "Centeredness," "one with the flow," "cool," "self-assured," and "together" are words or phrases we've heard used to describe this attribute.

We like the word "congruence." It means simply that thoughts, feelings, bodily reactions, and outward behavior are consistent—in harmony with one another. *Congruent* salespeople say what they feel and think; conversely, when they say they feel or think something, they really do.

To be sure, it's impossible, and in many instances inappropriate, to say *exactly* what you are thinking and feeling. There are times during a sales call, or any other encounter, when it is best to ignore or hold until later the expression of a particular emotion. And occasionally your body sends you signals that it is best to ignore at the time. But on the whole, consistency in thoughts, emotions, and actions is less stressful, and hence healthier, than holding dissonant beliefs, emotions, and actions. Some time ago psychologist Leon Festinger discovered that people are motivated to achieve consistency between their attitudes and their behaviors. That is, people generally find it difficult to say one thing while believing another. Either the belief or the behavior must change to resolve this state of "cognitive dissonance," as Festinger called this imbalance.[1]

On the surface, it seems easy and personally harmless to say, "The check is in the mail" or "Your order was on the train that jumped the track," or even "He's not here; I'm just the janitor," when there is a boiling-mad customer on the other end of the line. But whether we are conscious of it or not, we pay that particular piper—not in dollars and cents but with stress and tension. And the wider the gap between what we say and what we think, the greater the stress. Festinger makes the point this way:

> Suppose a good friend asks you to sign a petition advocating the legalization of marijuana. You are somewhat opposed to legalization but the good friend is very persuasive and you sign anyway. You now have two thoughts that are out of congruence or are inconsistent. One is "I oppose legalization of marijuana." Because of the dissonance in these two views, you become psychologically uncomfortable; stressed. To reduce the tension, one of the two thoughts must change. Since you did sign the petition, it would be difficult to persuade yourself that you didn't. The most likely outcome is that you will alter in some way your stand on marijuana. If you are only slightly against legalization, the shift will be fairly easy and you probably won't even be conscious of the change in your belief. Such dissonance-reducing changes in attitude are fairly frequent.[2]

The problem for the salesperson is that he or she meets ten prospects a week who in a sense want eight or ten different petitions signed. Seems far-fetched? Just consider this "hypothetical" example that is, by the way, based on truth:

CUSTOMER A likes you, your product, and your price. Customer A is also the campaign manager for the Republican candidate for mayor. To be comfortable, he wants to know that he's doing business with a "right thinking" person. Across town is Customer B who also likes you, your product, and your price. And guess what—yep, B is the campaign treasurer for the Democratic mayoral candidate. And yes, he *too* wants to be sure that he is doing business with an appropriately enlightened person. It's situations like these that cause salespeople to say things like, "Selling is a great way to make a living. It would be even better if I didn't have to deal with all those damn people!"

So, thinking influences what you do, and what you do influences what you think and feel. When beliefs and actions are out of concert, when they lack congruence, the dissonance is stress producing with its disastrous effects on your body. When your inner messages—your self-instructions, as we call them—are stress producing, they get in the way. They can take the edge off your effectiveness and erect an emotional barrier between you and your prospect or customer. They can also make you ill! Eventually, unresolved dissonance simply reduces the quality of life both on and off the job. Small wonder that one of the top reasons given for leaving sales is characterized by this sad statement from a departing sales rep:

> I can't take being pulled in all directions at once. I have to do what the company wants, what my boss wants, what my customer wants, what my family wants, and there's no space left for what I want. There has to be a more honest way to make a living.

The Cognitive Cartoon®

The Cognitive Cartoon® in Exercise 6 is an ingenious technique developed by Dr. Stern to help people look at the congruence between their thoughts and feelings and their actions. Use this exercise to help you to answer these questions:

- Is there a gap between what I say and what I do that is stress-inducing for me?
- Does disharmony between my thinking and feeling and my actions occur often enough to be a problem for me?

- Is it possible—and necessary—to decrease the distance between what I say and what I do?
- Would closing the gap between thought and action be too risky and stress-producing?

Ask yourself the following questions to provide insight into the potential problem and focus on finding solutions instead of recycling the problem and turning it into a stressor.

EXERCISE 6. Looking at Your Thinking

Figure 8-1 depicts a Cognitive Cartoon® salespeople have found useful when looking at their think-speak congruence. The instructions on the left are self-explanatory. Just look at the cartoon for a moment, imagine that you are the person in the cartoon, and ask yourself how you would respond. Fill in the two balloons—"thinking" and "saying"—with what you would be thinking and saying in this situation.

The cartoon in Figure 8-1 illustrates a situation many salespeople view as stressful. Put yourself in the picture. Ask yourself:

1. What is happening? _____

_____

_____

_____

_____

2. What am I thinking? _____

_____

_____

_____

_____

3. What am I saying? _____

_____

_____

_____

4. In the cartoon situation, my stress comes from _____

_____

_____

_____

After you've filled in your responses, ask yourself these questions:

1. Was I able to identify what I was thinking?
   ☐ Yes ☐ Yes, but it was difficult ☐ No

2. How great is the disparity between what I *said* and what I *thought* in the cartoon situation?
   ☐ Great disparity ☐ Some disparity
   ☐ Almost no disparity

3. How uncomfortable does this disparity make me feel?
   ☐ Very uncomfortable ☐ Not very uncomfortable
   ☐ Uncomfortable ☐ No discomfort at all

4. Would saying what I am thinking be even more stressful than living with the discomfort of the disparity between what I think and what I say?
   ☐ Yes ☐ No ☐ I'm not sure

5. What price do I pay for *not* "calling it as I see it?"
   ☐ I feel bad at the time
   ☐ I am losing respect for myself
   ☐ I feel bad later
   ☐ Doesn't bother me at all as far as I can tell

6. Is the price worth the disparity?
   □ Yes □ Yes, but changing □ No
7. Do I need to:
   □ Bring thoughts in line with actions
   □ Bring action in line with thoughts

The Cognitive Cartoon® in Figure 8-1 grew out of the experience of Jerry, a successful work-uniform salesman who was one of Dr. Stern's clients. Jerry's family physician had diagnosed him as hypertensive. His physician had also suggested that although hypertension tended to run in the family, Jerry's highly stressful job and life-style were aggravating the situation. Jerry then contacted Dr. Stern. Dr. Stern continues the story this way:

JERRY'S company was notorious for late deliveries. Materials came from out of the country and often were tied up on the docks and in customs. Jerry tried to give realistic delivery dates, but as often as not he was inaccurate. As a result, Jerry had frequent calls from irate customers. These calls were very stressful to Jerry. His reaction was a "kick the cat" syndrome. Jerry threw things a lot and screamed and hollered at the people in his office. The hubbub continued when Jerry arrived at home. Frequent arguments with his wife led to frequent arguments with the kids, which led to frequent arguments *among* the kids, which led to a lot of kicking of the family cat.

Jerry also manifested his stress in his body. His blood pressure was constantly elevated; he knew it, was afraid of it, knew he had to change it, but couldn't stop focusing on the problem and help look for solutions.

So I hit upon the idea of focusing his attention on the problem through a neutral medium, the cognitive cartoon. [*Figure 8-2 shows Jerry's response to the cartoon.*]

Text continues on page 106

Figure 8-1. Cognitive Cartoon® A.

Figure 8-2. Jerry's response to Cognitive Cartoon® A.

The cartoon at the right illustrates a situation many salespeople view as stressful. Put yourself in the picture. Ask yourself:

1. What is happening? _The customer is upset about a late delivery and is hollering at the salesman_

2. What am I thinking? _Why is he bugging me? If I've told him once I've told him a thousand times, orders are slow right now. He knew that when he placed the order. He was aware of the situation. So why is he carrying on so?_

3. What am I saying? _I understand how you feel, but this is the best we can do. Don't you think I'm upset too? It doesn't help my blood pressure when you call me all the time. OK, ok. I'll try to rush things along!_

4. In the cartoon situation, my stress comes from _Knowing we are doing the best we can but promising the client that I will do something for him . . . . . and I really can't._

Dr. Stern describes Jerry's responses to the Cognitive Cartoon®:

JERRY found himself in this situation frequently, and the dialogue he produced for the cartoon was his stock reply, with twists on the theme now and then for variety's sake. Nothing was accomplished. And note that Jerry concluded by making a promise to "rush things along"—a promise he obviously couldn't keep. He was *thinking*, "Why doesn't this guy get lost? He know the score before he got into the game!"

Needless to say, the dissonance between what Jerry was *saying* and was *thinking* was great. And he was very much unaware of it. He knew he was upset by these phone calls and dreaded having to talk with customers, but he saw no connection between what he was saying on the phone and how tense he felt after dealing with two or three upset accounts—until he did the Cognitive Cartoon® exercise.

Once Jerry clearly saw the disharmony between what he said and what he thought, he saw the options: bringing what he was saying into line with what he was thinking, or bringing his thinking into line with what he was saying. Either works; the choice depends on how a person evaluates the consequences and outcomes. In some cases it is more effective to change thinking; in others, speaking or doing should be altered.

Together we decided that it would be faster and more effective for Jerry to tune in to his customers' feelings and refrain from making promises. In essence, he chose to stop thinking of his customers as nags and complainers and reflect that in what he said to them. Jerry was a little hesitant, since he wasn't sure what specifically to say when a customer started hollering. He was sure he could learn to listen to emotions and change his thinking, but the words were going to be, he felt, a stumbling block. Jerry's hesitancy over this point isn't unique. What he and I did was to develop a set of *standard sentences*: specific prescribed responses for when the customer is upset over delayed orders. For example, Jerry decided to modify his behavior this way when a customer was doing a real rant-and-rave act on the telephone:

NEW THOUGHT: He's really upset. I guess I'd be ticked, too, if I were in his place. We're doing the best we can for him, and that's the truth.

REPHRASED REPLY
TO CUSTOMER: "I know how upset you are. I'd be, too, in your situation and I feel bad about it. I can't speed up the shipment, but we are doing all that can be done. You know how it is when you have to deal with a foreign country. Can you hold off for a few days [weeks] longer?"

Notice that there isn't a dramatic difference in the content of Jerry's new message, but repackaged in this manner, it had a new impact on the customer and, more importantly, on Jerry!

One other point. Jerry was a bit nervous at first about delivering the standard sentences. Even though the content and delivery were what he wanted to say, he couldn't always manage to get them out of his mouth when he was highly stressed. He felt the process wass too mechanical. It was— but Jerry was equating "mechanical" with "insincere." Do you doubt the sincerity of a friend or loved one's birthday greeting because it was written by Hallmark rather than the sender? Of course not, and as Jerry quickly found out, standard sentences become integrated into your "natural" repertoire in a very short time. Jerry reported that after two weeks he no longer had to have written standard sentences in front of him, and after three weeks he no longer needed to pause and instruct himself mentally to choose and use the sentences. They became a part of who he was. It was fairly easy because he had made a conscious, active decision about how he wanted to be with himself, the people around him, and his customers.

The trick Dr. Stern's client learned wasn't just the use of standard sentences. Jerry learned that you can't always control the environment around you. Some things just are, like the Rocky Mountains—immovable subjects. But you *can* control your response to the environment and, in the process, dig a win-win tunnel of communication through those mountains for yourself and your customers.

More Cartoons

Figures 8-3, 8-4, and 8-5 are three more Cognitive Cartoons®. If one of them rings a bell, if it reminds you of an all too familiar scene, work through the "thinking-saying" dilemma. Here is the setup for each:

COGNITIVE CARTOON® B   Saleswoman is about to ask for the order. A third party intrudes and diverts the prospect's attention.

COGNITIVE CARTOON® C   Sales manager is not providing enough support.

COGNITIVE CARTOON® D   Co-worker comes to salesperson's home late at night to drop off new-product brochures.

As you work through these cartoons, you might find useful a mnemonic developed by Dr. Michael J. Mahoney, of the University of Pennsylvania. He suggests that the acronym ADAPT (acknowledge, discriminate, access, present alternatives, think praise) can be useful in bringing thought and action into congruence, especially the "think and say" part (see Figure 8-6).[3] It is based on the Albert Ellis premise that thought leads to feeling and feeling leads to action.[4]

For example, you are thinking about a long lost love. That thought stimulates feelings of happiness or sadness or anger. Those emotions and feelings could prompt calling a friend for a talk, whistling a happy tune, crying, taking a good stiff drink, or going for a walk in the park. The Ellis "trick" and the usefulness of the ADAPT approach, is that it prompts you to sep-

Text continues on page 113

Figure 8-3. Cognitive Cartoon® B.

Figure 8-4. Cognitive Cartoon® C.

Figure 8-5. Cognitive Cartoon® D.

Figure 8-6. Acronym for resolving thought-feeling conflicts.

ADAPT stands for:

A ACKNOWLEDGE: Admit to yourself that you are upset when
                    you are upset, angry when you are angry,
                    and fearful when you are afraid.

                    It is impossible to change how you feel
                    about something until you identify and label
                    what you are feeling when you are feel-
                    ing it.

                    If you are suddenly feeling stressed,
                    stop and ask yourself, "What emotions am
                    I feeling? What was I feeling just before I
                    began to feel stressed?"

D DISCRIMINATE: Before you feel, you think. Once you have
                    identified the emotions you are, or just were,
                    experiencing, you are ready to look for the
                    thoughts and/or images that triggered the
                    emotional response, that led to the stress re-
                    sponse.

                    "Discriminate" means to sort through
                    the thoughts and images occurring just prior
                    to the emotional response. Once you start
                    practicing "thinking about thinking," it's
                    fairly easy to find the thought, image, or idea
                    that just preceded an emotional response.

A ASSESS: Examine the logical or rational basis for the
                    thoughts and images that are leading to the
                    unpleasant feelings and eventually to the
                    stress.

                    If you are worried and anxious because
                    "they are out to get you," and they *are*, your
                    concerns are logical and rational.

                    If, however, you are walking around
                    worried about DC-10s falling on your head,
                    it's safe to say that the odds against such an
                    occurrence make that fear an illogical and
                    irrational one. Even if you live on an airport
                    approach, the odds are so low that such
                    thoughts and resultant feelings would be un-
                    helpful and counter to your adaptive efforts.

Figure 8-6. (*continued*)

| P PRESENT ALTERNATIVES: | Once you have found the irrational thoughts leading to the bad feelings, you can replace them with more rational, logical thoughts or "self-statements." You can only think one thought at a time. So, when you substitute a rational for an irrational thought, you begin to gain control over the thoughts and emotions that lead to the stress.

Sounds artificial? It is! But it works. It doesn't matter whether you are skeptical or not; it is simply enough to practice thinking the more appropriate, more rational thought. |
| T THINK PRAISE: | Reward yourself every time you successfully stop an irrational thought and replace it with a more adaptive one. Mahoney suggests telling yourself how good a job you have done. We'll suggest that it is also a good idea to reward yourself in a more tangible way. We prefer chocolate as a tangible self-reward. |

arate thoughts, feelings, and actions and guides you to, in essence, think about your thinking—something people tend not to do. In the Ellis model, stress looks as shown in Figure 8-7.

Mahoney's ADAPT represents one of the Rethinking techniques discussed in Part Three. The premise is simple: Thoughts and mental images lead to feelings. Thoughts of positive ideas and images of past and future successes usually lead to feelings

Figure 8-7. The thought-feelings-stress process.

of happiness, joy, and pleasure. Negative thoughts and images of past failures can lead to sadness, unhappiness, and anxiety. Change occurs when you can:

1. Acknowledge and label your feelings
2. Identify the thoughts and images leading to the feelings
3. Replace the thoughts

9

STRESS AND HUMOR: NO LAUGHING MATTER

REMEMBER the last time a good laugh broke the tension of a situation? Every salesperson has told a story, joke, or anecdote to break the ice with a prospect or re-enter the good graces of an old customer. Humor is a proven strategy for managing stress in interpersonal situations.

But humor is no laughing matter. There may be a strong correlation between seeing humor in life's events and controlling them. Distress is most severe when it seems inescapable and unexpected—in other words, beyond our ability to control or contain it. Humor can help inoculate us against the ill effects of distress. It encourages us to take time out—in effect, to step away from the stressor. Laughter allows us to rethink our perceptions and perhaps view events from a less stressful perspective. Humor can grease the skis of life or make you fall flat on your face. Unfortunately, humor can also be used as a weapon. In angry hands, humor dished out on a regular basis has a tremendous capacity to hurt. Unlike healing humor, which allows us to laugh at ourselves and at the human condition, hostile humor finds jokes at the expense of other people.

Sick humor, when it reflects a way of being, really *can* make people psychologically and physically ill. It also turns others off, so here's a caution: When using humor on purpose, with a prospect or a customer, take care not to offend. You know this, but like the Saturday night bath, it "bares" repeating from time to time. Remember, humor at its best pokes fun at the human condition, not at the condition of humans. For example, the gag "In my part of the country there are two seasons—winter and road under repair" offends no one. But this one—"Know why it takes three (ethnic group of your choice) to change a light bulb? One to hold the ladder, another to read the instructions, and the third to replace the bulk—offends many people, regardless of the nationality ridiculed.

By the way, don't trust your audience and its immediate reactions. Audiences laugh first and are offended later. Many a public speaker has limited his or her career by letting audience laughter selectively reinforce the humor chosen. We know a fine gentleman who was nearly wiped out on the speaking circuit because of his misuse of humor. His audiences howled at the off-color stories when he first tried them. But during the six-month interval between the first and second times we heard him, his stories had gone from spicy to rude to downright disgusting. Audiences can provide powerful reinforcers. Without being conscious of it, our friend had let his audiences selectively shape his humor and speech content. Unfortunately for him, word of his bawdy material began affecting his bookings, and as a result, we've all been deprived of the opportunity to hear the ideas of a fine thinker.

Humor can be a thinly disguised expression of hostility, anger, unhappiness, or other negative emotions. If you want to send a message, fax it. A good rule of thumb is, Jokes should be strokes.

There is a B-T-A interaction in the effects of humor. For example, it's clear that negative emotions such as depression (as shown in studies on grieving) can manipulate the immune system in a downward direction. Likewise, it seems that positive emotions—released by a healthy dose of humor—may have positive effects on the immune system. Feeling good affects how we act and react; so does feeling bad. Laughter, while not today's all-purpose cure-all elixir, does seem to facilitate healing, reduce pain, accentuate the positive, and possibly "inoculate" against illness. The jury is still out on whether positive emotions can influence the onset or progression of disease, but the direction of medical research indicates that positive emotions have an influence on the physiology of the human body.

Many people are not waiting for all the answers. For some, the amazing observed effects of humor on healing and well-being are enough to get them doing something. For example:

- Patients in Duke University's cancer ward are greeted by a Laughmobile cart which brings them humorous cassette tapes, carton books, and toys and games of every description.
- A hospital in Houston, Texas, provides a living room that features a piano, television, games, toys, and live stand-up comedians, magicians, and musicians.
- An AIDS organization has received a grant to explore how humor can help AIDS patients and the people who care for them.

Humor and Healing Your Body

Interest in the healing potential of humor was sparked by a book written in 1979 by Norman Cousins, former editor of *Saturday Review*, in which he revealed that he walked away from his death-bed in large measure because of humor. Cousins was suffering from a painful nerve disorder that was destroying the connective tissues of his body. His doctors were convinced that the end was near. But Cousins devised his own "cure." He reasoned that, since he felt relief from the pain when lost in laughter, he would spend several hours a day laughing. He checked out of the hospital, moved into a hotel, and spent four hours a day watching films of comedians and old television shows. He listened to the tapes of famous old radio sketches and read joke books from cover to cover. If depression can bring on disease, he decided, perhaps enjoyment can bring on health. And he believes it did, although he did not give up on medication or his doctors, who treated him in his hotel.[1] Today Cousins is healthy, hearty, and still laughing. He lectures at medical schools around the world, extolling the body's miraculous power to heal itself when body and mind cooperate. For at least one person, then, humor isn't simply a joke.

Cousins felt that laughter may help protect against the negative emotions that accompany disease. He did not, however, suggest that laughter is a substitute for competent medical attention.

Laughter may indeed be one of the best medicines. Few question the fact that humor, or being in a good mood, affects their bodies, thoughts, feelings, and subsequent actions. A good belly laugh, taken many times a day, seems to pick up metabolism, massage the muscles, and release neurochemicals into the blood. The result? Increasingly, physicians, psychologists, and hospital personnel feel that laughter helps mind and body guard against depression, heart disease, and pain. Some medical researchers think that laughter may bolster the immune system as well.

The Humor-Emotions-Thought Connection

Humor is often used to deflect or dissipate negative emotions such as anger and frustration. In working with people on reducing the fallout from negative emotions—getting it out of the way of their selling and their lives—we've found four ways to do it: (1) by exaggerating the feeling to dispel it; (2) by staying with a feeling until it dissipates; (3) by debating a feeling to remove it; and (4) by reversing a feeling to eliminate it. Humor is uniquely suited to quickly and hilariously accomplish the task; it is counterconditioning to negative emotions and anxious thoughts—a fancy way of saying you can't feel or think angry when you're laughing.

For example, as Dr. Stern has found, a little levity aimed at oneself can help sort the real from the unreal and operate as a personal stress reliever. Dr. Stern uses the humor of exaggeration for herself and her private clients. She tells it this way:

WHEN I was contemplating leaving academia and starting the institute, I was really pretty apprehensive. I kept seeing catastrophic images of doom and despair before my eyes. I got bored with being "uptight" quickly, so I moved on to a game I call "What's the Worst Thing That Can Happen?" I'll spare you the details, but I started with things like:

ME: I could fail!

MYSELF: And what's the worst thing that could happen if you failed?

ME: I could go broke.

MYSELF: So what's the worst thing that could happen if you went broke?

I'll spare you the twists and turns of this inner dialogue, but give you the punch line. I finally came to the conclusion that the very, very worst thing that could befall me would be to end up fat and ugly, living alone by myself with no friends in a one-room, four-story walk-up cold-water flat so poor that there is a second mortgage on the toilet seat.

At that point I had a great laugh at the whole preposterous calamity I had invented. I figured the probability of my worst fear occurring was 1 in 2 million, and I went to work building the business.

Here is the dialogue of a similar encounter I had, not with myself, but with a very worried client who was stressed over a selling situation. He was having a terrible time prospecting over the telephone:

FMS: You hate calling prospects on the phone.

CLIENT: Like the plague.

FMS: What's the worst thing that can happen to you calling somebody on the phone?

CLIENT: I'll be rebuffed, turned down, insulted; and I won't get an appointment.

FMS: Pick *one*.

CLEINT: I don't like the rebuffs.

FMS: What's the worst that can happen if you're rebuffed?

CLIENT: Hurt me. I'd feel bad.

FMS: Would you bleed?

CLIENT: No.

FMS: That's it? Hurt feeling is the worst?

CLIENT: No. Not getting the appointment is worse.

FMS: What's the worst that can happen if you don't get the appointment?

CLIENT: No appointments, no calls; no calls, no presentations; no presentations, no sales; no sales, I lose my job.

FMS: What's the worst thing that can happen if you lose your job?

CLIENT: I'll be broke and have no income.

FMS: What's the worst thing that can happen if you go broke and can't find a job?

CLIENT: I'll lose my car, I'll lose my house, and probably my wife will leave me and the kids will hate me!

FMS: So no house, no car, no wife, no kids. It all takes place. What's the worst thing that could happen?

CLIENT: I end up a drinker, a derelict on a park bench.

FSM: So now you're a drunken bum on a park bench, sleeping away the day. What's the worst that can happen then?

CLIENT: I could get mugged. I could go hungry. I could get rained on.

FMS: So you're sitting in the park on a park bench and you get rained on. Your clothes are wet and soggy and you're cold and tired. So what happens next?

CLIENT: I end up in a laundromat, smoking old cigar butts, with my only set of clothes in a dryer.

FMS: So there you are, in a laundromat naked, watching your clothes go round and round. So what happens next?

CLIENT: (Laughs, then finally speaks)
Oh, I don't know. I guess I could catch pneumonia or break a leg and end up in a charity ward in a hospital.

FMS: So there you are, in a bed in a hospital, coughing, leg up in a cast in a charity ward. What's the worst thing that can happen?

CLIENT: (Laughing) I could die—that's gotta be the only way to end this story.

FMS: So look at this. Do you see the sequence of events? You die of pneumonia with the world's worse hangover and all because you wouldn't pick up the telephone?

CLIENT: (Laughing) Okay, Okay. I get the point. So what am I supposed to do with all that?

FMS: Use your "catastrophies" constructively. The exaggeration can help put things in perspective.

CLIENT; How do I do that?

FMS: Step away from your catastrophe for a moment. What would you say to me if you were in this chair and I were in that one? What would you tell me the odds are if I had just told you the story that you just told me?

CLIENT: About a million to one, I guess.

FMS: So if you recognize that the catastrophizing is all a bad joke, let's see if we can do something about it.

CLIENT: I see what you mean.

FMS: So the next time you pick up the phone, think of the idiocy of sitting naked in a laundromat smoking a second-hand cigar, watching your clothes go around. It may even give your voice a lilt and you'll get through to the prospect more easily.

CLIENT: Okay.

The object here wasn't to belittle or make fun of the man with the call-reluctance problem, but simply by exaggerating it to help him move away, distance himself, from the problem and thereby reduce his catastrophic thought and negative feelings in order to see the problem with a broader perspective. Incidentally, it worked.

A super stockbroker had been dealing with a most difficult client for a number of years, although she dreaded every lengthy, aggravating phone call. One day she said, "That clown is driving me up a wall! It's gotten so I spend half my waking hours focused on him!" Using the clown image, she quickly learned to envision him as a clown in whiteface and floppy shoes, and wearing a wide, foolish grin. The picture tickled her funny bone, reversing her feelings from anger to pleasure. It made her transactions with this stress-carrying client more manageable. Humor and imagery did the trick!

Activate Your Funny Bone

By now the message should be clear: humor can lift your spirits and make that next sales call easier. It can help put "no sale" problems in perspective. Humor can connect you—to parts of yourself, your customers, your co-workers; your friends and lovers. So here is a prescription to help you activate your funny bone—to act and be humorous:

1. *Develop your skill.* Keep an eye open for the funny things in life. A sense of humor is a human capacity, but it takes a bit of fine-tuning. You needn't be the best joke teller to have a good sense of humor, but you do need to be open to humor in your life and capitalize on it.

2. *Be an active humorist.* Where would Bob Hope be if he hadn't taken his brand of humor on the road? Would Rodney Dangerfield have been funny if he didn't get into "no respect" situations? Many successful sales pros learn some good jokes and tuck them into their briefcases.

3. *Practice controlled silliness.* Allow yourself to be part of the foolishness of life. It will keep you from becoming stiff, unyielding, and humorless. A naturally clumsy salesman we know raises his clumsiness to a fine art. It helps break the ice at a sales presentation and turns a sticky situation around. So, do something silly; let go, but control it.

4. *Invite humor from others.* Whenever possible and appropriate, watch for what puts a twinkle in someone's eye and then go for it. There's a wise lady who sells a lot of houses with that approach. There are times when her ability to bring forth laughter in a client makes the sale, especially with nervous first-time buyers.

5. *Lighten up your life.* Rediscover toys and games. Invite others to join you. Trivial Pursuit isn't trivial at all, for laughter and fun can pave the way to better communication. Figure out what amuses you and expose yourself to these things or situations on a regular basis. Dr. Stern has enshrined Erma Bombeck's words on the refrigerator door: "Laughter works much better than cookies, and it's less calories, too."

6. *Laugh at your own risk.* Beware! Don't laugh if you can't take it. Laughing can be risky because it can open up new ways of looking at the world and give the world new ways to look at you. Rather than view joking around as undignified, see it as opening doors for us to creativity, constructive change, and health.

7. *Don't laugh at what's not funny.* The perpetual "fun-nyman" who tells just one more joke about the traveling sales-man is boring and annoying. Similarly, sarcastic humor or forced jollyness falls flat. Remember your reaction to tasteless or inappropriate humor and avoid the pitfalls yourself.

EXERCISE 7. How's Your Sense of Humor?

Are you looking at the world through doom-colored glasses? Do you see storm clouds around every silver lining? Are you walking around expecting the worst and disappointed when it doesn't happen? The following thirteen true-false items are in-tended to let you see if you have a sense of humor about yourself and your work. Check off True or False.

True-False Quiz for Salespeople

	True	False
1. If there are four possible ways for a sale to fall through and you circumvent these, then a fifth way will promptly develop.	___	___
2. It is impossible to make any product or service foolproof because fools are so ingenious.	___	___
3. There is an inverse relationship between farmers' daughter jokes and available farmers' daughters.	___	___
4. In the performance of your product or service, nature will always side with the hidden flaw.	___	___
5. Miracles don't happen—but it helps to rely on them when considering delivery dates.	___	___
6. In case of doubt, make it sound convincing.	___	___
7. Badness comes in waves, called sales slumps.	___	___

	True	*False*
8. Under the most rigorously controlled conditions, the prospect will do exactly as he or she damn well pleases.	___	___
9. The salesperson who can smile when things go wrong has found someone else to blame it on.	___	___
10. Progress is made on alternate Wednesdays.	___	___
11. Your customers' paperwork is profit. Your own paperwork is loss.	___	___
12. Twenty percent of your customers account for 80 percent of the turnover.	___	___
13. Sales managers will act rationally when all other possibilities have been exhausted.	___	___

This baker's dozen true-false items are either (1) all true, (2) all false, (3) neither true nor false, or (4) just a piece of comic relief. You decide. If none of these items strikes you as even mildly funny, you either have *no* sense of humor or your sense of humor is different from ours. In any case, enough jokes about humor.

10

SPEAK UP: STRESS AND COMMUNICATION

S TRESSFUL situations can pop up unexpectedly nearly every day, and often they call for an assertive response. But asserting yourself can be difficult. For example:

YOU'RE standing in line at a very expensive and impressive restaurant with an important prospect. You're chatting and someone jumps in front of the line just as the maitre d' asks, "Who's next, please?" You know you were next, and everyone in line—including your prospect—knows you were next. You're furious. Your stomach is in knots and your palms are sweaty. And you know that no matter how you handle the situation, you aren't going to feel very good about it.

You're attending an important national sales meeting. You offer a brilliant idea for marketing the new Green Widget that has just been introduced. Your suggestion goes over like a burp in church. Twenty minutes later, the executive vice-president of marketing announces, "Say, George, that idea wasn't half-bad." Your name is Bill, but before you can claim credit where credit is due, George grabs the lead and is off and running. Your ears are bright red and you don't dare look up because you know that everyone in the room *knows* that you have been. . . .

These and similar situations occur every day: at home with the spouse, the kids, the in-laws, and the neighbors; with peers, prospects, and bosses; even with total strangers. These situations have two things in common. First, your wants and needs conflict with the wants and needs of others. Second, you must assert yourself in the face of perceived adversity, making your opinions, thoughts, and feelings directly and immediately known.

Assertive! What Do You Mean I'm Not Assertive?

You're probably thinking:

> Now wait a minute! Salespeople never have trouble communicating with people. That's their "thing," right? Why, right there in the irrefutable *Good Book of Salesmanship* it says in big gold letters:

SELLING IS COMMUNICATION

> Salespeople never have trouble communicating.

Let's do each other a favor and call that preceding dialogue exactly what it is: sliced baloney! Sure, salespeople *are* better communicators than 95 percent of the population. So what? Does that mean they don't have off days or that there isn't room to improve? Or that stress doesn't interfere with their ability to communicate? That communication isn't often stressful? Certainly not. In fact, many salespeople report a decrease in their communication skills as the first sign of mounting stress. Most important, being a salesperson and a professional communicator doesn't mean that you automatically know when and how to be an appropriately assertive communicator—that you know when to ask for what you want in a reasonable and calm manner.

If you have an association with the term "assertiveness," it probably derives from one of those Sunday-supplement stories of Shy Violet, Wilbur Milquetoast, and other 95-pound weaklings being turned into raving, fire-breathing, world-beaters with "Don't tread on me" tatooed across their chests in Day-Glo orange. A recent *New Yorker* cartoon captured it perfectly. Two surly, scowling fellows are seated at the bar, and one says to the other, "Oh yeah! Well, *my* assertiveness seminar can lick *your* assertiveness seminar any day!" Cute, but wide of the mark.

Assertiveness coaching isn't limited to those who wince at leading a group in silent prayer. It's for anyone who has to deal with communicative conflict. It works like this. Remember Walter Cannon and the fight/flight response? Well, the fight response to communicative conflict takes the form of aggressive verbal behavior, or defending oneself in a way that the rights of others are violated in the process. Aggressive verbal behavior is an attempt to win by humiliation and put-down. Generally it's a dishonest, manipulative process. How do you violate a prospect's rights? Here's a mild example:

MR. PROSPECTIVE Buyer, I know your boss's boss is very much in favor of this project and he would be pretty upset if he thought you were challenging him on this.

The flight response translates to nonassertive, or *passive*, behavior. Backing off, giving in, and showing undue deference to others' opinions are inappropriate passive or underassertive responses. Failing to stand up for your reasonable rights, or standing up in such an ineffectual manner that your rights are easily violated, characterizes the underassertive reply to communicative conflict and confrontation. For example:

YOU'VE scheduled a forty-minute appointment with Tom Customer. The account and this new product presentation are important to you. You arrive on time. He keeps you waiting twenty-five minutes. He walks into the reception area and tells you, "Got tied up in a meeting, Sam. Look, just give me something to read and I'll call you about it in a week or so." You say,

"I understand how that can happen, Tom. Here are our specs and the new configuration and the summary notes I made for our meeting. If you have any questions, don't hesitate to call me." You *know* this falls short of your goal, and you walk away feeling really rotten. You haven't said what you wanted to say, what you feel you should have said.

Dr. Joseph Wolpe and others suggest that humans have a third choice, an alternative to fight/flight, and that choice is reasoned *problem solving* or *assertive behavior.*[1] The problem-solving assertive response is the win-win position. This is characterized as standing up for your rights in such a way that you do not violate the basic rights of others but express your feelings, opinions, and/or needs directly, honestly, reasonably, and appropriately.

The Stress Connection

The most obvious stress is felt by the underassertive or passive communicator. Some people simply are quieter, less verbally assertive than others. But many "quiet" and underassertive people suffer from communication anxiety. They are stressed by situations requiring them to communicate with strangers or with people they know only slightly. While it would seem that communication anxiety is the *last* problem a salesperson suffers from, that assumption is false. A substantial number of salespeople lose their voice or become restricted and defensive communicators when they experience conflict with customers, prospects, peers, supervisors, and loved ones. People who are communicatively anxious—and who act passively in a confrontation—may cover their passivity by telling witnesses that they are "making the customer *think* he got his way." But the truth is that the passive secretly beat themselves because of their failure to assert, and they end up quite stressed. These people often do a "should have said" rerun in their heads, generating additional stress.

The aggressive communicator, on the other hand, gets hit with stress in the self-respect arena. People who verbally assault others are often held at arms length, abandoned. As a result, they often end up feeling isolated and deserted. They can never figure out why everyone in the office is always too busy for lunch, coffee, or any other situation that brings them face-to-face with the tiger. Additionally, aggression brings out the aggression in others. They then engage in guerrilla tactis. A customer may be badgered into a one-time buy—but at the expense of the salesperson's reputation. Negative word of mouth can keep an aggressive sales pro off of a lot of appointment calendars. Aggression gets short-term compliance but never long-term commitment.

How assertive are you? The following self-tests will give you a feel for your assertiveness level. Take both inventories, then follow the scoring and interpretation instructions.

EXERCISE 8. Communication Comfort Inventory

The following items refer to situations and experiences that may make you uncomfortable, uneasy, nervous, or slightly fearful. For each item, circle the number that most accurately describes the extent of discomfort you experience in the described situation. For example, if "asking for an order" causes you moderate discomfort, you circle 3. If you have not experienced the situation, circle the number that describes the extent of discomfort you think you would experience if you were in it.

The five degrees of discomfort are as follows: 1 = no discomfort; 2 = a little discomfort; 3 = moderate discomfort; 4 = much discomfort; 5 = a great deal of discomfort.

1. Arguing with customers or clients.   1 2 3 4 5
2. Asking for an order.   1 2 3 4 5
3. Starting a conversation with a stranger. 1 2 3 4 5
4. Disappointing close friends.   1 2 3 4 5
5. Looking foolish in front of prospects/
   clients.   1 2 3 4 5
6. Losing control of yourself.   1 2 3 4 5
7. Getting angry with members of the op-
   posite sex.   1 2 3 4 5

8. Not being able to say the right thing.   1 2 3 4 5
9. Acting natural around business acquaintances.   1 2 3 4 5
10. "Dropping" or "breaking" with a friend.   1 2 3 4 5
11. Expressing your opinions in a discussion group or a meeting.   1 2 3 4 5
12. Making a bad impression.   1 2 3 4 5
13. Having a lot of authority over others.   1 2 3 4 5
14. Talking with people who are smarter than you are.   1 2 3 4 5
15. Sounding artificial when you compliment someone.   1 2 3 4 5
16. Having to introduce people.   1 2 3 4 5
17. Getting angry with people you love and respect.   1 2 3 4 5
18. Refusing requests made by family and friends.   1 2 3 4 5
19. Giving opinions about which you are not sure.   1 2 3 4 5
20. Talking about personal matters with a customer.   1 2 3 4 5
21. Returning a gift given by a close friend or relative.   1 2 3 4 5
22. Feeling guilty about getting angry.   1 2 3 4 5
23. Looking bad on personality tests.   1 2 3 4 5
24. Dealing with pushy customers.   1 2 3 4 5
25. Disagreeing with supervisors.   1 2 3 4 5
26. Asking directions when lost.   1 2 3 4 5
27. Taking a sexual initiative.   1 2 3 4 5
28. Telling others the truth about your earnings.   1 2 3 4 5
29. Asking a favor from a stranger.   1 2 3 4 5
30. Asking a prospect for an appointment.   1 2 3 4 5

EXERCISE 9. Interpersonal Importance Inventory

The following statements refer to attitudes and beliefs you may have about a number of situations and experiences. Indicate your relative agreement with each statement by circling the number that corresponds to your degree of agreement, using the following scale: 1 = strongly agree; 2 = agree; 3 = neither agree nor disagree; 4 = disagree; 5 = strongly disagree.

1. Contradicting a domineering person doesn't pay since you will just make him angry.   1 2 3 4 5

2. It's seldom, if ever, necessary to insist on having things my own way.   1 2 3 4 5

3. It's improper for a man to argue with a woman.   1 2 3 4 5

4. It's never right to ignore the feelings of others, even if you're trying to accomplish something worthwhile.   1 2 3 4 5

5. If you really care for people, they'll know it even if you don't directly tell them so.   1 2 3 4 5

6. If a close friend or relative annoys you, it's best to keep quiet for the sake of peace.   1 2 3 4 5

7. It's usually expedient to do things without regard to what others may think.   1 2 3 4 5

8. If you aren't sure of your opinion, it's better to keep quiet.   1 2 3 4 5

9. Before doing something, you should consider how your customers will react to it.   1 2 3 4 5

10. Arguing makes people feel bad and it doesn't change anyone's mind.   1 2 3 4 5

11. A tolerant person tries to fulfill a customer/client request even if it's unreasonable.   1 2 3 4 5

12. It's important to be courteous to every-
    one, even disagreeable people.   1 2 3 4 5
13. Everyone must have a close confidant
    to discuss things with.   1 2 3 4 5
14. Insisting on having your own way inev-
    itably hurts someone's feelings.   1 2 3 4 5
15. Sometimes a person needs to pretend
    to know more than he or she really
    does.   1 2 3 4 5
16. If you're not being given enough credit
    for your work, you should complain to
    the boss.   1 2 3 4 5
17. You dislike doing things on the spur of
    the moment.   1 2 3 4 5
18. You enjoy saying what you feel at the
    moment.   1 2 3 4 5
19. You would be very unhappy if you were
    prevented from making numerous so-
    cial contacts.   1 2 3 4 5
20. It's pretty easy for people to win an ar-
    gument with you.   1 2 3 4 5

Scoring and Interpretation

THE COMMUNICATION COMFORT INVENTORY

Total the numbers you circled on the Communication
Comfort Inventory. Be sure you've circled one number for each
of the thirty items. Record the total here.

• *Scores Between 120 and 150.* Scores in this range suggest
that you may experience some degree of communication anxiety. Many people who score in this range find communication
stressful. There's a tendency for these people to be passive or
underassertive communicators. Salespeople scoring in this
range tend to be more stressed by communication than other
people, owing to self-expectations. As a salesperson, you think

face-to-face communications should be less stressful—after all, you're a pro. Facing up to that conflict between reality and expectation will help. Part Three will have some specific "do's" for you.

• *Scores Between 70 and 120.* Generally, salespeople tend to score in this range. Experience with people and communication stress tends to make most salespeople less stressed by communication than nonsalespeople. If you scored in this range, chances are that you are able to handle the stress of communication pretty well. That does not mean that you are automatically appropriately assertive; just that anxiousness and stress probably don't interfere with your attempts to communicate. You may, for example, have learned that salespeople must be tough and autocratic with customers; that position is what we call aggressive. Your score simply says that you are not stressed by your approach to communicating with others. You should be able to adjust your communication style as situations demand. You would be quite comfortable in the assertive communication posture.

• *Scores Between 30 and 70.* If you score in this range, you may be appropriately assertive, but there's also a chance that you're an aggressive communicator. The reason is simple. You tend to be less stressed and anxious about communications than most people. You must be careful to use the feedback—especially nonverbal—you get from others. Coming on like gangbusters with a prospect who is much less assertive than you are, someone who's anxious about communication, can kill your sale. You need to develop a sensitivity to other people's stress levels—which you will do in Part Two—*and* you need to guard against being too aggressive and unduly forceful with prospects and customers.

THE INTERPERSONAL IMPORTANCE INVENTORY

Total the numbers you circled on the Interpersonal Importance Inventory. Be sure you've circled one number for each of the twenty items. Record the total here. ☐

• *Scores Between 20 and 50.* If you scored in this range, you're probably very sensitive to communication conflict and try to avoid it. You may be communicatively anxious or stressed by conflict with others. You might be an avoider. Harmony at almost any cost may be important to you.

• *Scores Between 50 and 80.* Most salespeople score in this range. People who score here are sensitive to extremes of conflict but are tolerant of differences between themselves and others. Communication is fun for you and so may be disagreements— as long as they are not too extreme. You're probably aware that assertiveness keeps conflict manageable; passive and aggressive communications do not. Learning to be assertive rather than aggressive is a fairly easy task for you.

• *Scores Between 80 and 100.* People who score in this range tend to be insensitive to other people's communication comfort needs. Some are so stressed by *not* getting their own way that they shut out all other information. Others simply are insensitive to feedback. You may well be an aggressive communicator who has a tendency to promote communication conflict.

COMBINING YOUR SCORES

The scores from these two self-quizzes can be combined to give you a picture of your communication style.

Interpersonal
Importance Score

		20–50	50–80	80–100
Communication Comfort Score	120–150	A	B	C
	70–120	D	E	F
	30–70	G	H	I

Pick the cell your two scores fall into.

A B C D E F G H I

Then interpret the cell as follows:

Cell A. You are the communication-anxious person who avoids conflict like the plague.

Cells B and C. You are the communication-anxious person who nonetheless does communicate with others. The Cell 3 person tends to be both overaggressive and anxious—probably a stress carrier.

Cells D, E, and F. If you scored here, you are sensitive to communications and your own feelings in communication situations; you use your feelings for feedback. If you were either D or F, you should consider becoming more assertive and less passive or aggressive. You could easily learn and use win-win face-to-face communications.

Cell G. It's almost impossible to land in this cell. Re-check your score. If you're sure of your answers, consider this description. You come on like gangbusters and are very stressed by the way you communicate. Modification of your approach is critical to getting control of your stress.

Cell H. You're probably more assertive than most, bordering on aggressive. You should consider learning to modify your approach to others. It will take some practice and perhaps feedback from a third party.

Cell I. If you scored here, you are probably an aggressive person. You are both insensitive to communication tension and believe getting your own way and making your point are more important than making a sale. You're going to need to make a heavy change if you decide to try assertive communication. You will need a good source of feedback and an exploration of how you really feel during communication conflict.

Some Closing Words

According to Dr. Patricia Jakubowski, a University of Missouri-St. Louis assertiveness training pioneer, passive and aggressive communications are costly to both buyer and seller. Passive or nonassertive communications, characterized by indirectness, self-denial, inhibition, and emotional dishonesty, leave the sender with hurt feelings, anxiety, and anger toward himself. Equally important, the receiver frequently feels irritation, pity, and disgust for the passive sender. The receiver of nonassertive communications sometimes feels guilty and sometimes superior to the sender.

Aggressive communications also have unacceptable outcomes for both parties. The aggressive sender is direct all right, but also domineering at others' expense. His or her aggressiveness often cuts off communication at the outset. When stressed, the aggressive communicator issues demands and makes deprecating, chaffing statements that leave others feeling hurt and humiliated, angry and vengeful. The aggressive communicator tends not to get repeat appointments or repeat sales. Aggressors pay the price of isolation. After all, if others are so inferior and they are so righteous, who would dare be honest and open with them? The upshot is that aggressive communicators are often stressed by feelings of isolation or guilt.

Both aggressive and passive communicators cheat themselves of the opportunity to experience win-win communications. But not so the assertive person, who communicates directly and expressively and who treats others as equals. The assertive communicator tends to feel confident and "self-respecting" during the sales interview *and* afterward. The recipient of assertive communications feels respected and valued, and has reciprocal feelings toward the assertive communicator.

Assertive communication is risky, both personally and professionally. But the payoff for a salesperson can be great. It is also suggested that assertive communicators develop an assertive mind-set that leads to an enhanced ability to perform effectively and deliver results. Part of this effect comes from eliminating "meaning games." The "What did he mean by that?" and "Do I dare ask her to explain that to me?" questions promote anxiety and interfere with productive problem identification and solution finding.

Assertive communication *is* risky and takes practice to develop. It even takes away such standard sales tools as bullying prospects or giving away the store. But the goal is obvious: clear communication between buyer and seller, rep and manager, parent and child, and spouse and spouse. The need for assertive communication arises when people are in honest disagreement, in conflict. Proper assertiveness helps you face conflict or confront disagreement and lets both parties walk away with their self-respect intact, without bad feelings or bitterness. What more could you ask of such a simple idea?

11

ROLE JUGGLING: THE INESCAPABLE "PUSH ME-PULL YOU"

P RESSURE! Does this scenario sound familiar?

MY son is calling on line one to tell me he forgot his baseball uniform at home, while my customer on line two wants to know why we missed the promised delivery date. My husband on line three is waiting to find out what I want to do about fixing the car, and my secretary steps in to remind me that my mother has to be at the doctor's office by two thirty. My work day has just begun!

Welcome to a thoroughly modern stressor: role conflict. More than ever, salesmen and women must make ever-increasing and ever-more complex choices. "Will I attend that extra but useful sales conference, or go home in time to see Billy play in the regional playoffs?" "Can I skip the last day of my itinerary so that I get home in time for our anniversary?" These forced choices are increasingly stressful, since there is no solution to having one's cake and eating it too. To make things worse, you're told not to take your home problems with you on a sales call— an impossible request since people don't compartmentalize themselves. A sick child at home or a decision to be made about an aged parent, an unexpected outlay of cash or a problem with a customer's promised delivery date act upon each other and take their toll.

As sales pros demand a better quality of life on the job and integration of home and work life, the stress of reaching this goal increases. In fact, sales pros have told us just that. They rank *home and family pressures* as their number 4 stressor from a list of fifty possibilities. When we talk to these people at seminars and workshops, they complain about constantly having to be a parent, professional, playmate, and a community elder all at the same time. They lament about the wear and tear of having to juggle, trade off, and compromise the demands each of these and other roles make against one another. They express anger, sorrow, and disappointment—and the feeling that they are unable to do any one thing fully or well. They tell us that it is particularly stressful when one or more of their roles is not of their own choosing.

Research on general populations supports what our sales pros tell us: role conflicts can be very stressful. Psychologist Leonard Pearlin and his associates surveyed 2,300 Chicago-area adults to find out what they found stressful. Three of the top four items were associated with life roles—marriage, parenthood, and work.[1] In short, the more demands we perceive others make of us, the less we feel in control of our lives and the more we feel pressured and stressed by life in general.

A "role," or pattern of expected behavior, may be formal or informal, temporary or permanent, deeply embedded or superficial. Whether the role is as son, lover, mother, hotshot sales pro, or friend, it requires time, energy, and focus—all of which are in short supply. So people make choices among them, often requiring sacrifices. It is this juggling act that produces the thought and action stress responses that were virtually unknown in our grandparents' day.

Employers are beginning to recognize the bite that "role stress" takes out of profits and are trying to do something about it. Indeed, Stanford University Business School offers a workshop on the biological clock as part of its Happily Ever After series. It seems strange to have a business-school course dealing with when to have children until one realizes that becoming a mother affects a woman's personal and business life, and that half the students in graduate business schools today are women.

The armed forces, the nation's leading employer, find themselves faced with the fallout of role conflict. Despite the $16 million spent annually on child care for personnel, demand is running far ahead of supply. Military experts and civilian lawmakers suggest that a crisis exists because, as they see it, inadequate child care could undermine morale and readiness as the armed forces add more women, single parents, dual-service military couples, and enlisted men and women whose spouses also work outside the home. They link adequate child care with military-force readiness and psychological willingness of personnel to go to war on a moment's notice!

Employers are beginning to ask employees how their parental roles affect them on the job. A study of 6,600 male DuPont workers were asked if they wanted the option of part-time work to allow them to stay home with the kids. In 1985, 18 percent would have liked that option. In 1988, the percentage increased to 33 percent. The statistics suggest that the role of father is shifting to "good parent," away from the breadwinner aspect focused on previously. Redefining the role of father increases stress, on and off the job.

The Family Medical Leave Act now before Congress, which allows employees ten weeks of unpaid leave to cope with elderly parents, an ill spouse, or a new child, is likely to be passed by the time you read this. The fact that the bill has such wide support underscores the impact of role conflict on American life.

An enterprising New Jersey child-care organization, which services over 1,000 children daily in three New Jersey counties, responds to working parents' needs by providing take-out family meal service as well as full-day care and after-school programs. They also offer "lunchbag seminars" on many aspects of parenting and advise corporations as to the feasibility of on-site child care. A parent could conceivably leave his or her child from age six weeks through ten years, from 6:30 A.M. until 7:00 P.M. in the organization's care. Such centers, impossible to even conceive of fifteen or twenty years ago, are filling a growing need today. Their services are being sought by both men and women. That isn't surprising, since role conflict hits both sexes, though somewhat differently.

Women, who now constitute 44.8 percent of the work force, according to the U.S. Department of Labor, find that they must frequently sacrifice one role for another. They feel that they must concentrate either on their career or on their family, although they often try to do both at the same time. Worse yet, when they try to succeed at more than one role at once, they often feel they're not successful in either. They frequently find that when they perform the responsibilities of one role they worry about the things they are not doing, thus robbing themselves of the satisfaction of their immediate accomplishments. Sometimes humorous situations result, but more often the mounting tension is no laughing matter.

Men, too, say they increasingly feel that they have to sacrifice time with their families in order to be good providers and to advance their careers. And many fear that when they achieve their professional goals and refocus attention on their families, their roles as husband and father will have disappeared; that their families will have found ways of filling the vacuum that leave us no room on their return.

A CRACKERJACK "outside man" who helped catapult a small family-owned business into the big time, was stopped short in his workaholic ways when he discovered his wife was having an affair. He said, "I thought that being a good provider was enough. It sounds strange now, but I really didn't stop to think about what my wife wanted or what the kids needed, or even what was important to me for myself. I just thought about making a living and building this big business, and this big house that I may have to live in alone. This isn't how I thought it would work out. I really love my family. It wasn't worth sacrificing them to the business.

Dual-career couples face even greater role challenges. They must cope with a new life-style for which there is neither roadmap nor signs. Many couples find that when they make it up as they go along, they experience suffocating pressure personally, professionally, and between themselves.

Single parents are a new and growing headache on the corporate and personal horizon. Men and women who are single heads of household are sailing in largely unchartered, highly stressful waters. The single-parent sales pro has to tackle even greater challenges. What with uncertain cash flow, travel, and late working hours, it is only a very flexible person who can be effective across the board for very long. As a single parent told us,

> You may not believe this, but I actually found a client's file in the refrigerator and the kid's bottle on my desk one night. I went crazy looking for that file. I couldn't have remembered doing that if my life depended on it. I didn't even notice the bottle sitting on my messed-up desk. If I hadn't gotten frustrated and reached for something cold to drink, who knows when I would have found the file?

People today face problems unknown to previous generations and are increasingly feeling trapped, caught in the middle of role conflict. They find that they are parents longer, since they may have to care for adult children, and they are children longer, since they may have to provide for aging parents. In addition, rapid social changes have redefined these roles, making them less clear and bringing them in conflict with one another.

MARTIN, a heavy-duty heavy machinery sales pro, commented about the frustration he experienced in trying to accommodate his personal and professional world despite a heavy travel commitment. "I really feel boxed in," he said one evening after a workshop. "I've got to travel to get the job done—and that's what helps put bread on the table and keep the boys in college. But boy, do those walls close in when I try to play catch up with the paperwork, with my family, and with the everyday business of selling and servicing the customer. I feel the pressure from all sides. Everything needs attention. I try, but it's getting so that there is barely time to get a decent haircut or talk to my wife for more than a few minutes. It's like batting your head against a brick wall. Sometimes I ask myself why I'm willing to keep at it."

I'm sure it sounds as familiar to you as it did to us. Over the years we'd heard many variations of the "boxed in" theme. A box has four walls, but they're not all made of brick. Three walls are movable, less constraining. One wall often is a true brick wall, unyielding and totally immovable—a flat-out constraint. You can only get battered and bruised if you butt your head against this wall. A second wall, also pretty rigid, consists of basic company policy—those things that exist, locked in place. But the nature of this wall does alter, very slowly. It's stressful and unproductive to try to move this wall while it's still firmly in place, but it pays to check it out from time to time since policy does change. The third wall is a flexible one. It represents "standard operating procedure" at any given time. This constraint is a result of current expediency, but it represents the "right now." You can focus on what the existing conditions are. Make sure you understand the components that make up this wall and check your beliefs about them. This wall can be moved if you are careful. (See figure below.)

You can completely remove the fourth wall of the box because it is self-imposed, the wall you personally have erected. Ironically, this wall has the most give, yet it is often the hardest

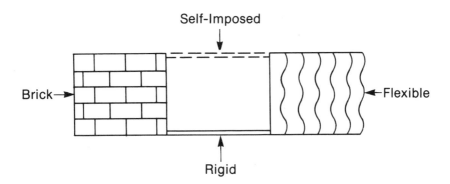

one to tackle. A self-imposed wall contains our personal assumptions, beliefs, and ways of doing things, many of which haven't been tested for years. We're closest to this wall—so close, in fact, that we may fail to see its potential. And it's a pity, too, since you only have to move one wall to get out of the box—any one. Self-imposed walls move quickly and easily once we see them, because we *control* them.

In the previous example, Martin *did* have to travel. He *did* have to attend trade shows, entertain overseas customers, and the like. They were true constraints. However, he found that some things had changed, including the addition of a sales vice-president who understood the problem and was looking for more flexible solutions himself. When testing the self-imposed wall, Martin was able to rethink "time" and "travel," resulting in his using both in larger blocks. He decided that he didn't have to travel as frequently or in the existing setup. Martin restructured his thinking and his routine. He traveled for a longer period of time, usually built around trade shows, and was home for larger blocks of time, which allowed for some continuity in his roles as father, husband, and golf buddy. He then was able to figure out a system for staying in touch with his life and work while on the road.

After Martin understood what the walls were made of, he went on to assess the *source* of his stressfulness. He found some stresses were self-created and set about re-evaluating his own attitudes and actions. Some "walls" (and the tension they brought) came from the attitudes and actions of others. Martin had to decide whom he could influence and whom he had to walk around. When circumstances created the tension, Martin had to learn to reduce his frustration by letting go of what he couldn't control or influence. Using techniques similar to those outlined later in this book, he learned to pick his shots. "It took a while, but I'm finally seeing the light at the end of the tunnel—and it's not a train coming at me," he laughed.

The roles that we assign ourselves (M), that other people assign us (O), and that situations dictate (S) have physical, emotional, and behavioral consequences. When people are not able to deal with their simultaneous multiple roles, they become angry, anxious, and depressed and they begin to function poorly.

The reality is that they perform poorly or, at best, mediocre in all those rolls. This creates the spiral of stress. If someone doesn't recognize a headache, backache, or short fuse as symptom of a role problem, the attempts to cope are inappropriate. The solutions don't work, they feel more frustrated, angry, and demotivated—which, of course, creates more stress—and they slump.

People who manage their multiple roles well use their bodies, thoughts, and actions to keep the pressure down and keep their heads screwed on straight. They take a few minutes to slow down and "daydream" at their desks, or they go for a walk around the block (often in their minds). They breathe deeply, often without knowing what they are doing or why it works. They remove the "shoulds" and "have to's" from their thinking. They step back and ask themselves questions that help them make decisions that generate workable solutions. They figure out which role needs to be juggled right now and which ball can be dropped without harmful effects.

The case of Mary Ellen shows that there is a solution to this dilemma:

MARY ELLEN, a once-successful software salesperson, suddenly found herself, as she put it, "in deep trouble and sinking fast." Insomnia, backaches, and blistering headaches sent her to the family physician, who suspected stress and referred her to Dr. Stern. After talking with her for a while, Dr. Stern noted that Mary Ellen's medical symptoms were indeed stress related, as she and her doctor suspected.

Not unlike many of today's "gotta have it all" professionals, Mary Ellen was frozen in place by her role conflicts. This once top sales pro was in trouble. Recently returned to work after an extended maternity leave (twin girls), she found her key accounts assigned elsewhere and herself, in effect, having to start from scratch to build contented clients. Worse yet, her production quotas were at the same high level as when she left—quotas more appropriate to a mature client book.

On top of these obvious work pressures, things were now different on the home front. First, and most obvious, was the pressure of being mother of twins and the family's consulting domestic engineer. Not far behind was her recently developed role of successful corporate-attorney spouse; during her maternity leave, her husband had come to depend on her as full-time hostess, social secretary, and loving, attentive partner. And while he had said not a word about her returning to work, it was obvious that he was having a tough time re-adjusting.

In a way, Mary Ellen was lucky. Her physical symptoms warned her that she was headed for trouble. The obvious changes in her life were easy to pinpoint, and the conflicts were obvious. Caught in suspension, she was turning her focus continuously and endlessly from role to role. As she talked about the frustrations she was experiencing, it became obvious that the hours she would have to devote to regaining her position as a top salesperson were in direct conflict with the time available as mother and as spouse-hostess.

Mary Ellen came quickly to see that there simply weren't enough hours in a week—or a year—for her to be successful at all her roles—at least not in the way she was defining "successful." Her breakthrough came only when she was willing to redefine her levels of achievement and the relative value of each role. Assessing the relative value of each role reduced Mary Ellen's possibility of dropping the same ball too often.

Zero In: Assess Your Roles

Take some time right now to zero in on yourself. Ask yourself the question, "Who Am I?" Pose the question at least five times (or until you run out of responses). Jot down your answers before reading any further.

How many "selves" did you discover? How many roles do they reflect? You may have found that the admonition "Know Thyself" is easier said than done, especially since there are so many "selves" to know: sales pro, parent, brother or sister, peacemaker, big spender, intellectual, game player, golfer, go-getter, friend, fool, lover—just to name a few. Clearly, the view we have of our roles influences how we see ourselves and how we respond to the environment—personally and professionally.

To evaluate your roles, complete the following exercise.

EXERCISE 10. Role Analysis

Write down your answers to the question "Who Am I?" Then ask yourself these four basic questions and write down your responses.

1. a. Is there any pattern to the responses? What do your descriptive statements reflect—social roles, personal roles, or what?
   b. Ask yourself what degree of consistency exists among your responses. Is there harmony among your various roles? If not, which roles are out of sync? Does one role seem to define you more than the others? Which one?

2. a. On a scale of 1 to 10, with 1 being the least and 10 being most, rate your current level of effectiveness.
   b. Ask yourself if the assessed level of effectiveness is good enough to get the job done (rather than perfect or close to perfect).

3. a. How comfortable are you with the role image you've reflected back at yourself? On the same 1 to 10 scale, rate how satisfied you are with each role.
   b. Is the picture one you'd like to see five years from now? Why or why not?

4. a. What importance does each role have for you? Could you let go of one of them without undue negative effect? Ask yourself, "If I stopped being that tomorrow, what would happen?"
   b. Evaluate your answer on the basis of how you'd feel as well as what would (could) happen. Come up with

as many possible scenarios, from best to worse, and then assess the likelihood of each one's occurring.

Turn Brick Walls Into Open Doors

In the complicated lives we lead, at times we're all faced with feelings of being boxed in and bound up by "brick walls." We often overlook the fact that a box has four walls. Here's how to identify each wall and determine who or what sets off the problem and how to handle what you find.

To test the factors in any role-conflict problem, it's necessary to identify which walls are most constraining and to figure out who or what is contributing to boxing you in. The figure that follows shows the situation:

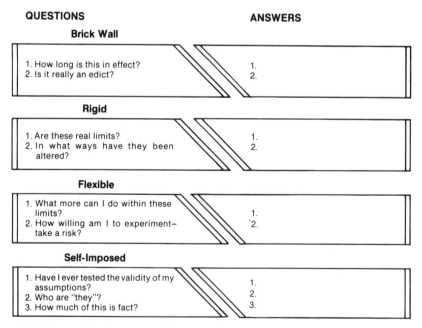

QUESTIONS   **ANSWERS**

Brick Wall

1. How long is this in effect?   1.
2. Is it really an edict?   2.

Rigid

1. Are these real limits?   1.
2. In what ways have they been   2.
   altered?

Flexible

1. What more can I do within these   1.
   limits?   2.
2. How willing am I to experiment—
   take a risk?

Self-Imposed

1. Have I ever tested the validity of my   1.
   assumptions?   2.
2. Who are "they"?   3.
3. How much of this is fact?

(Adopted from a collaboration between Dr. Stern and Dick Colvin, who was with GE in the early 1970 s.)

Now ask yourself who or what set up this wall. Was it you, other people, or a result of circumstances? Identifying the source of the "walls" of your role conflict also helps reduce feelings of frustration and helplessness. Ask yourself, "Where is the stress coming from? Is that wall made up mainly of the stress you create by your own thoughts or actions? (The MYSELF of the M-O-S). Is it generated by other people? (OTHERS). Or do circumstances and existing situations play a large part in tying your hands (SITUATIONS)? By determining the answers to these questions you begin to focus on the solution rather than the problem, come to see the extent to which your own actions box you in, evaluate the impact of other forces, and assess the potential for success in moving a particular wall. Thus you can identify goals that are achievable rather than continue to bat your head against a brick wall.

Personal and professional identity, as reflected in one's roles, is a life-and-growth issue. As we strive, grow, and change, we continuously define and redefine ourselves through our roles and how we choose to live them. Zeroing in helps clarify these roles and illuminates your available life choices. For example, if there are any roles that are out of sync with the main ones, offer low satisfaction, or make you uncomfortable, you might consider dropping them or reducing their impact.

Zeroing in on the source of the stressful "wall" helps to direct your efforts for maximum impact. Zeroing in also helps you see existing patterns and evaluate their usefulness. For example, overidentification with performance in the sales role is limiting. It keeps you from experiencing and enjoying all of who you are. It also fosters a distorted self-image. Underidentification with the professional side of who you are undermines confidence, inhibits productivity, and also keeps you from enjoying one important facet of yourself.

12

FRIEND OR FOE?
THE TWO FACES OF
STRESS

S O far, we've talked mostly about stress as the enemy. But, like nuclear energy, stress can be an ally as well as a hazard. Do you work harder and longer when you have a deadline to meet? Do you seem to get more done under pressure? If your answer is yes, then you already know the friendly, working-for-you side of stress. Stress is only an enemy when it goads you into working night and day, causes you mental anguish or unhappiness, and precipitates mental and physical discomfort, illness, or permanent damage. The goal of any stress-management program should be to help you learn to manage negative stress—to hold the enemy at bay—and help you maximize positive stress—to arm you with the best equipment available. We've said quite enough about stress that's out of control; now let's look at the way managed stress can be an asset.

Understress, Positive Stress, and Selling

Believe it or not, there is a malady referred to as understress. A light workload that does not challenge your potential is under-stressing and can be a psychological stressor of the first order. We have met bureaucrats who complain of boredom and underwork, saying things like, "I know it sounds crazy, but I have so little to do that I'm tired all the time. I feel guilty about the

narrowness of this job and how little I have to put out to do it."
If you think that could never happen in selling, you're dead
wrong! Take the case of a mortgage banker, an individual whose
forte is putting property development specialists together with
risk capital. Jim is a mortgage banker who hasn't grossed less
than $80,000 in the last ten years. Last year he was at $98,000
and ended up in consultation with Dr. Stern—not because of
overwork, anxiety, or tension, but because of boredom, blues,
and lack of challenge.

JIM would get himself revved up—stressed—for a sale, and
then bottom out—rest on his laurels; that would spiral to a
down energy level. He was making "a decent living"—everyone giving him feedback on it. He was earning as much money
as many of his office buddies "without killing himself" and
actually had more disposable income since he only had to
support himself. He was divorced: no kids and a professional
ex-wife who was self-supporting. What did he really need more
money for? Friends told him how lucky he was.

Jim came to see me, asking himself "So what's my problem? I should be happy. I'm doing okay, making a decent living, and yet I feel bored, down, and not good about myself. I
don't even want to make my usual effort." In my work with
Jim, it became clear that he did not respect himself for the job
he was doing. Always an achiever, he'd allowed himself to
take the easy way the last few years, with an accompanying
lowered sense of personal integrity. Others said he was doing
okay, but he did not really feel that way about it.

Dimly aware of the lack of congruence among his feelings,
thoughts, and productivity level, Jim just slid along—until the
day he could no longer motivate himself to get out of bed to
go to the office and shuffle papers. Over a period of ten weeks,
Jim became aware of what was getting to him and how his
low productivity, as he viewed it, was reinforced by the people
around him. He really knew what was getting to him all
along—he just didn't know he knew. He needed to face it and
verbalize it for himself. He'd been marching to the drummer

of his office peers, not to his own. Together, we developed a plan for mobilizing his inner resources.

In sequential steps, Jim began to make more calls and enjoy talking to more people. He targeted three buddies in his office to do the same, thus providing a do-it-yourself support system. He looked at the little nasties of his job and divided them into those things he could change or influence, such as hours worked, types of clients worked with, and amount of paperwork he was willing to do, then concentrated on changing those. We also looked at what he could to that was pleasurable. Did he make a million? No, but that wasn't his objective. Jim did find living—and selling—more exciting. He began to get support from his work buddies (they formed an Action-team study group). He experienced a significant increase in positive tension and increased his income rather substantially—a natural result of getting one's act together.

How do you know if you're suffering from work underload? Not an easy question to answer. Most of us are reticent to admit we aren't working up to our potential. We once polled an audience at a speaking engagement and fully one-third of those in attendance raised their hands when asked, "How many of you believe you use 100 percent of your potential on your job?" People suffering from work underload often report:

- The need for a pick-me-up at work (food, caffeinated drinks, cigarettes)
- Their minds wandering during meetings as well as when working alone
- Sometimes staring blankly and thinking of nothing at all for periods of time
- Feeling low or "flat" when at work
- Being tired at work but re-energized by the time they reach home or a social event
- Dragging themselves out of bed in the morning
- Job dissatisfaction with no obvious cause
- Few feelings of pride about tasks accomplished on the job

Lack of stress helps explain why telephone operators complain of boredom during off-peak call periods and why airline pilots get angry or bored when their aircraft are on autopilot. These people are temporarily lacking or being deprived of the stimulation—stress—that is normal for their job—the stress level they are used to and the tension that is part of the expectations they have of the job.

We bring up the understress, work underload problem here to make a point:

> WE ALL NEED STRESS AND PRESSURE IN MANAGEABLE FORMS
> TO DO A GOOD JOB AND TO EXPERIENCE AN INTERESTING, FUN
> LIFE.

Only when stress becomes excessive does it gives rise to strain and sickness. A regular shot of adrenaline can do wonders for boredom and listlessness. A government-funded study, another of those white-mice projects, found that even rodents need some dynamic tension in their lives. The researchers built an environment you could call Mouse Heaven. The place was stocked with everything a little mouse's heart could desire, from cheese to members of the opposite sex. The youngest mice in the group became listless, lethargic, and lost interest in both food and sex. The older rodents stalked about their cages very stressed. The researchers reported that these rodents displayed typical stress responses.

An article in *Business Week* had a title proclaiming "Executive Stress May Not Be All That Bad." It made the point that studies of top managers suggest that executives expect stress on the job and take it in stride. They either have learned on their own to manage stress or have been innoculated against it through experience.[1] This may explain why many organizations are surprised to see their top people not taking advantage of stress-management programs.

But be warned. There are plenty of stressed people in managerial ranks, for whom the example of unflappable seniors and peers is a trap. Even those top dogs who can handle large amounts of stress have to maintain a balance *and* limit how much even they can take. Their thresholds for stress are just higher.

And don't be fooled by breezy articles that confer a "Natural Stress Handler" title on high-power managers and salespeople. Even the heavies had to learn to manage stress; they just went to the School of Hard Knocks for their lessons. It's a good school, but one with incredibly high tuition and a high failure rate.

People who experience stress but who manage it so that it activates instead of debilitates report the positive effects of being under positive pressure:

• *Positive stress can take you that extra mile.* Star athletes like Brian Boitano, Olympic gold medal skater, and Jackie Joyner-Kersee, gold medal runner and gymnast, both credit their extraordinary performance to their mental as well as to their physical abilities. They credit stress-reducing strategies such as deep breathing, visualization, and thought rehearsals for their seeming ability to "go beyond" and perform amazing physical feats.

One of the most startling uses of psychology in sports involved Denise Parker, a 1988 Olympic champion at age 12. With the help of a sports psychologist, Denise, only four foot ten and weighing under a hundred pounds, was a star at archery—no easy feat for someone that size and weight. What set Denise apart, in addition to her determination and competitive urge, was her willingness and ability to train her psychological self. Denise learned to tense and relax her muscles (a common stress-reducing procedure). She also learned to stay on target by learning to block everything else out, no matter where she was or what was occurring. Most interestingly, Denise took to visualization. She created a room in her head where she could relax and practice winning archery. She described it as having stairs leading up to it. The room itself had brown wall-to-wall carpeting and a king-size waterbed. Denise said she would lie down on the bed and watch tapes of herself (on her VCR and big-screen TV, both with which the room was equipped). Other things Denise described the room as having were posters of Tom Cruise on the walls and a fireplace that was always blazing. Denise said that later, when she got to the tournament, everything seemed familiar to her. She said that even at the Olympics she was calm when she began to shoot.

• *Time pressure can get the creative juice flowing.* Creative people, from scientists and artists through sellers, suggest that they only achieve breakthroughs, make progress, and develop win-win compromises when under the threat of a deadline or commitment.

• *Stress can be exciting.* Some people, referred to as stress seekers, need to cause a general uproar around them or precipitate a crisis to get mobilized. These are the same people who jump out of airplanes and enter demolition derbys to "relax."

• *Stress is the basis for some jobs.* Studies of air-traffic controllers, frontier radar-surveillance people, and others responsible for life and limb of fellow humans show that these high-stress victims don't perform at their best unless they are in fact stressed. Air-traffic controllers *do* suffer from stress overload, but the stress is also a positive part of their job and an integral aspect of their success.

Orchestrating Stress in the Selling Cycle

A psychological stress principle, sometimes referred to as the Yerkes-Dodson Law, is often employed by successful salespeople to orchestrate the stress in a sale. According to this principle, tension, anxiety, stress—call it what you will—has to exist for work to get done. As stress increases, performance improves until a certain optimum level of tension has been reached. Above that point, performance deteriorates; below it, nothing much happens. Sales-training specialist Larry Wilson paraphrases the principle when he suggests that a sale only takes place when Task Tension (the need to get work done) is high and Relationship Tension (the need to trust the sales rep) is low or fulfilled.[2] The important thing is to recognize and control where you and the prospect are on those two tension scales. Then selling really *can* take place.

The issue of managing the tensions of both buyer and seller was brought home most vividly by one of Dr. Stern's clients.

JANE M. sells heavy machinery: road graders, cranes, hoists, mobile construction gear. She came in complaining of a poor closing ratio. As she described it, everything would be great right up to the close. But Jane was never sure when to close. Her standard routine was to run out of things to say and leave. For three sessions we rehearsed closing statements and stress control. After one or two field trials, it looked as if Jane had overcome her closing fears and had developed some closing statements that worked for her.

A month later Jane was back. She was still having a closing problem. She wasn't afraid of trying to close anymore and, indeed, some of the closing statements we had made up and rehearsed together worked for her. She *had* made one sale in the month, but her closing ratio was still the lowest in the office.

After some pondering and discussion, Jane made a passing reference that, "Some of them [her prospects] seem too relaxed to buy anything." And that, of course, was the literal truth. Jane had, in a way, learned to handle her own tension level too well. The result was that she was inadvertently holding her tension or stress level so low that prospects found her to be a comfortable, relaxing person to be around. The consequence was that the stress levels of the prospective buyers were below a level I call the "buying threshold"—that level of excitation necessary for a sale to occur. Jane and her prospects were both understressed!

With that concept in mind, Jane was at last able to track the specifics of her closing problem. It turned out that Jane was being underassertive when she asked for the order, which she compounded by not building toward the close with her prospects. The solution to Jane's problem was for her to raise her own stress level as she moved toward the close and then to close in a more forceful manner. Specifically, Jane started using a "summary close." That is, she moved toward asking for the order by first briefly summarizing her understanding of the prospect's needs and the fit between those needs and her company's products. As she delivered this verbal summary she also consciously changed her body language from informal to formal, modifying the tone, pitch, and volume of her voice. In essence, she learned to lead her prospect to a higher tension level.

We won't try to convince you that Jane's learning to move herself from relaxed and nurturing to forceful and energetic was what made her the number 1 salesperson in her office. Jane is a very capable, bright person. She has a mechanical-engineering background and her family has been in the construction business for three generations. Second, Jane is in an industry where women are still a novelty. That gets her a lot of appointments, but occasionally costs her sales. The point is that Jane has a lot of horsepower. Learning to orchestrate the tension levels of the close simply redirected some of that energy. When we last heard, she was still selling and her closing ratio was improving.

Managing Sales Tension

We don't claim to be selling-skills experts. But the salespeople we have been working with on personal stress management have helped us develop a good feel for the appropriate stress levels to strive for during a face-to-face sale. Figure 12-1, showing desirable sales stress levels, was developed from a workshop exercise we have been using for about six months. First we ask the participants to list the steps of a face-to-face sale—whatever system they are comfortable with—then we ask them to estimate the stress or tension level they should be at in each of the selling postures and the tension level they would like to see in their prospect at the same sales step.

As mentioned earlier, the kind of sale involved limits the applicability of these guidelines. With that in mind, here are the parameters for the kind of sale to which Figure 12-1 applies:

1. The salesperson is selling an intangible; for example, something in personal finance management.
2. The prospect must see the need and take some action for the sale to be consumated: consult an accountant or lawyer, take a physical examination, notify the company of the arrangement, or the like.
3. After the close and after the prospect has qualified for the service, the contract will be signed.

Text continues on page 162

Figure 12-1. Desirable sales stress levels (intangible financial service).

Point in the Sale	Focus of Stress-Management Effort	Desirable Stress Level
1. Initial face-to-face contact	• Reducing prospect tension resulting from rep's presence and prospect uncertainty over the rep's intent, competence, etc.	• Move prospect from where he/she is to moderate stress level* or lower end of apparent comfort zone. • Rep needs to be at a moderate stress level: relaxed enough to work and be pleasant but obviously in an attentive and alert state.
	• Maintaining rep's tension at an even, comfortable level—comfortable for both self and prospect. • Rep's tension level kept nonintrusive in the relationship-building effort. • Rep consciously "reading" prospect's tension level.	
2. Information-gathering mode; looking for facts and feelings.	• Moving prospect's tension level up during information-gathering process. • Prospect needs to be seriously attending to the fact-finding process.	• Rep maintains moderate to low-moderate stress level except when doing verification-feedback. Center to lower center of rep's comfort zone. • Prospect in upper half
	• Moving interview focus from objective to subjective, from factual to emotional level. • Rep monitoring prospect's tension level, looking for success at increasing it gradually.	

		• Rep monitoring own level to keep it even and unobtrusive. • Rep feeds back or reintroduces subjects that "up-tick" prospect's tension level. Verifying importance of issue.	of apparent comfort zone, except when answering specific questions. Rise in tension level is indication of importance of question. Leave "room" to move up in prospect level.
3. Information giving; case "workup"; initial proposal of options.	• Moving prospect from comfortable to uncomfortable. • Prospect aroused and "motivated" by felt tension at end of presentation meeting.	• Rep controlled and lower slightly in level than prospect. • "Shadowing" prospect changes in tension level. • Rep does not go out of upper quarter of comfort zone.	• Rep wants medium to medium-high stress level. Moves slightly from slightly above center of comfort zone to center of upper quarter. • Client starts at low and moves to high end of comfort zone by final crescendo of presentation.
4. Asking for action; first close; proposal acceptance.	• Prospect moved to and maintained at upper limit of tolerance/	• Rep maintains own tension level. Does not shadow prospect if he/	• Prospect's tension quite high—at or above tolerance level. Should

Figure 12-1 (continued)

Point in the Sale	Focus of Stress-Management Effort	Desirable Stress Level
	comfort zone. Want prospect's tension high enough to moderate own actions to reduce tension.	be some psychological distress.
	she leaves own comfort zone.	• Rep's tension level kept even in upper part of tolerance zone.
		• Rep keeps tension level even after close. Prospect's level must stay up, thus rep's level must stay up.
5. Signing of contract, accepting first payment; reinforcing/	• Prospect's tension brought up at opening of interview, brought down again somewhat	• Prospect tension brought to upper part of comfort zone early in meeting.
	• Rep starting meeting at higher tension level than prospect.	
	• Moving prospect	

supporting buying
decision.

- after signing of
  contract.
- Tension reduced to
  reinforce buying
  decision.

tension level up by
reviewing situation.
- Bringing own tension
  level down after
  contract is signed and
  first payment received.

- Prospect/buyer brought
  down to center/lower
  half of tension
  tolerance zone.
- Rep's tension level
  starts moderately high;
  moves up to top of
  comfort zone during
  review and
  presentation of
  contract.
- Rep tension level near
  center of comfort zone
  as interview ends.

---

* In Part Two you will learn to do Subjective Level of Stress (SLS) estimates. "Comfort zone" is used to indicate the range of stress levels that are work enhancing for the rep but neither relaxed nor debilitatingly high. The center of your comfort zone is your best working edge.

These parameters are important to keep in mind as you review the figure. For example, in this type of sale, it is desirable to bring the prospect's tension level up during the information phase and keep it there through the close. Since the prospect must take action for the sale to be made, it is important that he or she be energized and motivated to perform that task. In other situations, however, it is more appropriate to bring the prospect's tension level down after the close. As you read the table, think of a scene in which the seller is suggesting something like an insurance-funded living trust to a high-net-worth individual. Also assume a three-meeting sale. The dotted lines indicate the end of each call.

You may not agree totally with our analysis of where the stress levels should be during these five phases of the selling cycle. That's fine. We just want you to be aware of the way managed stress can be your ally during selling. After all, stress is a part of who you are and how you work. Your goal in selling is to hold your stress and your prospective buyer's stress at the level most conducive to your game plan. Sometimes you must make a conscious effort to keep the tensions from getting out of hand, from going beyond the level you deem constructive for your purposes. Other times, the process just flows. In order to express yourself fully, you must first find your optimum stress level.

So far, we have been taking snapshots of you and your stress tendencies, and sharing these images with you. In Part Two we'll resolve the issues of what your current stress level is and how you personally manifest stress; in Part Three we'll explain the techniques you can use to manage the two-edged sword that is stress. The ability to see your stress, manage it, and use it constructively and creatively—without harmful side effects—is what separates the winners from the also-rans. Winners accept the challenge and the risk of sales stress. Also-rans, true to their names, simply run away from challenge. The ancient Chinese character for the concept of crisis is a combination of the caligraphs for "danger" and "opportunity," symbolizing the belief that every crisis is also an opportunity. People who can stretch and develop their ability to manage, control, and orchestrate stress will succeed. They will live better and happier, with released energy for life's challenges. These are the men and women who attack life's opportunities without paying too high a price or depleting their psychic funds. These are the men and women for whom this book was written.

TWO

Four Exercises to Develop Your Personal Stress Profile and Your Personal Stress-Management Prescription

Introduction

EVEN though people all experience stress, they may be overstressed by different stressors. Responses to stress are also quite individual. Age, sex, heredity, and previous learning combine to make people unique in matters of stress, stressors, and stress responses.

To help you catch hold of this personal quicksilver, we have developed the Personal Stress Profile and the Stress Management Prescription. You already have begun developing your Personal Stress Profile through the self-tests in Chapters 1, 4, 5, 6, 7, 8, 9, 10, 11. If you skipped any of those self-tests, go back and complete them *now*.

A word of caution. You probably took the self-tests alone while you were reading the book. Great! That's what they were there for. However, be cautious about something we call the self-labeling paradox.

The classic classroom example of this phenomenon is a trick psychology professors play on first-year students. It is known informally as the old handwriting-analysis gambit and it works this way: After some especially important test, the professor announces to the class, "I have done an experimental personality analysis of each of you based on your handwriting in the essay section of the midterm. I will now hand the summaries back to you. Please don't show your profile to anyone else. Look it over and decide how accurate, on a scale of one to ten, the analysis is."

Two things invariably happen. First, the class rates the professor's analysis to be right on target. Second, the professor asks the class to exchange profiles. You guessed it. The profiles are exactly the same. The point is that we too readily and uncritically accept information about ourselves. Interns and graduate students in medicine and psychology invariably catch the diseases they study. It seems, at least in part, to be an important step in the process of developing empathy.

If you suspect that you may have responded too empathically to some of the self-tests, ask a spouse, close friend, or colleague—someone whose opinions you respect—to go over your responses and give you feedback on accuracy. Of course, you are the final arbiter of what you choose to believe about yourself; but be aware that you can probably never see your own behavior in a completely objective way. As the Scottish poet Robert Burns put it,

> Oh w'ad some power the giftie gie us,
> To see oursels as others see us!
>
> —"To a Louse"

Asking a trusted "other" to help you develop your Personal Stress Profile is as close as you will probably get to having that "Mirror, Mirror, on the wall" that Burns pined for in his famous lament for objective self-knowledge.

Before you bring forward the scores from the earlier self-tests, there are three more exercises to complete. Two of them, the Stressor Identification Matrix and the B-T-A Inventory, are based on the three-step model of becoming stressed, discussed in Chapter 3. The first part of that model suggested that all stressors are classifiable as M, O, or S in origin, as follows:

M	MYSELF	Stressors you make up yourself; these are basically thoughts, ideas, and images you conjure up in your head and which act as stress cues or triggers for the stress response
O	OTHERS	The behavior, actions, words, and deeds of other people, which act as potential stressors
S	SITUATION	Things you can't avoid, which bring on a stress response: traffic jams, airline delays, long lines

The Stressor Identification Matrix will lead you through the task of determining the M-O-S of your ten most significant personal stressors.

The second part of the three-step process emphasizes that stress responses tend to come in three forms: Body, Thought, and Action, or B-T-A. The B-T-A Inventory will help you determine whether you are more likely to manifest stress in your body, in your thoughts, or in your actions.

The third and final exercise is the SLS Measurement Profile. SLS, or Subjective Level of Stress, is a quantitative measure of felt stress. Once you have worked through the SLS Measurement Profile, you will be able to assess your stress level at any time or in any place. In addition, you will be able to determine your ideal stress level for specific occasions and also your ideal work and play stress range, or comfort zone.

When you have worked through these three exercises you will be ready to compile your Personal Stress Profile and begin the interpretation that will prescribe appropriate stress-management techniques and exercises for your unique problems.

EXERCISE 11. The Stressor Identification Matrix

Directions

It should take you about 30 minutes to work the six steps (A through F) that follow. Don't rush through this exercise. Take your time and follow instructions carefully. Some people have suggested that the specific instructions for this exercise are too complete. But the matrix exercise is a little tricky, so we have provided very complete guidelines. If the instructions seem overcareful or redundant, be patient. The results are worth it.

Scoring and interpretation follow the sixth step.

Step A

You took a preliminary step in analyzing your personal stressors in Chapter 4, when you went through the list of fifty frequent stressors and picked the ten that seemed most stressful to you. List those 10 stressors below. Be sure to include the *item numbers* from the original list in Chapter 4. You will need to refer to those item numbers as part of this analysis.

_No._	_Item_
____	_____
____	_____
____	_____
____	_____
____	_____
____	_____
____	_____
____	_____
____	_____
____	_____

Step B

Now you are ready to use the Stressor Weighting Matrix. Enter the number of each item in the boxes that run along both the top and left edges of the matrix. For example, if Item *17*, *Personal production that is low*, is one of your stressors, write number 17 twice, first on the top and then on the left.

Item	15	17		
15	X			
17		X		
			X	

Now enter the remaining nine item numbers for your top stressors.

STRESSOR WEIGHTING MATRIX

Step C

Compare the items you entered on the Stressor Weighting Matrix, one at a time. For example, suppose you have items 17, *Personal production that is low*, and 33, *Low morale in the com-*

pany, as two of your top stressors, entered on the matrix as shown below:

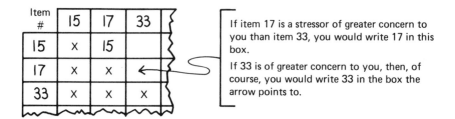

If item 17 is a stressor of greater concern to you than item 33, you would write 17 in this box.

If 33 is of greater concern to you, then, of course, you would write 33 in the box the arrow points to.

In other words, compare each of the items this way on the descending diagonal, writing the item number of the stressor of more concern in each comparison.

Step D

In the Summary Box on the next page, enter the stressor item number and number of times you entered that number on the matrix. List them in order, from *most* frequently to *least* frequently chosen. For example, if you choose item 17 as the stressor of most concern eight times, your entry of item 17 into the Summary Box will look like this:

Summary Box

Item #	Times Chosen	Class.		
15	11	M	O	S
17	8	M	O	S
33	5	M	O	S

Summary Box

Item No.	Times Chosen	Classification		
_____	_____	M	O	S
_____	_____	M	O	S
_____	_____	M	O	S
_____	_____	M	O	S
_____	_____	M	O	S
_____	_____	M	O	S
_____	_____	M	O	S
_____	_____	M	O	S
_____	_____	M	O	S
_____	_____	M	O	S
Totals		_____	_____	_____

Step E

Now you are ready to code, or classify, your top stressors as either M (Myself), O (Others), or S (Situation). Use the M-O-S Key to circle the appropriate code for each item in the Summary Box.

For example, Item 17, *Personal production that is low,* is an M item. If you have picked item 17 as one of your top stressors, you would circle M in the Summary Box on the line where 17 is entered.

Summary Box

Item #	Times Chosen	Class.		
15	11	M	O	S
17	8	M	O	S
33	5	M	O	S

When you have finished coding each of your top stressors, total the number of M's, O's, and S's. Then use the codes in the figure on page 000 to classify the M-O-S of the items in your Summary Box.

The M-O-S Key

M items	1, 4, 5, 9, 10, 15, 17, 22, 24, 38, 43, 47, 48, 49, 50
O items	2, 6, 7, 18, 20, 21, 23, 25, 32, 34, 35, 37, 39, 40, 41, 42, 45
S items	8, 12, 14, 16, 26, 28, 30, 31, 33, 34, 36, 46

Special Items

We have found that six items can only be correctly classified by taking into account your interpretation of the specific item.

Item   *Classification Options*

3 • If you suspected all along that the prospect was *not* the decision maker but you *chose* to make the presentation anyway, you're probably upset with *yourself.* That's an M.

• If the situation demands you make the presentation, the non-decision maker is an *influencer* or *gatekeeper* and you need to get by him to get to the power; that's an S.

• If the person reveals to you during the presentation that he isn't the power, and that upsets you, code this stressor as O.

Item	*Classification Options*

11 • If you assume *you* did something to muff the sales, code this stressor as M.
  • If you believe someone else blew it for you, "Sorry, Jim but the boss's brother is going to get the contract," code this stressor as O.
  • If your bid, design, or delivery just couldn't make sparks, then the stressor is an S.

13 • If the new sales manager is an old enemy or the old sales manager a special friend, classify this item as O.
  • If you are just rankled by a new face or player to get the feel for, call it S.

19 • If performance reviews make you feel jumpy in general, call it M.
  • If you consider performance reviews to be a chance for the boss to get in a "one up" position, code this one O.

29 • If the client died, was fired, etc., call it S.
  • If the client "betrayed your trust," call it O.
  • If you made a pass at the client's spouse and that cost you the account, it is M.

44 • If the bad territory is luck of the draw, call it S.
  • If you were given a "bad farm" on purpose and you know who did it and why, and are steamed, call this stressor O.

Step F

You are now ready to begin scoring and interpreting the information you have generated about your personal stressors. First, look again at your list of top stressors in the Summary Box, and pay particular attention to the "Time Chosen" column. Chances are, there will be clusters of items with very similar weights.

For example, if items 15, 21, 47, and 48 have similar numbers in the "Time Chosen" column, then these are probably equally stressful and can be considered a cluster.

Re-organize your list of top stressors by apparent clusters, using the "Time Chosen" column. Look at these clusters, especially the top cluster (those top items with similar weights) and see if there is an obvious theme in the nature of the items.

For example, suppose your top cluster looked like this:

Top Stressors

Times Chosen	Item #	Stressor
13	15	*Conflict* between customer and company policy
12	21	*Argument* with sales manager
12	47	Accidentally *offended* client
10	48	*Losing temper* in a meeting

THEME POSSIBILITY

You might conclude that at least one common theme in items 15, 21, 47, and 48 is conflict. That's an important awareness. You now know that you must either learn to head off conflict or learn a less stressful response to it when it comes.

Top Stressors   **Theme Possibilities**

Times Chosen	Item #	Stressor
_____	_____	
_____	_____	
_____	_____	
_____	_____	
_____	_____	

CLUSTER ANALYSIS

Let's take a close look at the M-O-S classifications. The proportion of times you chose a particular classification reveals a lot about your tendency to be stressed by certain types of stressors. Enter the number of M's, O's, and S's here.

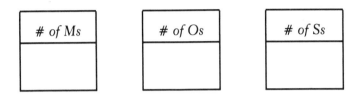

Since we're working with your top stressors, you can think of these as percentages, or proportions. For example, if five of your top stressors are M, 50 percent of the things that stress you are self-generated, or things you do to yourself.

Interpretation of Scores

•   *Understanding M. If 50 percent or more* of your top stressors are M, it is fair to say that you may be your own worst enemy. You probably let your own behavior, choices, thoughts, and emotions make you tense. It's likely that you stress yourself by being demanding and tough in your self-expectations and unforgiving of yourself when you fall short. If you are *also* a high Internal on the quiz you took in Chapter 5, then you closely fit the classic pattern. We have noticed that many salespeople who are high Internals also report many M stressors.

If 20 percent or fewer of your top stressors are M, it is fair to say that you tend *not* to stress yourself very frequently. If you were mid-range or high External on the quiz in Chapter 5, then it's a good bet that you focus your attention away from yourself and are more stressed by O and S.

•   *Understanding O. If 50 percent or more* of your stressors are O, the source of your stress is the people you deal with. Quite likely this also means that you are stressed by interpersonal situations and communication issues. If you found in Chapter 10 that you are less assertive and either more passive or aggressive than is good for you, then interpersonal situations, especially communications, are a problem for you. But be aware also that quite often, when we are upset with others and point to "them guys" as culprits, it is our own negative interpretation of their behavior that is the real stressor. In short, don't rule out the cognitive part of M as a contributor to your stressor picture.

If 20 percent or fewer of the stressors you listed are O, then it is possible that you are a person who doesn't get especially upset by the actions of others in interpersonal situations. But caution. It is also possible that either you are a little too insensitive to feedback from others or you are what is sometimes referred to as a "stamp saver." In the former case—insensitive to feedback—it is desirable to have a thick skin but not so thick that appropriate and constructive information from others bounces off. "Stamp savers" are people who don't get mad but do get even. If you don't ever get mad at others, or if you usually find yourself patiently waiting your turn at bat, you may be a stamp saver. Unfortunately, when it comes, the explosion can be a stress-filled dandy; and bottling up all that stuff you're saving can have negative side effects.

• *Understanding S. If 50 percent or more* of your stressors are S, you let the immovable objects of the world get to you the most. Highway traffic jams, late airplanes, or the state of the economy are the sort of things that stress you. If you also are a high Internal person, as measured in chapter 5, it makes sense that being in control of events—being the Chess King of your environment—is important to you. There is also a possible cognitive factor here. You may be one of those people with an unending "instant replay" capacity, continuously replaying old "love scenes" and sales calls that have gone awry. We can learn from the past, but regardless of how often we roll the tape back, we can't change what happened.

If 20 percent or fewer of your stressors are S, then quite likely you are a "let bygones be bygones" person. Just be careful that you accept the situation as having taken place and that the outcome wasn't that great. Denying that a bad thing ever happened or cheating on your memory denies you a valuable possible learning opportunity.

• *When M-O-S Scores Are Even or Mixed.* If your M-O-S

scores are about even, then you tend to be stressed by all three sources at one time or another. It's likely you were midrange on a number of the other self-tests. If you have moderately high scores on two of the factors—40 percent or better for M and O, M and S, or O and S—then consider that both are likely sources of stressors. It's a good idea to list the stressors from both moderately high groups and see if there is an overriding theme—a common thread that explains why both factors rate high. For instance, items 1, 15, 47, and 48 are all M items; items 18, 20, 21, and 23 all deal with O. But a thoughtful reading of these eight items—considering them to be a cluster—gives special meaning. Each has to do with a face-to-face conflict, either with customer, prospect, peer, or supervisor.

• *Summing Up M-O-S.* Stress can come from almost any place. But as you now see, you are selective about what you let get to you. Knowing where stress comes from and what your high stressors are are important steps in our approach to stressless selling.

EXERCISE 12. The B-T-A Inventory

The B-T-A Inventory is composed of three checklists of twenty items each: (1) the Body Stress, or "B," checklist, which gives you a reading of your tendency to manifest stress physiologically; (2) the cognitive, or "T," checklist, which gives you a reading of your tendency to manifest stress psychologically; and (3) the Behavior Stress, or "A," checklist, which gives you a reading of your tendency to manifest stress through your actions.

It should take you twenty to thirty minutes to work through this inventory. Scoring instructions and interpretation follow the third checklist.

The Body Stress, or "B," Checklist

This inventory is designed to assess your tendency to experience body stress. Each of the items has been shown to be potentially related to stress. Read each statement carefully, then circle the number of the statement to the right that best reflects what has been typical for you over the last few months.

In the last few months I have experienced:	Frequently	Often	Sometimes	Occasionally	Rarely or Never
1. Headaches	5	4	3	2	1
2. Dizziness	5	4	3	2	1
3. Back pain or tightness	5	4	3	2	1
4. Trembling in parts of body	5	4	3	2	1
5. Rapid or irregular heartbeat	5	4	3	2	1
6. Elevated blood pressure	5	4	3	2	1
7. Chest pains	5	4	3	2	1
8. Stomach trouble	5	4	3	2	1
9. Internal jitters or the shakes	5	4	3	2	1
10. Nausea	5	4	3	2	1
11. A lump in the throat	5	4	3	2	1
12. Hot or cold spells	5	4	3	2	1
13. Loss of energy or general tiredness	5	4	3	2	1
14. Joint or muscle stiffness or soreness	5	4	3	2	1
15. Tingling in body extremities	5	4	3	2	1
16. Sudden and rapid hair loss	5	4	3	2	1
17. Bowel disturbances	5	4	3	2	1
18. Frequent colds	5	4	3	2	1
19. Sudden skin rashes or blotches	5	4	3	2	1
20. Frequent or recurring nonspecific infections	5	4	3	2	1

Add the numbers you circled and enter the total here.

The Cognitive Stress, or "T," Checklist

This inventory is designed to assess your tendency to experience stress in your thoughts and feelings. Each of the items has been shown to be potentially related to stress. Read each item carefully, then circle the number of the statement to the right that best reflects what has been typical for you over the last few months.

In the last few months I have:	Frequently	Often	Sometimes	Occasionally	Rarely or Never
1. Experienced a sense of dread and foreboding	5	4	3	2	1
2. Thought catastrophic thoughts	5	4	3	2	1
3. Felt isolated or distant from people	5	4	3	2	1
4. Had ideas that make me feel panicky	5	4	3	2	1
5. Felt lonely	5	4	3	2	1
6. Believed I move from crisis to crisis	5	4	3	2	1
7. Worried too much	5	4	3	2	1
8. Have not been able to "shut off" my head	5	4	3	2	1
9. Thought of myself as helpless, being victimized	5	4	3	2	1
10. Thought about "packing it all in"	5	4	3	2	1
11. Doubted my abilities	5	4	3	2	1
12. Dwelled on thoughts that won't go away	5	4	3	2	1
13. Believed things were usually my fault or usually someone else's fault	5	4	3	2	1
14. Believed that things should be "right" or "perfect" or "fair"	5	4	3	2	1
15. Thought I was losing my mind	5	4	3	2	1

In the last few months I have:	Frequently	Often	Sometimes	Occasionally	Rarely or Never
16. Been generally bored or disinterested in things	5	4	3	2	1
17. Had many conflicting thoughts or ideas	5	4	3	2	1
18. Had feelings of anger or frustration	5	4	3	2	1
19. Believed most people are not to be trusted	5	4	3	2	1
20. Had thoughts or images that frightened me	5	4	3	2	1

Add the numbers you circled and enter the total here. ☐

The Behavior Stress, or "A," Checklist

This inventory is designed to assess your tendency to experience stress in your actions. Each of the items has been shown to be potentially related to stress. Read each item carefully, then circle the number of the statement to the right that best reflects what has been typical for you over the past few months.

In the past few months I have:	Frequently	Often	Sometimes	Occasionally	Rarely or Never
1. Made more errors than usual	5	4	3	2	1
2. Ate, drank (alcoholic beverages), or smoked more than I should	5	4	3	2	1
3. Took tranquilizers or sedatives	5	4	3	2	1
4. Drove myself too hard	5	4	3	2	1
5. Been unable to use or enjoy leisure time with others	5	4	3	2	1

In the past few months I have:	Frequently	Often	Sometimes	Occasionally	Rarely or Never
6. Had trouble concentrating	5	4	3	2	1
7. Slept too much or too little	5	4	3	2	1
8. Withdrawn or acted underassertive	5	4	3	2	1
9. Lost my appetite	5	4	3	2	1
10. Been accident-prone	5	4	3	2	1
11. Lost interest in sex or had sexual performance difficulties	5	4	3	2	1
12. Been absent from work more than usual	5	4	3	2	1
13. Had difficulties communicating with others	5	4	3	2	1
14. Experienced a decrease in my productivity	5	4	3	2	1
15. Worked at a reduced pace	5	4	3	2	1
16. Had difficulty making decisions	5	4	3	2	1
17. Had uncontrollable outbursts of temper	5	4	3	2	1
18. Made excessive or unrealistic demands of others	5	4	3	2	1
19. Been unable to accept feedback from others	5	4	3	2	1
20. Displayed emotional responses out of proportion to the situations	5	4	3	2	1

Add the numbers you circled and enter the total here.

Interpreting Your B-T-A Scores

You should have completed each of the three checklists and totaled the points. In each case your total could range from a low of 20 to a high of 100. If you had totals lower than 20 or higher than 100, check your addition and be sure you answered all the items. Transfer your scores below:

B   Body Stress Score

T   Cognitive Stress Score

A   Behavior Stress Score

THE "B," OR BODY STRESS, SCORE

• *Scores Between 60 and 100.* If you scored between 60 and 100, you probably don't need to be told that your body is on overload. If you answered the questions accurately, your body may seem to be under siege a great deal of the time. You may be experiencing acute stress and experiencing it somatically. You probably notice yourself trying to "shake it off" or "loosen up" in some fashion. You are probably experiencing more tension than your arousal system can typically cope with. You may have had trouble sitting still long enough to fill out the inventory. If you ignore these warning signs, your health and job performance may be diminished. At this point you should consider seeking competent medical advice if you have not done so already.

• *Scores Between 36 and 59.* If you scored between 40 and 76, it is less likely you are being victimized by debilitating somatic (bodily) expression of tension. In other words, your tension may be a figurative pain in the neck but not necessarily a literal one.

However, if you scored 60 or greater, there is a chance you are feeling some discomfort. This is especially true if you have a physical weak link, or a history of some somatic ailment. ("Weak link" simply refers to possible inherited weaknesses. If your family has a history of lower back problems and they aren't galley slaves by trade, you might be susceptible to these problems too, especially if you are carrying a long-term stress load. Tension seems to cluster about these weak links when they exist, and they do for most of us.)

In addition, we have found that individuals who maintain a high activity level (people who walk instead of ride, engage in active sports, jog, or climb stairs as a matter of course) suffer less from somatically expressed manifestations of stress.

• *Scores Between 20 and 35.* If you score on this lower end of the scale, one of three possibilities exists:

1. Any somatic stress you are experiencing is probably well within your personal tolerance for body discomfort.
2. You tend *not* to experience somatic manifestations of stress and tension in general.
3. You are not used to paying attention to your body signals and ignore them.

Note: If you rated one or more of the listed symptoms as a "5," you are high "B" or have body stress. You should consider consulting a physician if you are not doing so now.

THE "T," OR COGNITIVE, STRESS SCORE

• *Scores Between 79 and 100.* If you scored in this range you may be trapped in stressful thinking. Stressful thinking tends to trigger negative emotions, which in turn can compound feelings of mental distress. This is the "worry cycle": mentally induced stress feeding back on itself in a seemingly never-ending upward spiral. This cycle is breakable and preventable. We'll send you to the right procedure for making that happen as soon as you have completed this section.

Cognitive, or thought/feeling-related, stress in this range of impact can block the road to important sales, interfere with your relationships with others, and take the joy and zest out of living.

• *Scores Between 40 and 76.* If you scored in this range you are probably able to keep your worry thoughts, emotional concerns, and perceptions of the world in good balance. You are likely to be one of those people who are able to stand back, or "distance yourself," and look from afar at immediate situations when you are cognitively stressed by them. You seem to be able to remain within your capacity to tolerate stress-induced or stress-producing thinking.

However, if your score was 60 or greater, the possibility exists that your thoughts can begin to "run away with you." You need to exercise control over these thoughts, images, and feelings. It is possible—at the 60+ level—to experience counter-productive thoughts and disturbing feelings.

If you exercise caution and control, fine; but there is a possibility that you could slip into a "worry cycle" that could quickly elevate your stress level.

• *Scores Between 20 and 39.* If you scored in this range, two possibilities exit. First, you may be tuned into your mental life, comfortable with it, and able to tolerate the disharmony that exists within all of us. Or, you may be "out to lunch"; you may have learned to avoid facing stressful or disturbing thoughts and feelings. Unfortunately, the old psychological truth applies here:

> One can ignore the thought or idea, but the feelings ooze out elsewhere, resulting in inappropriate behavior and/or stressful somatic symptoms. Repressed stress still hurts; it hurts your body or your friends, loved ones, customers, and co-workers. Look closely again at both your T and B profiles and the answers you gave to specific questions.

THE "A," OR BEHAVIORAL STRESS, PROFILE

• *Scores Between 79 and 100.* If you scored in this range, it appears that your stress has broken through to your behavior. It may be affecting both your personal actions and your ability to get along with other people. You are temporarily unable to relate to friends, loved ones, superiors, and customers.

As a sales professional you know how important interpersonal relationships are and how easily a customer can misinterpret your nervousness and lack of rapport. Your success in the marketplace depends on being a cool, calm communicator and a counseling sort of person. If you don't get this problem under control in a big hurry, you could be in for real problems. This is the stuff sales slumps are made of.

• *Scores Between 40 and 76.* It's likely you are operating within an effective range. What stress you experience does not impede movement toward achieving your professional and day-to-day work goals.

However, if you scored over 60, it would be useful to look at each of the items in the Behavior Stress Inventory and determine whether your high scores are associated more with personal action (questions 1, 2, 3, 4, 6, 7, 9, 10, 12, 14, 15, 16) or with interpersonal behavior (5, 8, 11, 13, 17, 18, 19, 20). Add those separately and put the scores in the boxes below.

Percentage of personal-action items $\left(\dfrac{?}{12}\right)$ □

Percentage of interpersonal-action items $\left(\dfrac{?}{8}\right)$ □

If either of the items above is disproportionately larger than the other—twice the other—there is cause for alarm. Though your total behavior stress score is in a typically safe range, an exceptionally high score on personal or interpersonal stressors could indicate a problem in that area.

• *Scores Between 20 and 39.* If you scored in this range, you are in the enviable position of already being able to manage your stress and tension so that it does not interfere with your selling efforts. It's unlikely you are a stress carrier, and you are controlling and using your tension as a positive sales tool to energize yourself and others. Your behavioral or action stress falls within an optimal coping range. You will want to take advantage of this fortunate state by learning to orchestrate the total tension flow in the sale. In Part Three you will learn the technique for doing that.

There is an outside chance that you are not fully aware of the impact your behavior or actions have on yourself and others. If that is the case, you may be misinterpreting the feedback you are getting from the environment around you, and your Behavior Stress score is low because you have a low awareness of your stress. If that is the case, you could be unaware of the effect of your behavior on others and on your effectiveness. If you have any doubts about your perceptiveness of your own Behavior Stress level, ask one of your third-party references—a colleague, friend, co-worker, or spouse—to go through your ratings with you and verify them. *If you choose this course of action*, be careful not to turn the exercise into an argument. You are asking another person to perform a risky favor; respect his or her efforts on your behalf.

EXERCISE 13. The SLS Measurement Profile

You are now going to determine

- Your optimal, or best for you, stress level
- Your stress range, or comfort zone
- Your maximum stress tolerance level

You will be going through a series of six (A through F) SLS, or Subjective Level of Stress, exercises to determine these measures.

Only you can really know how stressed you feel or how much tension you need to do your best work. These exercises are designed to help you determine both. At one point (F) you will need some volunteer helpers to give you feedback on your SLS. You will be given detailed instructions for choosing your helpers.

There is no interpretation section. Interpretations are interspersed with the exercises.

Exercise A

Lean back and think of a time when you were selling up a storm, when you were at your best. That revved up, with-it feeling was positive stress. You were energized rather than debilitated by stress because you were working at a stress level within your comfort zone.

You knew you were up, and you enjoyed it because the tension you were experiencing was within your ability to manage.

Visualize that level of stress as a point on the line below. Zero stands for *total absence of stress* and 100 for *complete overwhelming stress.*

MARK THAT POINT ON THE LINE.

Now visualize that level of stress as a *number.* Write that number above the point you marked on the line.

0   10   20   30   40   50   60   70   80   90   100
Complete   Overwhelm-
absence of   ing
stress   amount of
                                            stress

Simple first step, right? But it's an important one. People sometimes have a hard time thinking of stress as a quantifiable commodity, yet you've just done that. It's the first step in learning to consider stress in a quantifiable way—so that at any time, at any place, or in any situation you can immediately and accurately evaluate the amount of stress you are experiencing and relate it to your stress tolerance threshold. We call this your Subjective Level of Stress (SLS) because only *you* can determine what you are experiencing. Learning to name and quantify the things you experience is a critical step toward control over these things. When you give stress a number, you have the start of an early-warning feedback system that will let you adjust to the situation at hand.

Exercise B

Focus your attention on your curent stress level. How stressed do you feel *right now?* Imagine a number from 0 to 100 for the SLS you are feeling right this moment and enter it on the stress line below.

0   10   20   30   40   50   60   70   80   90   100

Focus your attention on the amount of stress you think you *should* be experiencing now. Enter that SLS number on the 0 to 100 line below.

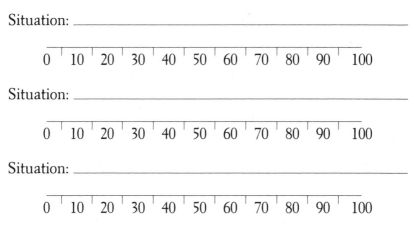

0 ' 10 ' 20 ' 30 ' 40 ' 50 ' 60 ' 70 ' 80 ' 90 ' 100

Now you have had your first experience at comparing your actual SLS with your estimate of appropriate SLS for a situation in which you are actively involved. Unless you are hang gliding as you read this book, or under very severe stress of some sort, the two levels you just estimated are probably fairly close. If desired, pause now and estimate your best stress level for other situations. Use the three lines below for this optional part of the exercise.

Situation: _____

0 ' 10 ' 20 ' 30 ' 40 ' 50 ' 60 ' 70 ' 80 ' 90 ' 100

Situation: _____

0 ' 10 ' 20 ' 30 ' 40 ' 50 ' 60 ' 70 ' 80 ' 90 ' 100

Situation: _____

0 ' 10 ' 20 ' 30 ' 40 ' 50 ' 60 ' 70 ' 80 ' 90 ' 100

Exercise C

DETERMINING YOUR GENERAL SLS RANGE

You're now going to expand your stress awareness beyond present time and specific incidents. The task is to generate an SLS level that reflects the amount of stress you *typically* feel.

Reflect on the last six months. Take a few minutes and mentally run through the events, pace, and feel of the last half-year. When you are ready, form an estimate of the range of stress you have typically experienced during this time. Think about the intensity of what you've experienced, the duration, the length of time the stress lasted, the pervasiveness of the stress, the amount of your life that was affected by the stress. When you're ready, record the range of stress you typically experienced during this six months on the stress line below, as shown in the example.

Example: A person decides his stress has ranged from 30 to 90 in the last six months. He records that estimate this way:

0 10 20 30 40 50 60 70 80 90 100

Now record the range of your last 6 months SLS:

0 10 20 30 40 50 60 70 80 90 100

The range you identify reflects your general state of felt tension—in effect, the amount of stress you typically feel over time. Your general state of tension is influenced by three factors:

1. *Frequency.* How often do you feel a given amount of stress?
2. *Duration.* How long does the stressed feeling last?
3. *Pervasiveness.* How many areas of your life and work does that stress touch?

Exercise D

DETERMINING YOUR OPTIMAL SLS

Think for a moment about the stress tolerance range, or comfort zone, you would consider optimal for someone in your industry with your experience, background, life-style, and age. Record it on the line below.

0 10 20 30 40 50 60 70 80 90 100

The average SLS range reported to us by a sample of 250 male and female salespeople was *40 to 65*. When their SLS dipped below 40, efficiency and effectiveness were impaired; call this a condition of understimulation. When the SLS moves above 65, they reported stress or tension that exceeded their comfort zone.

How does your comfort zone compare to our average? If your upper limit is higher than 65, you may be capable of functioning effectively at a higher SLS level than most. If your comfort zone is not as broad as the average (25 points), *or* if your upper limit is significantly lower than 65 (less than 58), you need to increase your tolerance level. There is an exercise in Part Three that will help.

At the same time, if your SLS lower limit is significantly below 40—say, as low as 30—customers might perceive you as inattentive or too laid back.. You need to monitor your SLS for a few sales calls. If you find you are functioning at a level lower than your prospect, or if your prospect seems too laid back to do business with, consider consciously moving your SLS up a few notches. Don't forget; your behavior can move your SLS up. It's the old "whistling in the graveyard" routine. Act more alert and you will *be* more alert. More important, if you act more alert you will be *perceived* by your prospect as more alert. Your prospect will, in turn, become more alert. It's a positive use of the stress cycle–stress carrier phenomenon.

Exercise E

UNDERSTANDING YOUR GENERAL SLS RANGE

Compare your general SLS range and the stress tolerance range you said someone like you should have.

• If your estimate of your *actual* stress tolerance range is relatively close to that of your optimal or desirable range, you may well be operating at a stress level you believe to be appropriate and reasonable.

• A large difference between your actual and optimal ranges could mean that you are operating under too little or too much tension to be at your best; you are spending most of your time outside your comfort zone, or you have an unrealistic view of how much stress a human being should be able to handle.

> Sometimes we encounter people who suggest that a salesperson should be able to function effectively in a 20 to 80 SLS range. That's unrealistic. At the low end, 20 is the SLS people usually indicate as "just about right" for sitting back with their feet up, reading or watching the wind blow; 80, on the other hand, is the SLS people report for close calls on the highway and intense arguments. If your stress tolerance range did go that high, you need to face a charging bull before your fight/flight is kicked into gear. That would be dangerous unless you are a bullfighter or a stuntperson.

Exercise F

SEE YOUR STRESS AS OTHERS SEE IT

Stress is often interpersonal, therefore it is valuable to know how other people perceive your level of tension. It is especially helpful to know how people who see you in very different situations perceive your tension level. This is one of those times you need to use others for feedback. Ask a number of people to evaluate your apparent stress level. We say "apparent," since only you can judge your actual SLS, but others can tell you how alert or stressed you appear to be.

We suggest that you ask these four people to evaluate your apparent stress level:

A work peer	Someone who has seen you working with clients. If possible someone who has seen you make a client presentation.
Sales manager/supervisor	Be sure that this is someone you have worked with in the last six months.

Spouse or significant other   Someone who sees you at
                                 social events and in
                                 relaxed, private situations.

A friend   Someone you see or talk to
                                 regularly—at least once a
                                 week.

Ask each of these people this question: "On a scale of 0 to 100, with 0 as completely relaxed with no tension and 100 as complete panic, what number would you give to label how stressed I generally am?" (You can assist them by drawing a 0 to 100 scale.)

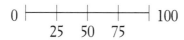

Some people work better in a visual mode. After they have placed your stress level on the line, ask them to estimate the number that point on the line represents. Record the answers you get here:

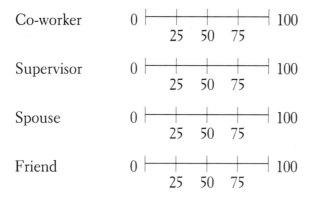

Co-worker

Supervisor

Spouse

Friend

The agreement and disagreement among these ratings offers potentially important feedback. If people in this wide variety of settings and caliber of contact see you as quite differently stressed, it's a good bet that some of your important stressors depend on where you are and whom you're with. If you seem low-stress to spouse and friend but high-stress to co-worker and supervisor, look at your job and sort out the stressors. What is going on in your office or your territory may be keeping you continually aroused. While you will seldom be as relaxed at work as you are at home, there will be times of lower tension. So, the average SLS reported by people you work with should be in the lower third of your stress comfort zone. If you are high at work but much lower at home—lower than your own lower stress range limits would predict—then think about where your energy is being dissipated.

If your major weeknight activities are sleeping, eating, and watching television, and a midweek social event is something you dread, it's an indicator that something about your job is keeping you both aroused during the day and debilitated in the evenings. Take another look at your stressor list to see if any items are giving you "drip drip" stress, such as an unresolved conflict with a supervisor.

One caveat: your optimal stress level is different in different situations, which will influence the raters somewhat. After all, an SLS of 20 is hardly appropriate for sexual activity or making a group sales presentation. On the other hand, an SLS of 80 at bedtime makes sleeping or even closing your eyes difficult. Be cognizant of the context in which your raters generally see you. But on the whole, an old Russian maxim applies to the situation:

If nine sober men tell you you're drunk . . . lie down!

Summary

You are the best and most appropriate source of information on how stressed you are under given circumstances. If you have followed the routines in this section, you are now an accurate source of information about your stress. You can take an SLS reading whenever and wherever you choose, and you can make decisions about where you want your SLS at any given time. By the time you finish *Stressless Selling*, you will also be able to adjust your SLS as you see fit.

Being able to do an accurate SLS helps you:

- Focus your attention on the stress and quickly identify the stressor in the situation.
- Validate, through feedback, the effectiveness of your efforts to modify your own stress.
- Assert control over what's happening within you in potentially stressful situations.

You have completed the final self-test. Your next step is to compile all your self-test scores and see what stress-management techniques you need to learn.

EXERCISE 14. The Prescription for Stressless Selling: Building Your Profile and Selecting Your Strategies

Now is the time to pull together all the things you have been learning about your personal stress tendencies and characteristics, and generate prescriptions for dealing with your specific stress. This is a two-step process. The first step is to collect and summarize the results of the self-quizzes and then assess their stress-management implications. The second step is to weigh the implications of the quizzes and develop a plan of treatment.

EXERCISE 1. The Role-Values Inventory (Chapter 1)

Answer the following three questions. Base your answers on the scoring and interpretation of your answers to the Role-Values Inventory. Circle the *number* of the choice that best answers each question.

My self-concept is:

Positive	*Negative*
1	2

My view of the professional salesperson is:

Positive   *Negative*
1   2

The overlap between my view of myself as a *person* and my view of myself as a *sales professional* is:

Just Right   *Too Little Overlap*   *Too Much Overlap*
1   2   3

Add the numbers you circled and put the total here. ☐

If your total is 5 or greater, the following stress-management strategies are preliminarily indicated. Put an X next to each of the strategies. (This may sound silly, but later on you will count up the number of X's so bear with us.)

Strategy No. and Name

_____	3	"Thought Reprogramming"
_____	4	"Six Ways to Get High on Yourself"
_____	7	"The Sales Call Postmortem"
_____	13	"Overcoming Call Reluctance"

EXERCISE 3. Internal-External Belief Inventory (Chapter 5)

Transfer your score from the box at the end of the exercise to here. ☐

If your total was 20 or less, you are an External, and the following stress-management strategies are preliminarily indicated.

Strategy No. and Name

_____	5	"Desensitization"
_____	7	"The Sales Call Postmortem"
_____	8	"Asserting Yourself"

If your total was 50 or greater, you tend to be an Internal, and the following stress-management strategies are indicated.

	Strategy No. and Name
_____ 3	"Thought Reprogramming"
_____ 7	"The Sales Call Postmortem"
_____ 11	"Giving and Getting Feedback"

EXERCISE 4. Type A Behavior Inventory (Chapter 6)

Transfer your score from the box at the end of the exercise to this box. ☐

If you rated 70 or higher, you are probably a Type A. The following strategies are preliminarily indicated in modifying Type A behavior toward Type C.

	Strategy No. and Name
_____ 4	"Six Ways to Get High on Yourself"
_____ 6	"Reducing Type A Behavior"
_____ 8	"Asserting Yourself"
_____ 11	"Giving and Getting Feedback"

If you rated yourself 40 or less, you are probably Type B. To make sure you can move toward Type A when you need to, and can handle the special tensions of Type B, the following are preliminarily indicated.

	Strategy No. and Name
_____ 7	"The Sales Call Postmortem"
_____ 9	"Increasing Your Comfort Zone" *

* This only applies to Type B's who can't raise their tension level enough to induce movement in a prospect or to show enthusiasm and interest.

EXERCISE 5. Are You a Stress Carrier? (Chapter 7)

In this exercise you assessed your stress-carrier tendencies. If you decided that you probably are a stress carrier, the following strategies are preliminarily indicated.

		Strategy No. and Name
_____	6	"Reducing Type A Behavior"
_____	7	"The Sales Call Postmortem"
_____	11	"Giving and Getting Feedback"

EXERCISE 6. Looking at Your Thinking (Chapter 8)

In this chapter you worked through a series of exercises. Based on those exercises, make the following judgment about yourself: "I believe I need more practice on making my thoughts, what I say, and how I feel more 'congruent,' more in line with one another."

_____ Yes   _____ No   _____ Not Sure

If you answered Yes or Not Sure, the following strategies are preliminarily indicated.

		Strategy No. and Name
_____	3	"Thought Reprogramming"
_____	7	"The Sales Call Postmortem"
_____	8	"Asserting Yourself"

EXERCISES 8 AND 9. Communication Comfort and Interpersonal Importance Inventories (Chapter 10)

There were two inventories in this chapter. The scores formed a nine-cell matrix and each cell indicated a slightly different stress-management need. Find your cell in the list below, and mark it with an X for future reference.

	Cell	Indicated Strategy
_____	A	2, 3, 9
_____	B, C	8, 9
_____	D, F	8
_____	E	None
_____	G	6, 8, 11, 12
_____	H	8, 11, 12
_____	I	6, 8, 11, 12

EXERCISE 11. The Stressor Identification Matrix (Part Two)

You used the matrix to determine whether you are stressed by M, O, or S—Myself, Others, or Situations.

If you had a high M score—that is, 50 percent or more, the following strategies are preliminarily indicated.

	Strategy No. and Name	
_____	2	"Breaking the Worry Cycle"
_____	3	"Thought Reprogramming"
_____	4	"Six Ways to Get High on Yourself"

If you had a high O score—that is, 50 percent or more, the following strategies are preliminarily indicated.

	Strategy No. and Name	
_____	5	"Desensitization"
_____	8	"Asserting Yourself"
_____	12	"Overcoming Call Reluctance" †

† Only indicated if your "O" stressors are predominately of an interpersonal nature.

If you had a high S score—that is, 50 percent or more, the following strategies are preliminarily indicated.

Strategy No. and Name	
_____ 3	"Thought Reprogramming"
_____ 5	"Desensitization"
_____ 13	"Body Relaxation"

EXERCISE 12. The B-T-A Inventory (Part Two)

The B-T-A assessment is actually three inventories, each measuring a separate tendency to manifest stress. Refer to your scores to decide which prescriptions apply.

High B. If your B inventory (Body Stress) score was between 60 and 100, or if you rated one or more symptoms a 5 in frequency, the following are preliminarily indicated.

Strategy No. and Name	
_____ 10	"Physical Exercise"
_____ 13	"Body Relaxation"

High T. If your T inventory (Cognitive Stress) score was between 79 and 100, the following are preliminarily indicated.

Strategy No. and Name	
_____ 2	"Breaking the Worry Cycle"
_____ 3	"Thought Reprogramming"
_____ 4	"Six Ways to Get High on Yourself"
_____ 7	"The Sales Call Postmortem"

High A. If your A inventory (Behavioral Stress) score was between 79 and 100, the following are preliminarily indicated.

	Strategy No. and Name
_____ 10	"Physical Exercise"
_____ 13	"Body Relaxation"

In addition, if you found that your high A score is concentrated heavily in *interpersonal-action* items, the following are also preliminarily indicated.

	Strategy No. and Name
_____ 8	"Asserting Yourself"
_____ 11	"Giving and Getting Feedback"

EXERCISE 13. The SLS Measurement Profile (Part Two)

If you found that (a) the upper limit of your stress tolerance range, or comfort zone, is lower than 58; or (b) your comfort zone spanned fewer than 25 points, then the following is indicated:

	Strategy No. and Name
_____ 9	"Increasing Your Comfort Zone"

Next, pull these scores and strategy recommendations together, and decide on your greatest stress-management need. Do this by:

- Counting the number of times each strategy was recommended.
- Circling that number on the Strategy Selection Chart on page 201, on the same line with the name and the number of the strategy.

If the number you circle lies in the gray zone, then that strategy is the particular one you need to master stress. If the number you circle falls short of the gray zone, then you can consider postponing this strategy.

Strategy Selection Chart

Strategy	*Number of Times Indicated*
1. Stress-Attack First-Aid Kit	This technique is a must for everyone needing control.
2. Breaking the Worry Cycle	1 2 3 4 5 6 7 8 9
3. Thought Reprogramming	1 2 3 4 5 6 7 8 9
4. Six Ways to Get High on Yourself	1 2 3 4 5 6 7 8 9
5. Desensitization	1 2 3 4 5 6 7 8 9
6. Reducing Type A Behavior	1 2 3 4 5 6 7 8 9
7. The Sales Call Postmortem	1 2 3 4 5 6 7 8 9
8. Asserting Yourself	1 2 3 4 5 6 7 8 9
9. Increasing Your Comfort Zone	1 2 3 4 5 6 7 8 9
10. Physical Exercise	1 2 3 4 5 6 7 8 9
11. Giving and Getting Feedback	1 2 3 4 5 6 7 8 9
12. Body Relaxation	1 2 3 4 5 6 7 8 9
13. Overcoming Call Reluctance	1 2 3 4 5 6 7 8 9

For example, suppose you found that "Breaking the Worry Cycle" was indicated three times. Line 2 would look like this:

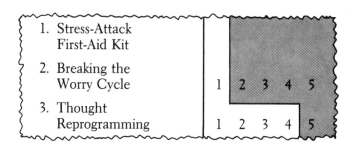

This means that, after you have learned to use the Stress-Attack First-Aid Kit, a primer for *all* other techniques, you would then master Breaking the Worry Cycle.

Now go ahead and count the number of *X's* for each technique, and enter the totals on the chart. Now you are ready to write your prescription. List each of the strategies for which the "count" falls in the gray area of the chart:

- _____

- _____

- _____

- _____

- _____

- _____

- _____

- _____

Fill in your prescription pad with the strategies that most need your attention, in descending order:

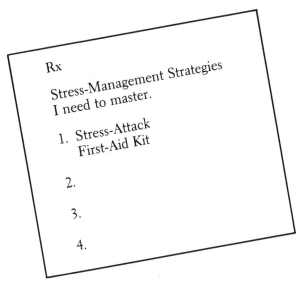

Rx
Stress-Management Strategies
I need to master.

1. Stress-Attack
   First-Aid Kit

2.

3.

4.

The Stress-Attack First-Aid Kit heads every prescription. It is the key strategy about which every other one revolves. The second strategy for you to master is, naturally, the one that is highest on your list. Make the third highest count number 3, and so on.

You are now ready to turn to Part Three and begin the process of learning and practicing the stress-management strategies most appropriate for your personal stress.

THREE

Stress-Management Strategies That Work

Introduction

THE stress-management techniques detailed in this section meet three criteria:

1. They work.
2. They are portable.
3. They bring rapid relief.

We have tried every technique in this part and have taught others to use them—successfully. Salespeople report the techniques work, making a considerable difference in their selling effort. For example, an insurance rep who learned these techniques in a workshop recently wrote:

Dear Frances:

You will be pleased to hear the effect on me has been quite remarkable and I really do not know myself; my stress levels are down completely. . . . I have been able to maintain very strict control over any possible stress situation that may arise. I continually remind myself of the basic rules that you gave me and find that they are rather easy to follow. The obvious effect has been that I am quite relaxed at all times and do not find myself in a situation that creates stress.

The results have had a far-reaching effect on my relationship with my family and my staff, who have, incidentally, complimented me on the remarkable change in my attitude towards stress problems. They very much appreciate this change and find that it is far easier to work under these new conditions.

Kind regards,

Sender Lees
Johannesburg, South Africa

You need no special equipment or complicated gadgetry to augment these techniques. We won't ask you to chant mystical phrases, take to wearing saffron robes, or lie down on your office floor twice a day. These techniques are strictly portable: you can use them at home, in your car, in a prospect's waiting room, or, if need be, in the midst of a face-to-face situation. Once you have learned the techniques and know your stress profile, or a particular stress problem, they will literally be at your fingertips for life.

The trade-off is that these techniques are not instant soup. A few people have reported learning them in a flash of insight, but they are the exceptions. For most of us, learning a new skill takes time and practice. But that's not news. Habits change slowly. Move your wastebasket from the right side of your desk to the left side and—guaranteed—you will throw paper on the floor for the next sixty days. Eventually, tossing to the left becomes as automatic as was tossing to the right.

Most people go through three phases when learning any new skill, as shown in the figure on page 207.

The Three Phases of Learning a New Skill

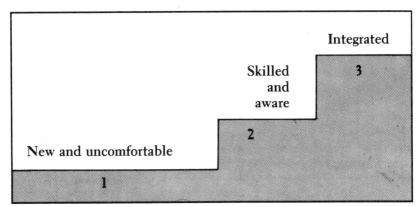

Let's take a closer look at these three steps:

1. *The New and Uncomfortable Phase.* When you first start practicing a new skill, it feels all wrong. It feels more like you are *playing at* using the new skill than actually using it. The new skill doesn't feel the way you thought it would, it doesn't look the way it did when the pro demonstrated it, and the whole thing takes a lot of concentration and energy. Be it playing tennis, sailing a boat, speaking French, typing from dictation, "active listening" to prospects, or playing the tuba, the first phase is the toughest to overcome. It doesn't feel a part of you yet—but it *will.*

2. *The Skilled and Aware Phase.* This is the phase you've been waiting for! It holds some of the most rewarding feelings you can have. You have mastered the new skill, you know it, and you are aware when you use it. A good backhand volley, a well-answered question, or a snazzy stem christie in powdery snow makes you proud and gives you cause to celebrate within yourself. At last the reward is in the doing. The new skill has become part of a polished performance and—at least in your eyes—a thing of beauty.

3. *The Integrated Phase.* After a while, every new skill becomes so much a part of who you are that it is difficult to imagine

a time when you didn't have the skill. You get the feeling that it was "in there someplace" lying dormant all along. It is difficult to remember that you actually had to learn it. Playing a musical instrument, performing a magic trick, serving a tennis ball, or using an interpersonal skill can become so ingrained and integrated that it seems as natural as reading, writing, talking, and making love.

You know when you have reached this phase by what you *don't* think about. A phase 3 tennis player thinks about where the other players are and what strategy to employ. The phase 3 musician watches the audience and listens to the piece he or she is playing. The phase 3 communicator listens to the content of someone's talk and responds to the problem to be solved. You know you are in phase 3 when the new skill is no longer something you do but something you *are*.

When you have had sufficient practice with stress-management skills, they will become part of who you are. They will be as integrated as your question-asking skills and your timing for a close.

Develop the Stressless Selling Habit

What does it take to make stress-management skills an integrated part of who you are and how you sell? There are both general and specific answers to that question.

The general answer is a model borrowed from the American Cancer Society's Stop Smoking Program. They use the acronyms HABIT and TIP to explain the process of learning a new skill, of making a new skill a HABIT. Any well-honed skill, be it smoking, reading, or managing stress, exists because it has become a HABIT, a:

Highly
Automatic
Behavior
Intensively conditioned over a period of
Time

To make a new skill an integrated habit, the program suggests this TIP: habits develop because of:

Time
Incentive, and
Practice

How much TIP, you ask? The incentive has to come from you. We will suggest ways to reward yourself as you learn, but basically, nothing is going to happen until you *need* and *want* it to happen. What about time? The practice routines we suggest for each technique take no more than ten minutes a day. The repetition is a more variable matter. Some techniques—like respiratory relaxation—can be learned in one practice period. One or two of the routines take more than a week to master. But two weeks of practice times ten minutes a day is still less than two hours of actual work.

Be aware: discarding old habits and learning new ones *is* work. Giving up old habits—even when you know you must— is uncomfortable. Be prepared for the discomfort; we all go through it. Building a new habit can also be—you guessed it— a little stressful. You have to be prepared for both the discomfort and the stress of learning new behaviors, new habits, new ways of dealing with yourself, the world, and other people.

How hard is the practice? If you can count to 10 on your fingers and hold your breath for seven seconds, you have the basic qualifications. The specifics aren't much more complex. To guarantee success, follow these suggestions:

1. Follow the instructions as closely as possible.
2. Practice the skills. You cannot expect to use them only when you are tense, at least not right away. Practice at a convenient time and on a regular basis.
3. Focus on the skill. Learning new skills takes time, effort, and self-absorption. Practicing a new skill goes slowly at first, but speeds up and eventually becomes a solid habit.
4. Keep a log. It's not critical, but it is useful to record your stress levels and briefly describe stressor situations and

sneak attacks. Writing things down helps you spot patterns, increases awareness, and informs you of progress.

5. Make the commitment. Tell somebody important what you are up to. Public acknowledgment of a plan helps you stick to it. In any case, your willingness to consistently work at helping yourself is crucial.

6. Get someone to join you. Shared efforts can firm resolve, offer opportunities to practice in a safe environement, help perfect skills, and also add encouragement. Study groups are a natural stress-management support group.

Specific Procedures for Using Part Three

By now you should have (1) developed your Personal Stress Profile and (2) written your first Stress Management Prescription. From here on, it's all techniques, practice routines, and tips for handling specific stressors and situations.

Strategy 1 is to learn to use the Stress-Attack First-Aid Kit. The kit contains some of the basic techniques you need for your prescriptions. They are also the routines you must master to handle those sneak panic attacks and stress overloads that just happen from time to time. They are designed to bring you back down after you have been in a high-stress situation.*

Here is how to maximize your utilization of Part Three.

1. Read through the Stress-Attack First-Aid Kit. Practice the techniques according to the instructions. You cannot overpractice or "overlearn" this routine. It is a core routine composed of techniques you must master.

2. The section immediately following the kit, "Getting Your Act Together: Behavioral Rehearsal and the Ten Finger Exercise," is the basic practice routine. Draw on it for

---

* Almost all the techniques and routines in Part Three have stress-relief value. But most of the uses we detail are for *stress prevention* rather than *stress relief.* Attacking the source of your stress has long-term benefits that cannot be achieved through procedures designed solely to lower the immediate tension level. Treating symptoms doesn't cure the problem; you need to be able to do *both.*

practicing *all* the techniques and routines. It is, therefore, also a *must master* routine.

3. When you have mastered the First-Aid Kit, you are ready
   to work on your first prescription. Locate the techniques
   or routines for your Stress Management Prescription.

4. Read quickly through the first strategy in your prescription to get a feel for it. If the instructions suggest a technique you are unfamiliar with, look that technique up
   in the index. Practice the technique before going ahead
   with the prescription.

STRATEGY 1

STRESS-ATTACK FIRST-AID KIT

OBJECTIVE: To "bring yourself down" when you are highly stressed.

USAGE:
- *Before* an event or call when anticipation raises tensions that don't automatically subside after a few minutes
- *After* a call or encounter has raised your stress level and the level does not come down automatically
- *During* a call or encounter when attack from another person—or just surprise—threatens to escalate your stress out of control

Introduction

THE Stress-Attack First-Aid Kit is composed of four techniques, *used in this order:*

1. *Deep breathing*—A proven technique for quickly bringing physical arousal, especially hyperventilation, under control.
2. *Mental imagery*—The nervous system can't differentiate between real and imagined experiences. Playing non-stressful pictures on the movie screen in your mind brings your subjective stress level down.
3. *Thought stopping*—A stress-producing thought, image,

213

or idea can go cycling in the mind. Once you learn how, you can tell it to stop—and it will!

4. *Self-coaching*—Not a pep talk, but a four-step method for telling yourself what to think. The emphasis is on stress-controlling thoughts.

Together these four techniques in this sequence can bring you from a post-call SLS in the overload range to an SLS in the upper half of your comfort zone in less than five minutes. The key is having the routine down pat *before* you need it.

EXERCISE 15. Deep Breathing (Respiratory Relaxation)

Overview

High stress and panic have at least one thing in common: both are associated with too little oxygen and too much carbon dioxide. In the laboratory, anxiety attacks are commonly induced by having students breathe a mixture that is 70 percent CO_2 and 30 percent oxygen. This mixture is the reverse of normal air.

Highly stressed and panicked people take shallow, rapid breaths through the mouth. This breathing pattern tends to hold carbon dioxide in the lungs and keep oxygen out. In both laboratory experiments and during real stress attacks, the oxygen–carbon dioxide mixture can be corrected by inhaling through the nose, holding the breath for seven seconds, and exhaling through the mouth. We have added instructions so that you can get a jump on controlling the panic thinking that usually accompanies a stress attack.

Specific Steps

1. Take a deep breath through your nose.
2. Hold it for a count of seven (no more).
3. Release the breathe slowly through the mouth.
4. Repeat three to six times, focusing on your breathing as you do.

If done as described, you will bring your stress level down in less than three minutes just by deep breathing. Some people have reported extra stress reduction when they use their imagination while deep breathing. Others report that visualizing the air in their lungs rising all the way to the top of their head in little bubbles provides extra relief.

Practice

1. Practice the exercise three to six times right now.
2. Engage in an activity that normally causes you to breathe rapidly, such as running up a flight of stairs. Deep breathe until your rate of respiration returns to a comfortable level.
3. Practice the "breathe-hold-count-release" cycle three to six times in a meeting or at a social engagement. Do it as unobtrusively as you can. This is a good rehearsal for doing deep breathing during a stressful face-to-face encounter. Once you see that you can do it in public with no one being the wiser, you will be encouraged to use it in any number of stressful situations.
4. If, after a few days, you find that deep breathing doesn't bring quick control over a stress attack—that is, it doesn't bring your SLS down to a point where you can use imagery and thought stopping—you will need to add body relaxation to your Stress-Attack First-Aid Kit. If your muscles are very tight and you hold your body in a rigid or tense fashion during a stress attack, you definitely need to try the Body Relaxation technique, Strategy 12.

EXERCISE 16. Mental Imagery

Overview

Your imagination is a powerful tool for coping with problems. You have the ability to develop vivid mental scenes and "play" them for yourself whenever you wish. Some have referred to this skill as running inner motion pictures. Imagery is especially useful in stress management because your body can scarcely tell these mental images from the real thing; your mind, like your body, can't be in two places at once. Therefore, if you are in a stressful situation and you project a positive mind image on your motion picture screen, your tension level drops significantly.

One workshop participant developed a vivid image of himself snorkeling off a beautiful white-sand beach in the Caribbean. He worked on that scene until he experienced "being there," enjoying the interesting marine life, feeling comfortable and relaxed. He was able to lose all sense of time and place, even though the trip only lasted from 60 to 120 seconds. He reported that he continues to "go to this favorite place" while sitting in his car following a stressful call or before talking to particularly unpleasant or stress-inducing customers. He reports a 20-point SLS drop with this mental image.

In addition to affording time out from stress, imagery can be a reward for finishing a task or reinforcement for problem solving. The technique is also useful as a mental rehearsal, such as before a proposal presentation or a speech, and for goal setting.

Specific Steps

The following procedure is for developing and using a stress-relieving mind trip. Using this mind trip will give you mental distance from the stressful event and bring your SLS down. It can be used before or after a stressful event, such as a difficult sales call.

Developing the Favorite-Place Mind Trip

1. Choose a favorite place—a pleasant relaxing place you have enjoyed in the past or one you would enjoy visiting in the future. Typical favorite places are a beach, a museum, an island, a mountain valley, a rowboat in the middle of a tranquil lake, and a powdery ski slope at daybreak or dusk.

2. Close your eyes and think about the scene. If it's outdoors, what is the weather like? If you're developing a beach scene, try to feel the warm sun on your body. Think about the sounds, smells, colors, and shapes in your favorite place.

3. Put yourself in your favorite place. If your scene includes people, have them vague or at a distance, rather like part of the scenery. If you feel like moving about in your scene, just float—no need to walk or exert yourself unless that relaxes you.

4. You may find your mind wandering a bit. That's okay. You will find yourself drifting back to the scene again after a short while.

5. Practice developing your favorite place in one- and two-minute sessions twice a day. By the end of your fifth or sixth practice session, the image should be fairly well developed and clear.

6. Note: Your mind trip may never be as vivid as a photograph, but with practice you can get pretty close. If you are experiencing visualization problems after two or three attempts, start this exercise over and over, until its details became clear enough that you learn to build mental images.

Using the Favorite Place Mind Trip

1. Use your favorite-place image after you have done deep breathing and/or body relaxation.

2. Close your eyes or focus them on a fixed spot; your hands, a desk, or dashboard object will do.

3. Bring up the favorite-place image and go with it. See, feel, smell, and experience all the good things you can as vividly as possible. Don't force the images if they don't develop right away. They will come without effort once you cue them to come.

4. You don't need to set a time limit. A mind trip is not a hypnotic trance. You never lose touch with what's going on around you.

5. When you sense that your SLS has come down, erase

the mind trip. A good indicator of when to stop is noticeable body relaxation. Another is boredom or a sense
of completeness about the trip.

EXERCISE 17. Thought Stopping

Overview

Events, ideas, and images that trigger a stress response
sometimes linger in your mind the way a haunting refrain stays
with you long after the band has stopped playing. Concentration
is all but impossible, getting to sleep out of the question. It is a
distressing and rather common experience for sales professionals. In thought stopping, in a sense you startle yourself out of
the obsessive thought.

Specific Steps

In workshops this process is fast, simple, and fun.

1. We ask a volunteer worrier to sit in a chair facing away
   from the group. We tell the worrier to worry—out loud.
2. After about 10 seconds, we blow a police whistle. The
   worrier is startled, jumps, and stops talking.
3. We prompt him or her to continue worrying out loud
   and repeat the whistle blowing. We go through the whistle cycle two to four times, provided the volunteer stays
   with us.
4. Once again the worrier is encouraged to worry aloud.
   This time we interrupt by loudly hollering the word
   "stop!" We do this step twice.
5. Again the worrier is encouraged to worry aloud. This
   time we hold a stop sign in front of the worrier at eye
   level and we repeat this instruction:

   From now on whenever you begin to worry or stress
   yourself through constantly recurring thoughts,

blow the whistle on yourself, tell yourself *stop*, and visualize this stop sign.

From that point on, most participants report that they can perform the whistle and stop-sign routine in their mind to successfully thought-stop. This technique works, not only for the volunteer worrier, but for the rest of the workshop group as well. How? Through *vicarious learning*—experiencing the process along with the volunteer. It has to do with the empathy process you depend on as a salesperson when you ask feeling-finding questions.

Learning to Thought-Stop

Learning to thought-stop is a two-stage process. First, use your mental imagery skills. Read through the preceding six steps and visualize yourself as a workshop participant. The process will work best if you take the role of the volunteer, but it can also work if you take the role of observer; just make sure the imaginary volunteer is worrying your worry. When you finish, reward yourself with a favorite-place image. Second, go into a bedroom, den, office, or other private place and follow these steps. You can read them to yourself or ask another person to read them to you.

1. Start talking aloud about a business problem that is bothering you. (Allow 10 to 15 seconds.)
2. Shout the word "stop!"
3. Start talking about your problem again. (Allow 10 to 15 seconds.)
4. Shout the word "stop!" Repeat numbers 3 and 4 one more time.
5. Now say, "Close your eyes. Start talking about your problem again. When I say the word 'now,' visualize a stop sign." (Allow 10 seconds to pass.)
6. Say, "Now." (Pause three counts.) "You should be seeing a stop sign in your mind's eye." (Pause 10 seconds.)
7. Repeat numbers 5 and 6 twice more.
8. Say, "From now on whenever you begin to worry needlessly or stress yourself through constantly recurring

thoughts, mentally tell yourself to *stop*, and visualize the stop sign you are visualizing right now." (Pause 5 seconds.)

9. Say, "Very good. Reward yourself with a Favorite Place Mind Trip." (Pause 2 seconds.) "Come back when you are ready."

Make a Habit of the Thought-Stopping Technique

Next best to a workshop is having a friend or relative read the instructions to you. If there's someone who wants to help you learn, and who also wants to learn thought stopping, you might go all the way and get a whistle and a stop sign. Under those ideal conditions you should be able to master thought stopping if you practice three times a day for three days. That comes to about one half-hour of work apiece.

If you are reluctant to use a helper, record the instructions on tape. Then practice to the sound of your own voice, once in the morning and once in the evening for five days.

Some people use an actual whistle, shout, and hold up the stop sign as learning aids and then they mentally thought-stop. We know several sales professionals who keep a police whistle in their cars and blow it when thought stopping is necessary. Others continue to shout "Stop" aloud. Practice the thought-stopping sequence several times before you attempt to use it in an actual high-stress situation.

Integrate Thought-Stopping Into
Your Stress-Attack First-Aid Kit

You now have three of the four first-aid techniques under your belt. That brings your kit up to six steps.

1. Use deep breathing and mental imagery to bring your stress level down a bit.
2. Use the thought-stopping technique to identify the thought, image, idea, worry, or problem that is running wild in your mind.
3. Ask yourself, "Is there anything I can do about this right

here and now?" Ninety-nine times out of 100 the answer is *no way.*

4. Each time the thought occurs, go through the thought-stopping routine: These three steps should occur almost simultaneously: (1) blow the whistle on the thought; (2) mentally say "Stop!"; (3) show yourself the stop sign.
5. Repeat the thought-stopping routine until you have the offending thought at bay.
6. Reward yourself with a quick, positive mind trip.

EXERCISE 18. Self-Coaching

Overview

Thoughts can guide behavior. The thoughts we think affect what we do and what we feel. "Men are disturbed not by things but by the views they take of them," wrote the philosopher Epictetus in A.D. 60. Since the year 1, positive-thinking enthusiasts have insisted that the things we say *to* ourselves *about* ourselves determine what we achieve and how we feel about ourselves. It wasn't until quite recently that scientists studied and verified that belief.

Positive self-instructions are *not* positive thinking; they are more specific. If you say to yourself, "I can't cope," you're right. If you say to yourself, "I can cope by using the strategies in my first-aid kit," you'll be right again. Negative or unrealistic self-instructions increase stress. Positive, realistic self-instructions help manage stress. Thought-stopping is the strategy you use to turn off the negative self-instructions. Self-coaching is the strategy for generating the positive self-instructions that must replace the vanquished negative self-instructions.

Specific Steps

To be effective, your positive self-instructions must be:

- Short
- Clear

- Behaviorally specific
- Direct

Since the first-aid kit is strictly for bringing stress under control, the self-instructions presented here deal only with three specific situations:

1. Preparing for a stressful meeting
2. Confronting and handling a stressful situation
3. Coping with "after the fact" stress

The ideal is for you to generate your own positive self-instructions for each situation. Eventually you will, but for now, we provide you with (1) the stressful situation, (2) the rules for generating the positive self-instructions, and (3) four usable self-instructions.

Preparing for a Stressful Meeting

☐ Anticipating an important sales call can provoke a stress attack. If you are unprepared, are unsure of the politics and players, or believe that the sale isn't going your way, you can start generating negatives and stress before the call ever takes place.

☐ The guidelines or rules for generating coping statements for a pre-call stress attack are:

1. You can develop a plan to deal with the situation.
2. Just think about what you can do about the situation. That's better than getting anxious.
3. No negative self-statements; think rationally and logically.
4. Don't worry; worry won't help anything anyway.
5. Maybe what you think is anxiety actually is eagerness to confront the stressor.

☐ These four statements have been known to help others:

1. *I know I'm ready and prepared for this call. Let me just stick with what I have to do.*

2. *I've done it before, successfully. I can psyche myself up.*
3. *One step at a time. I won't get ahead of myself.*
4. *If I get a no, I'll still be okay.*

Confronting and Handling a Stressful Situation

☐ Things can happen during a call that bring on a stress attack. A customer who asks an unanticipated question or who has a novel and new objection can kick off a stress attack.

☐ The guidelines for this situation are:

1. Psych yourself up; you can meet this challenge.
2. You can convince yourself to do it; you can reason your fear away.
3. One step at a time; you can handle the situation.
4. Don't think about fear; just think about what you have to do. Stay relevant.
5. This anxiety is what they said you would feel; it's a reminder to use your coping exercises.
6. This tenseness can be an ally; it's a cue to cope.
7. Relax; you're in control. Take a slow, deep breath.

☐ These five statements can help you cope positively with "during the call" stress:

1. *This guy is tough, but he's human. Let me identify his stress level, too.*
2. *If the sale goes down the drain, I'll survive it.*
3. *I'm good at what I do. Let me remember to use my sales training skills.*
4. *Nobody is perfect. Let me focus on the customer and do the best I can.*
5. *I haven't got time for negative tension. I need to focus on what the prospect is saying.*

Coping With After-the-Fact Stress

☐ Many times you can keep yourself together before and during the call, only to fall apart after it's over.

☐ These are the guidelines or rule for coping with this situation:

1. Keep the focus on the present. What do you have to do next?
2. You can expect your stress level to increase after certain calls.
3. It wasn't as bad as you expected.
4. You held it together very well.
5. Put a number on your stress. When you name it, it goes away.
6. You survived a real toughy.

☐ One or more of these positive self-instructions should apply to your post-call stress attack:

1. *Wow! I survived that one. Just getting through it is terrific.*
2. *Don't get stressed. Focus on what I can learn from the call.*
3. *I should expect my tension level to change. It's okay. If I go with it, I control it.*
4. *Let me take a few minutes to fall apart and then get back to business.*

Practice Self-Coaching

You need to program yourself for using the positive self-instructions so that they are available during a stress attack. The best preparation is practice. We recommend the following method for practicing and using positive self-statements:

1. Obtain four 3- by 5-inch index cards.
2. Write a title on the top line of each card. You can use some version of our titles, e.g., "Preparing For," "Confronting and Handling," "After the Fact," but a more personalized tag might serve as a memory peg. Something like "Psyching Up" or "Pre-Call Warm Up" might work better for you than "Preparing for a Stressor."

3. Write the guidelines for each situation on the front of each card.
4. Write the positive self-instructions on the back of each card.
5. Find a comfortable place to practice. Read both sides of each card twice, then imagine a scene where you would be stressed—something related to the title of one of the cards. Let the image of the scene increase your stress level.
6. Focus your attention on reading the appropriate card to yourself. (Reading the card aloud will help focus your attention and block out the stress scene you conjured up from your imagination.) When you feel your stress level returning to a more comfortable level, reward yourself with a favorite-place mind trip.
7. Repeat step 6 until you have done a scene for each card.
8. Practice this procedure once a day for three to five days. Reading the guidelines will begin to trigger the positive self-instructions you've practiced. If you want to practice until the instructions are committed to memory, fine, but it is not essential.

Use Self-Coaching

In the Stress-Attack First-Aid Kit, use self-coaching after thought stopping, in this order:

1. Deep breathing
2. Mental imagery
3. Thought-stopping
4. Self-coaching

Carry the four 3- by 5-inch cards in your glove compartment, if you travel by car, or in your briefcase. For some, the handiest place is in their wallet or purse. When you have finished the thought-stopping technique, you are ready for the self-coaching routine.

1. Take out the card appropriate to the situation.

2. Focus your attention on the card.
3. Read the card to yourself. Don't just look at the words; read them slowly and carefully. The positive statements are *not* worry beads to be chanted through. Read them for meaning.
4. Try to make a mental image of the person—you—the positive self-instructions are describing.
5. After each card reading, stop and check your stress level. If the level is too high for comfort, add deep breathing and mental imagery to the end of each reading.
6. When your stress level is comfortable and the worst part of the stress attack is over, reward yourself with a mental image, preferably a favorite-place mind trip.

The Ten-Finger Exercise

Obviously, there will be times when pulling out your index cards will be neither possible nor appropriate. A prospect, for instance, might not understand if you started reading them in the midst of giving a presentation. You can, however, make the self-instruction statements portable. You can "program" them into your mental "computer" with the help of your ten fingers.

Select one positive statement from those on your index cards. Each night before going to bed, recite the chosen self-instruction ten times, ticking it off on each of your fingers beginning with the thumb on your dominant hand. Recite the statement five times, working through to your pinky finger. Then do the same with your other hand. Continue the ten-finger exercise with the same self-instruction statement for as many nights as it takes to "hear it" and integrate it into yourself. Then, when you need to use the statement with a customer, supervisor, or co-worker, merely put your thumb to the forefinger of your dominant hand, and the statement will just be there for you. Repeat the ten-finger exercise with as many self-statements as you've generated on the index cards.

Strategy Summary

The Stress-Attack First-Aid Kit is your best strategy for reducing a stress overload and bringing your SLS under control. It is most useful when you have been experiencing a stress overload for too long, when you feel your SLS starting to slide up above your comfort zone, or when a sudden shock occurs and you aren't coming down naturally. The four techniques are easy to remember and, when practiced sufficiently, quick and easy to perform:

1. *Do deep breathing*—until you feel your body simmering down and you are satisfied that you have reversed the SLS climb.
2. *Take time out for mental imagery*—until you feel a sense of distance from the stressor or stressful situation.
3. *Thought-stop the negatives*—when the negative self-statements and stressful thoughts are out, or at least whispers and not shouts, move on.
4. *Rebuild the positives through self-coaching*—fill in with positives the holes left when you eliminate the negative, stressful thoughts and images.

STRATEGY 2

BREAKING THE WORRY CYCLE

Worry vs. Problem Solving

WORRY is problem centered with attention focused on the "cause" rather than the "solution." When we learn to look back at the "solution" (the problem-solving aspect of the worrysome situation), you begin to concentrate on things over which you can have some control. It can help you move toward creating more positive, workable alternatives, in effect, better solutions.

The following juxtaposes a problem-solving approach with a worrying approach.

Problem-Solving

1. **Solution-oriented—**
   Attention focused on the outcomes or possible effects.

2. **Sequential—**
   Orderly progression of steps in thinking.

Worrying

1. **Problem-centered—**
   Attention focused on the cause or triggers mainly.

2. **Random—**
   Disorganized thinking patterns. Thoughts and ideas often circular.

Problem-Solving	*Worrying*
3. **Closed ended—** Has definite beginning and end. Efficient use of time.	3. **Open ended—** Recurrent, continuous thoughts. Often intermittent. Frequently takes great deal of time.
4. **Overt or covert—** Can be open, including others or occurring in thoughts and images (internally). Usually results in some overt action or behavior.	4. **Covert—** Mainly thoughts and images; solitary, but occasionally shared with others. Generally does not result in overt action.
5. **Produces perceived resourcefulness—** Individual sees self as able to cope effectively. Own actions viewed as causal in positive actions or reactions.	5. **Produces perceived helplessness—** Individual sees self as unable to cope. Own actions do not seem to bring positive change. Often views self as victim.
6. **Autonomic arousal—** Reduced as individual moves through the sequence.	6. **Autonomic arousal—** Sustained at high level; upward spirally. Catastrophic thinking often keeps the body tension high.
7. **Stress reducing**	7. **Stress producing**
8. **Appropriate coping device—** Enhances resourcefulness; goal directed; reinforces positive self-view.	8. **Inappropriate coping device—** Fosters helplessness; reduces personal effectiveness; reinforces negative self-view.

Introduction

An event seldom turns out the way we fear it will, yet we often continue the worry cycle. Why? Because we don't know how to *stop* worrying. Your worries won't disappear—that's unrealistic—however, you can reduce the cost of unproductive worry.

There's another factor, too. Worry takes its toll on your body as well as your mind. Remember the last time you became anxious about something? What happened to your body? If you're like most people, uncomfortable body tension accompanied the worrisome thoughts. The more heavy duty the thoughts, the more a toll they can take on your body. Many people report heavy smoking and drinking, ulcers, chronic back pain, and headaches as well as other debilitating physical responses. Vivid mental pictures of catastrophes require a good deal of time and energy; there's often little left for problem solving or doing one's best. One result is a real or imagined sales slump.

General Steps

1. Observe your worry pattern: It is necessary to learn what you are worrying about, when you worry, and how much time you spend worrying.
   a. In a small spiral notebook or on a set of index cards, record:
      - Worry topic
      - Time spent worrying
      - Where you were at the time
      - Where in your body you felt tense, if at all (if you rub a body part while worrying, that is likely to be a tension-carrying "spot")
2. Place your cards on the table:
   a. After a week of collecting data on yourself, sit down and review your cards or notebook. Place the cards or pages face up on your desk or a table.
   b. Answer the following questions:
      - What do I find to worry about with regularity?

- Do I worry at a specific time and/or in a specific place?
- Where in my body do I usually experience the tension?

c. Look for patterns. You will quickly see that worry is not random. We all have worry *topics*, worry *times*, and worry *places*. Many salespeople worry in their cars. Some do it in the shower and still others lie awake nights. Some worry about not being able to close a particular sale, others find quota a worry, and some see personal concerns to be worry topics. Almost all of us experience tension as a result of worry. We all have a physical weak link—some body part or area susceptible to stress. Body tension can be a cue to kick into a stress-reduction routine.

3. Build a worry ladder:
   a. Arrange your index cards in order, from the most to the least stressful worry.
   b. If you find one high-stress worry that seems overwhelming, break it into smaller parts.
   c. You are now ready to begin using specific worry-stopping techniques. Concentrate on concerns that seem to be circular, dead-end, and do not usually turn out the way you expected. For example:
      - Worrying about whether or not a shipment will arrive for a major customer, after you have done all you can to ensure its timely arrival.
      - Worrying about what the new sales manager really thinks about you.
      - Worrying about growing older, losing your vitality, and being replaced by younger salespeople.
      - Worrying about whether or not you will receive a call-back.
      - Catastrophic thoughts about not having enough active prospective buyers.

4. Break for deep breathing. Before you start working on your high-worry issues, you need to be calm and focused on the task. If sorting and ordering your cards has upped your stress level, deep breathe yourself down.

5. Blow the whistle on worry:
   a. Pick an item from your worry ladder that boomerangs on

you—one of those worry items that snowballs as you think about it.

b. Focus on the worry and allow your imagination to run with it. Really stew over it.

c. At some point, thought-stop the worry. Blow the whistle, scream "Stop" in your head, and visualize your stop sign.

d. Bring the worry to a complete halt.

e. Once the worry is stopped, relax a moment, deep breathe, then repeat b, c, d, and e.

6. Get bored. Repeat the 5b, 5c, 5d, 5e sequence until you get bored with it and your attention begins to drift. You will eventually reach a point where it will be difficult to even conjure up the worry. When you reach that point, stop.

7. Take a favorite-place mind trip. Either use the mental image you developed earlier for your first-aid kit or build a new one based on a highly pleasing work scene.

8. Set a timer for worry. A variation on the theme is to bring your worry out into the open and run it into the ground. This is especially helpful for heavy-duty worry. It goes like this:

a. Pick a heavy-duty worry from your list.

b. Set a kitchen timer or alarm clock for 15 minutes.

c. Start worrying. Think of nothing but your worry. If your attention starts to wander, read the notes you took while tracing your worries. Allow yourself no other thoughts or activities until the bell or buzzer goes off.

d. When the time period is over, thought-stop the worry to a standstill. Deep breathe until you are comfortable.

e. Reward yourself with food, drink, or a favorite-place image.

One of two things happens to your worries as a result of this exercise:

1. You may find that this approach "defangs" specific worries. If that happens, you can go on using this technique for working on specific worries.

2. You may be able to confine your worrying to a specific time and place. If that seems to be happening, start reducing your allowed worry time. Eventually you will

be able to confine your worrying to a specific two- or three-minute period once a day.

Create Positive Alternatives

Choose one worry from the worry ladder, concentrate on it, and escalate it. Carefully think through all the possible catastrophes that have been ricocheting through your head.

SUPPOSE you are worrying about a shipment that *must* be in Toledo no later than Monday. You are uncomfortable because you aren't able to light a fire under the shipping manager. You work yourself up and isolate five possible dire outcomes:

1. The shipment didn't leave the warehouse.
2. It was sent to Toledo via Peking.
3. It arrives Monday evening instead of Monday morning.
4. The wrong thing gets sent.
5. The merchandise is broken on arrival.

Now focus on possible alternatives to the catastrophe you envision. What solutions can you find for the worry? Expend at least as much time and energy on the alternatives as you did on envisioning the potential catastrophe. This step forces you to introduce a reality perspective. It is now possible for you to pair a positive alternative with the worry. Doing this often leads to a decrease in worrying and an increase in problem solving.

In our example, as you force positive alternatives, you decide:

1. I can call or go to the warehouse and verify shipment. Then I'll still have Sunday to panic. If it's necessary, I can always hire a plane.
2. I can call the customer and give him all the details so I know he knows.
3. I can put a trace on the shipment and have the trucking firm call me when they hit Toledo.

4. I can call the customer Sunday night, tell him where the shipment is, and make sure he puts a Monday A.M. pickup on it.
5. I can quit worrying. I've covered every possible base at least twice.

Rehearse for Success; Practice in Your Mind

Picture yourself confronting a sales situation you have been worrying about. This time, instead of rehearsing the worry outcome (as we tend to do), rehearse the possible positive outcomes. Then choose one or two of these positive outcomes and rehearse them in your imagination until you can perform them with confidence. Inner practice does tend to increase desired sales performance.

STRATEGY 3

THOUGHT REPROGRAMMING

Introduction

THE Thought Reprogramming strategy consists of three techniques used consecutively:

1. *Rethinking*—The process of examining the rational and irrational basis of your stressful and stressed thoughts, and selecting new nonstressful thoughts to replace stressful ones.
2. *Thought stopping*—The process of calling a halt to irrational thoughts. (See Exercise 17.)
3. *Ten-finger exercise*—The process of "drilling," or programming, a new thought or belief into your mind. The steps of the ten-finger exercise are detailed in Exercise 18.

You already know the thought-stopping technique, and if you have worked through the Stress-Attack First-Aid Kit, you also are familiar with the Ten-Finger Exercise. The additional technique you need for mastering the Thought-Reprogramming strategy is the rethinking technique.

235

EXERCISE 19. The Rethinking Process

Introduction

The Rethinking process has much in common with self-coaching. Both share the belief that thoughts have a direct and important impact on performance. Rethinking is a more analytical approach.

The Rethinking process is similar to our Chapter 3 discussion of the origin of stressors:

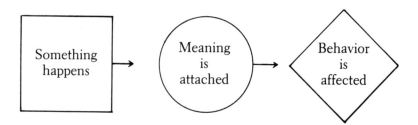

1. *Something Happens.* An event takes place. You make a sales call. You oversleep. A prospect cancels lunch. Your manager chews you out. You spill coffee on a report. A prospect buys from someone else. A cab driver honks and shouts at you. It's nothing more complex than an everyday event.

2. *Meaning Is Attached.* This is when the trouble starts. Because people are thinking beings, they try to make sense of the everyday events of life. To do this, they filter today's experiences through a screen of past experiences and beliefs.

Ellis believes that people often get in trouble right here. Many of the beliefs they use to measure experience are "irrational life philosophies" and they induce people to turn relatively insignificant events into catastrophies in their minds.

For example:

1. Joe's prospect calls and cancels lunch.
2. Joe interprets this to mean the prospect doesn't like him.
3. Joe infers that "I must not be very likable."

4. Joe has a rule in his head that says: "Everyone *must* like me."
5. Joe becomes sad, depressed, and stressed.

3. *Behavior Is Affected.* The frequent result of this tangled logic and overemotional reaction is some form of stress response and a decrease in sales efforts. Joe becomes emotionally stressed, these are the usual physical side effects, and his sales performance suffers; this boomerangs and it confirms Joe's assessment—and his fears. Welcome to the beginning of a stress cycle for Joe.

Ellis believes that when people go through this process they interpret events using one or more of 12 specific "irrational beliefs." Rethinking:

- Identifies the irrational belief that triggers the stress response.
- Replaces this tangled, stressful thinking with realistic, rational, and helpful self-instructions.

General Steps

1. *Isolate the Event That Is Triggering the Stressor.*

- This work is already done. When you identified your top stressors and classified them as M, O, or S, you isolated your stress triggers, or cues.
- The Rethinking process works best with the M stressors, but you can use it for O and S stressors as well. After all, we do think about other people and situations, and those thoughts are stress producers.
- If you scored a high T when you took the B-T-A Inventory, you are also in the right place.

2. *Debate and Challenge the Belief.* In a one-on-one counseling session, the stressed person and the counselor talk about the beliefs underlying the stressor isolated in Step 1. The call-

reluctance dialogue Dr. Stern used to lead a client through is typical.

Obviously, we can't debate beliefs in a book. We have replaced this discussion with a menu of possible irrational assumptions as they apply to sales. Sales professionals are pretty honest with themselves and can generally spot their irrational beliefs (see Twelve Common Erroneous Beliefs and Nine Common Reasoning Errors, later in this chapter).

3. *Replace the Irrational With the Rational.* Once the faulty assumptions or beliefs are identified, the task is to build more useful rules to live by. You won't be building new life rules here, but you *will* learn about alternative ways to interpret your identified high stressors.

Once you have what you consider an acceptable replacement for your interpretation of the stressor, you are ready to thought-stop the irrational interpretation and replace it with the new rational interpretation, using the ten-finger exercise (exercise 20, which follows later in this chapter).

Specific Steps

1. Write down the stressor that is causing the problem.
2. Write a short description of the reason that stressor is bothering you.
3. Refer to the Twelve Common Erroneous Beliefs and find an irrational belief that may be at the root of your dilemma. If none seems to fit your situation, compose the irrational belief statement you are using.
4. Refer to the Nine Common Reasoning Errors and find the reasoning error that took you off track.
5. Refer to the Alternative Thoughts and find the corrective statement that corresponds to your stressor. If none is to your liking, write your own. For example:

JOE is in a panic. He feels very stressed. He has completed the Stressor Identification Matrix and has identified "Personal production that is low" as his number-one current stressor. His analysis of the problem is shown in the figure on page 239.

Rethinking Worksheet

1. My most pressing M stressor is:

Personal Production is low

Here is my explanation of what is happening:

I have only one sale this month and it's the 3rd. I had planned on 3 sales and they didn't come. I'm lagging really behind and I don't know if I can do anything to recover momentum

2. After thinking things over and looking at the suggestions on page 242, I can see that my irrational belief in this situation can best be expressed this way:

#3 I have the belief that things must come out the way I planned them & feel bad and frustrated when they don't. I can't see what use planning is if the plans don't come out the way they are supposed to. I REALLY FEEL THAT WAY!

I have also spent the money from the three I didn't get   AM I IN TROUBLE!

3. I got to that belief through faulty reasoning. After looking at the suggestions on page 243, the way my reasoning went wrong was:

#4 & #5 I do overthink my problems and I don't look at things in perspective when I do that. I was doing OK til this month. maybe the problem isn't as big as I thought. Maybe I blew up.

4. After looking at the alternatives on pages 244–245, I believe a better way to view the situation, at least one that I can use to straighten my thinking out and use for building a standard sentence, is:

This is temporary (it better be!) I can sell my way out of it (I really can!) I know I have the skills. I really do too!

5. This makes sense to me because:

I do have some prospects in the pipe. I can push on them a little sooner than I had planned. If things get tight I can get a refund on the cruise I put the money down on I only lose a couple bucks

Review of Joe's Rethinking Efforts

1. Joe used a rethinking worksheet to look at his stressor, "Personal production that is low." He wrote down the circumstances of the low production, which hints at why he is stressed.

2. Joe looked over the list of irrational beliefs and found one that clicked for him. (By the way, when you read these irrational beliefs they sound a little comical. But if you listen to the "shoulds" and "musts" you use when you talk to yourself, you'll hear some silly-sounding phrases echoing around in your head. We all do it. Most of the time it doesn't hurt too much, but sometimes we get hooked by one and the panic sets in. That's when stress begins and things move into a stress cycle.) If none of these had made sense, Joe could have made up his own statement. The objective is to find the irrational belief that has you knotted up. Notice Joe's editorializing— that's great! It means Joe isn't just doing an exercise, he's thinking!

3. Joe moved on to look at the list of reasoning errors and decided that two of them had led him into this tense state. He wrote them down and added some ideas and comments. Great! These are more indicators that Joe is debating the problem with himself.

4. Joe looked at the list of alternative thoughts and decided that the statement for stressor 17 was a good replacement. He isn't 100 percent sure, as you can tell from the notes he made in parentheses. That's fine! Joe doesn't have to be a true believer to get better; he just has to counter his irrational thinking with a rational counterthought.

5. Joe has already started to make plans for getting back on the move. His irrational belief was that "things have to come out the way I plan them." That doesn't mean he has to give up planning. Far from it! But it means that Joe has to use his plan as a guide instead of as a god. He has even begun figuring out how to resolve his money problems.

Joe is going to have to drill those standard sentences using the ten-finger exercise, and he will have to thought-stop his irrational beliefs and panic. He has to work at getting hold of the problem. But problems like his generally get resolved in less than a week.

Rethinking Worksheet

1. My most pressing M stressor is:

   _____

   Here is my explanation of what is happening:

   _____

   _____

2. After thinking things over and looking at the suggestions on page 242, I can see that my irrational belief in this situation can best be expressed this way:

   _____

   _____

   _____

3. I got to that belief through faulty reasoning. After looking at the suggestions on page 243, the way my reasoning went wrong was:

_____

_____

_____

4. After looking at the alternatives on pages 244–245, I believe a better way to view the situation, at least one that I can use to straighten my thinking out and use for building a standard sentence is:

_____

_____

_____

5. This makes sense to me because:

_____

_____

_____

_____

Twelve Common Erroneous Beliefs

My erroneous belief probably is:

1. I must make everyone like me. If I can't get everyone to like me, I'm no good. I'm upset because they are telling me that they don't like me.
2. Certain acts are awful and the people who do them should be punished. I am being punished because I did something wrong; I must have.
3. Things *must* come out exactly as I planned and hoped they would. I'm a failure if things aren't perfect.
4. They are making my life miserable. I have no choice but to be upset and stressed; they won't get off me.
5. That stressor is a terrible thing to have happen. I'm *supposed* to be stressed by it.
6. I have to duck that. I can't handle it. If I can avoid it long enough it might clear up without me.
7. I need that [person, account, job, etc.]. Without [it] I'm nothing.

I'm a flop. It's my lifesaver.

8. I've got to be the best. Second place is no place. I have to strive to win every race, make every sale, know every answer. If I fall even a little short, lose even one sale, I'm a failure.

9. I can't change things. It happened to me and I'll never get over it. I can't recover from a fall like that. I *must* suffer forever.

10. I have to have all the bases covered. If anything can go wrong, it will. It will be a catastrophe if I don't cover every possibility.

11. I must change that [or them or him or her] to be the way I want and expect that [or them or him or her] to be. Everything depends on it. The way people are and the things they do have tremendous effect on my well-being.

12. I can't help feeling this way. That's the way I am. There is nothing I can do. There's nothing anyone can do.

Nine Common Reasoning Errors

The reason my belief is erroneous is that:

1. I am drawing a conclusion that doesn't gel with the data.
2. There are no data one way or the other.
3. I am exaggerating the importance of a very small piece of data.
4. I have blown a small incident into a catastrophe by overthinking it.
5. I am not looking at the problem in a wide context. It's a small part of a whole I am neglecting to look at.
6. I am only looking at the situation in black and white, success or fail, good or bad terms.
7. I am reacting the way I have been *told* to react, not the way I feel.
8. I'm not sure why my belief is erroneous.
9. I think my belief is rational.

Alternative Thoughts for the M Stressors

Stressor	*Rational Counterthoughts*
1. Being late for an appointment.	• Being late is uncomfortable. It won't cost me the sale.
4. Not feeling well.	• People understand when you are ill. I can reschedule the appointment.

Stressor	*Rational Counterthoughts*
5. Not being well prepared.	• It isn't the end of the world. I can handle any problems.
9. Having just made an error in judgment.	• Errors are unfortunate, not catastrophes.
10. Preparing to make a cold call.	Cold-call problems are handled in strategy 13.
11. Losing an important sale.	• This is not the worst thing that can happen to a person.
15. A conflict between what you see as customer needs and company policy.	• I *am* flexible. I can negotiate an acceptable compromise.
17. Personal production that is low.	• This is temporary. I can sell my way out. I have the skills.
19. Your performance being evaluated.	• I'm good. I know it. I can handle a simple evaluation.
22. Knowing your production is too low to win an important sales contest.	• Sales contests do not define my worth as a person.
24. Working more hours than are desirable.	• I choose what to do with my time. I can stop if I choose.
29. Losing an old, valued customer (buyer).	• It is inconvenient, but I'll live. I can get another one.
38. Doing things you know are wrong to make a sale.	• I can stop. I have other choices. There are better ways.
43. Selling a product or service that does not make you feel good about myself.	• I can sell something else. I can find a product I like. I can succeed with it as well.
47. Believing you accidentally offended a customer.	• Accidents like these happen. No one is perfect. He will get over it. So will I.
48. Losing your temper in a meeting.	• I have a right to express my feelings. My opinions have value.
49. Difficulty in asking for the order.	This is handled in Strategy 13.
50. Losing respect of peers.	• This will pass. I'm an O.K. person.

Summary

Now you have a model for doing the rethinking exercise on your own. The Rethinking Worksheet and the three charts, Twelve Common Erroneous Beliefs, Nine Common Reasoning Errors, and Alternate Thoughts for the M Stressors, are the tools to get you started. If the worksheet feels too structured, use a pad. And don't feel limited to our lists. They are only guides. It's important that you use the rethinking strategy to break free of thoughts that are making you stressed.

EXERCISE 20. Ten-Finger Exercise

Overview

The ten-finger exercise helps you drill new rules and positive coping statements into your memory bank; in other words, it helps you reprogram your mind. It may be useful to you in memorizing items to say to a prospect.

The exercise is quite ritualistic but when used consistently and quickly, these steps will help you memorize the new, non-stressful thoughts:

Specific Steps

1. Pick one or a series of related standard sentences you want to put into your new way of thinking.
2. Write them on 3- by 5-inch index cards.
3. Each night for one week, read the sentences to yourself 10 times. A mix of reading aloud and reading silently or to yourself is preferred.
4. Count the repetitions by touching a thumb to each finger. Touching thumb to fingers is important. Later, when you are under stress, you will be able to call up from memory the appropriate thoughts by touching your thumb and forefinger together.

Strategy Summary

The Thought Reprogramming strategy is your big gun for ending the stress caused by the things you say to yourself about yourself. When stressful thoughts have you all bound up, it's time to free yourself of those ties. The three steps are straightforward; practice plus patience is the formula for using them to your best advantage. But some soul searching and careful thought are necessary.

1. Rethink the way you view yourself, your work, your world, and your stressors ...

    until you have found the irrational base beneath your stressors and built more realistic things to say to yourself.

2. Thought-stop the irrational statements ...

    until the stressful thoughts are eliminated or quieted, and the mountainous catastrophes reduced to molehills.

3. Replace irrational thoughts with rational thoughts through the ten-finger exercise ...

    until you fill the open spaces where the irrational beliefs were eliminated with helpful, rational ideas.

You need only remember the simple statement of Descartes: I THINK THEREFORE I AM. A slight paraphrase brings us full circle:

> I AM WHAT I THINK.

STRATEGY 4

SIX WAYS TO GET HIGH ON YOURSELF

Introduction

YOUR self-esteem—the way you feel about *you*—is critical to your success as a person and as a professional. We know you wouldn't be reading this if you didn't already have the building blocks of personal worth and professional competence you need to win as a person and as a professional. You probably just need to get it together a bit better.

Low self-esteem is often based on perceived rather than real deficiencies, but they act as a self-fulfilling prophecy. You expect to do poorly, which cues you into failure, which reinforces your negative prophecy. It is possible to reverse that cycle. With a little effort you can elevate your image of yourself, learn to feel competent and confident, and become a winner in your own right. The following six rules will prime the pump and develop your taste for becoming as much as you can be.

Rule 1. Learn to Accept a Compliment

Somehow, many of us think there is something wrong with accepting a compliment. When an associate says "nice coat" or "great dress," we feel compelled to say "This old thing? Why it comes out of a Tide box," or "This old thing? I've had it for years." When we say "yes but" to the sincere compliments of customers, co-workers, and friends, in effect we tell them, "You dummy. I'm awful. Can't you see that?"

248

The rule is:

> KNOCK IT OFF!
> YOU DESERVE EVERY GOOD THING PEOPLE SAY
> ABOUT YOU AND *THEN* SOME!

False modesty is an easy habit to break. Here's how:

1. The next time someone compliments you or your work, accept it as their sincere view and say "Thank-you."
2. Tell yourself, "What she or he said is true and valid. It is something they see in me, so it must be true."
3. When someone compliments you for good taste in clothing, food, wine, or anything else, say "Thank-you. I like good things and I appreciate knowing that other people do, too."
4. When someone says "god job," tell them, "Thank-you. I worked hard on the project and it really did turn out well, didn't it?"

Start with 1 and 2. When you are comfortable with them—when you can say thank-you without flinching and feel good about agreeing with people, move on to 3 and 4. People are eager to have you know they appreciate you, your efforts, and your accomplishments. When you let down the barriers, hear the applause, and believe it, you can't help getting even better.

Rule 2. Avoid and Eliminate Self-Criticism

Listening to what you say to yourself about yourself can be revealing. The put-downs you mumble when you mess something up aren't simply "letting off steam" and "grousing"; they are low self-esteem. Listen to what you say to yourself when you are mad. Replace "How could I be so stupid?" with "Everybody makes mistakes. This one was a classic. What can I learn from it?" It isn't a trick or a con job. It's critical semantics of how you feel about yourself. These aren't word games we play. They are real expressions of how we view ourselves. Here's Rule 2:

KNOCK OFF THE KNOCKING!
REPLACE SELF-INSULTING REMARKS WITH
SELF-ACCEPTING COMMENTS.

Here are some common self-insults, with some recommended self-accepting statements:

Self-Insulting	*Self-Accepting*
1. *I blew that sale. Any dummy could have closed it; I'm a real turkey.*	1. "I lost that sale. I wasn't at my best. You have some good days and you have some bad days."
2. *I completely blew the close. I always cave in like that; I'm really incompetent. I'll never succeed.*	2. "I held back on the close. That needs work. I can use some practice; I'll get better."
3. *She looked at me like dirt. I don't have what it takes to attract a class woman. I'm not much of a catch. I'm not worth much, period.*	3. "Boy, did that approach not work. She really cooled me. I'll try her again later. She's OK; there are a lot of OK women around. I'll find one."

Now it's your turn. Write down one self-insult you frequently say to yourself—one you have used recently—and then write down a corrected self-accepting version. If you're not sure of what they are, ask your friends or family for feedback.

Self-Insulting	*Self-Accepting*
_____	_____
_____	_____
_____	_____
_____	_____

Rule 3. Learn to Say Something Nice About Yourself

You are A-OK. You are good at things, nice to be around, and a competent person. If somebody complimented you for an hour, they probably wouldn't come close to touching your best qualities. What? You can't think of a good thing to say about yourself? Then it's time for Rule 3:

> DEAL YOURSELF A WINNING HAND.

1. Obtain a deck of 3- by 5-inch index cards.
2. Every workday for at least two weeks, write two things you did well on the cards—one incident per card, one good work incident and one good personal incident.

Collect the cards until you have at least ten. Twenty would be even better.

3. Every day you should shuffle the deck, deal yourself a hand of five cards, and then read what it says on the cards.

After two weeks, ease up. Put the cards someplace where you won't lose them and they will be safe. Anytime you feel the need of an "upper" or you start having feelings of low competence, deal yourself a fresh hand.

Rule 4. Do Something Nice for Yourself

You deserve "nice." We all do. But waiting around for other people to notice is a fool's game. If you deserve, you should get. Who better to give it than you? And you get two kicks for one price: the thrill of getting and the joy of giving. Doing something nice for yourself—something that gives you a kick, that pampers you, or that is just plain different—is fun. Being able to treat yourself for your own progress toward your own goals is that added ounce of confidence that separates almost won from almost lost. Rule 4 is:

> PAY UP!
>
> YOU OWE YOURSELF A TREAT TODAY.

Now put this rule into effect:

1. Make a list of treats you would really like to have some-one give you. We've started the list with some of ours and have left space for some of yours:

Special Treats I Owe Myself

An afternoon movie
A bottle of good wine
A big, thick steak
An expensive facial
A weekend in Paris

One pound of Godiva
  chocolates
A catered breakfast in bed
A favorite-place mind trip

_____

_____

_____

_____

_____

_____

2. List the things you deserve treats for or will in the near future. We prime the pump again, using our own list of re-wardable performances, and leave space for yours:

Things I Deserve a Treat For

Just for being me
For finishing this book
For delivering a speech
For writing thank-you notes to our reviewers
For initiating a sales possibility

_____

_____

_____

_____

3. What you have just done is to develop the pieces of a performance contract. A good self-motivation strategy is to write a formal contract with yourself. For example, "When I finish proofreading Chapter 10, I am going to take myself to dinner at the Mountain Yen." Or, "After I make my presentation to Mr. X, I am going to talk to Reina on the phone for five minutes." Now write two behavioral contracts for yourself:

I. When I _____

   I will treat myself by _____

   _____

II. When I _____

   I will treat myself by _____

   _____

Rule 5. Use Positive Mental Imagery as a Reward

You have already learned how to use mental imagery (the favorite-place mind trip in the Stress-Attack First-Aid Kit). The variety of mind trips possible is almost limitless. If you like the concept, Dr. Stern's book _Mind Trips to Help You Lose Weight_ has dozens of mental imagery exercises. There are two mind trips especially helpful in shaping your self-view, based on Rule 5:

TREAT YOURSELF TO A MOVIE—
STARRING YOU.

Feature Number 1: The "Up" Scene

1. Recall a recent sales situation in which you felt good about the process *and* the outcome. In other words, pick a sale you are 100 percent proud of.
2. Picture the scene in your mind's eye. Use all your senses to make it vivid and real. Recall the dialogue—what you said, what the prospect said. Feel the exhilaration. Savor it.
3. Make this a call-up scene to use when your sense of self-worth is flogging and you feel down on yourself. Replay it for a pick-me-up; use it to move your tension level up; or use it when in doubt about a call.

Feature Number 2: The Testimonial Dinner

Everyone deserves a testimonial dinner—a celebration of the person's uniqueness and a tribute to his or her strengths and accomplishments. The easiest and cheapest bash to throw is a mind-trip testimonial dinner.

1. Picture yourself at a testimonial dinner where you are the guest of honor. People have come to speak about your good qualities. Experience the scene. Who is there? What are you wearing? What are you feeling?
2. A speaker is introduced. He or she begins a speech, saying some wonderful things about you, such as what a worthwhile person you are. What the person says makes you feel good because you know the speaker's feelings are genuine. Listen to the speech all the way through.
3. A second speaker is introduced who also says some very nice things he or she feels about you. Other speakers rise to pay tribute to you. Listen to everyone and don't contradict them. Recognize that the things they say are true.
4. Stand up before the group. Watch all the people smile and applaud. Enjoy the scene for a little while, then allow it to slowly fade out.
5. Play back this scene whenever you feel low, or perhaps when tempted to improve your mood by eating, drinking, or smoking.

6. Use this mind trip when you doubt your worth, feel low in competence, or are unsure of your skills.

Rule 6. Develop a Positive Self-Image

You are what you say you are and what you program yourself to be. The low-self-esteem salesperson often says, "It's me against the world and personally I think I'm going to get creamed." Your behavior with prospects can reflect this and can trigger a low productivity cycle. That, in turn, can reduce feelings of resourcefulness.

Use the ten-finger exercise to drill positive self-statements and new rules into your memory bank and to reprogram your mind. The ten-finger exercise is described on page 226.

It's time for Rule 6:

> TO LEARN TO BE A NEW YOU,
> LET YOUR FINGERS DO THE LEARNING.

1. Choose a significant but realistic improvement goal.
2. Construct one short self-instruction sentence.
3. Each night for a week, practice the sentence by repeating it to yourself 10 times.
4. Repeat the sentence once for every finger. Count the repetitions by touching your thumb to each finger.
5. Touch thumb and forefinger whenever you find yourself in a situation that requires the information or attitude you programmed into yourself with this exercise.
6. Use the ten-finger method to: program standard sentences, commit self-worth statements to memory, and buoy your spirits when you are down.

Some self-worth sentences you might consider are:

I am a worthwhile person.
People will pay me the price I set on myself.
I have value as a person.
My customers need my help.

I can help people meet their needs.
I have personal power. What I do matters.
Selling is important work and I am up to the responsibility.

Strategy Summary

This exercise is bound to incease your sense of self-esteem and positive self-feelings. Remember that it can help you pull through a "feeling bad about yourself" cycle and promote yourself to yourself as a better person and as a professional.

STRATEGY 5

DESENSITIZATION: TAKING THE STING OUT OF IRRITABLE FORCES

Introduction

THERE are situations and people we simply can't change. A boss who takes out the miseries of his or her home life on the staff needs more help than you can offer. A traffic jam won't go away because you get mad at it. Things that can't be changed can only be coped with. The Desensitization Strategy is a set of techniques for helping you cope with immovable objects and irresistible forces. It is based on three facts:

FACT 1. We are all born with the fight/flight response.
FACT 2. The events, people, and situations that trigger the fight/flight response—that trigger stress—are learned.
FACT 3. Stress triggers that are learned can also be unlearned.

Here's the way it works. Some things—loud noises, extremes of heat and cold, a sudden fall, someone's striking or hitting you—prompt your intense arousal the first time you encounter them. They are unlearned reactions. The problem is that other things become paired or associated with those natural

257

arousal triggers and take on the power to elicit fight/flight, thus causing stress, fear, and anxiety. For example:

JOANIE has a father who shouts a lot. He loves her, wants to protect her, but shouts a lot. Little Joanie is tottering on the kitchen counter trying to get the cookie tin from atop the refrigerator. Dad shouts, "Joanie Marie, get down from there!" She does, in one big step and lands on her head on the kitchen floor. A few repeats of this scenario and Joanie is likely to learn a fear response to authority figures. She might also become stressed by arguing and arguments.

Though Dad was simply trying to protect his "little girl," nature is so constructed that such side effects, such accidental learning, are pretty common. If, as an adult, Joanie still responds to all "big people" and all thoughts of risk taking as she did as a child, she will have a problem. To be able to take reasonable risks—such as asking for an order—or be able to cope with authority figures, Joanie will have to *unlearn* the arousal response or become desensitized to these two stressors.

The key to desensitization is that there are some situations that bug us which can't be changed; people who "fire our stress triggers" won't change. That is the way life is sometimes. Once we acknowledge that, we can go about the business of changing the way we respond or react to those situations and those people. That is the goal of desensitization.

The Technique

Desensitization is the technique best suited to:

- Lessening the stress of being in an uncomfortable, unchangeable situation.
- Dealing with obnoxious and stress-carrying customers, superiors, peers, and social contacts who can't be avoided.

Typical desensitization targets are:

- Bosses who seem to enjoy making life miserable for their salespeople.
- Obnoxious customers, office mates, and relatives.
- Traffic jams, train and airplane delays, and noisy parties.

The two desensitization routines are aimed at (1) lessening your emotional sensitivity to situations and (2) refocusing your energy and attention on things you *can* affect.

EXERCISE 21. Moving Immovable Objects

Overview

When you find yourself stuck in traffic, "socked in" in the Buffalo airport, or stranded in a prospect's waiting room, and you feel your SLS on the rise, the following routine can help you establish positive control.

Specific Steps

1. *Deep breathe.* Practice a standard deep-breathing cycle until you (1) feel your SLS coming down and (2) are focusing attention on yourself instead of on the situation.

2. *Erase the scene.*
   a. Picture the situation as it stands. Develop a vivid mental image. For example, see yourself seated in the airport or stranded on the highway. Visualize the scene as if you were watching yourself on television.
   b. Once the image is in your mind's eye, refocus your attention on estimating your SLS.
   c. When you have determined your SLS, return to the image of the situation and see yourself erasing it. Paint a giant red X through the scene with a paintbrush.
   d. Force the scene to "dissolve" before your mind's eye.
   e. Call up your favorite-place mind trip.
   f. Concentrate on your mind trip and deep breathe.

g. Repeat the step 2 sequence *once more* before going on to step 3.

3. *Picture yourself coping.* This time, see yourself using a coping strategy, such as:

Deep breathing;

Enjoying a favorite-place mind trip;

Self-coaching (You might, for instance, tell yourself things like: "There's nothing I can do to control this situation, but I can control me"; "It won't kill me to be late. People understand these things"; It's silly to be stressed by unavoidable things"; "I can do something better with my time than be tense."), or

Doing something else, such as reading, writing a memo or letter, or catching up on planning.

4. *Self-coaching.* Carry a card with three to five coping statements in your wallet, purse, or briefcase. When stuck someplace, take it out and read them to yourself, using the ten-finger exercise. Some possible coping statements are:

Hold on.
Stick with it.
I can handle this situation.
Being stressed solves nothing.
I can use this time constructively.
There are alternatives to worrying and being uptight.
I can use this time to
• *read* _____
• *write* _____
• _____
(fill in)

5. *Do something else.* Once you get your stress level back down and have decided to cope, and are coping, *do something else.* Pick one of the ideas you came up with in step 4, or carry a book or piece of work with you just for times like these.

EXERCISE 22. Learning to Live With the Devil

Overview

When a peer, boss, prospect, important customer, or obnoxious rich relative "sends you up"—when you feel your SLS rising—the following two-stage routine can help you regain your poise.

Stage 1: Homework

When the trigger person is someone you deal with three or more times a week, you need to develop an emotional dead space or buffer zone between you and that person. Build and climb a "desensitization ladder."

1. *Man Does She/He Bug Me!* List all the things the person does that stress you. Write down everything that bugs you, in the column on the right. The column on the left has some examples.

	Example List		*Your List*
SLS		*SLS*	
___	1. Smokes a cigar	___	1. _____
___	2. Sniffs all the time	___	2. _____
___	3. Calls me "You"	___	3. _____
___	4. Criticizes my work — Never acknowleges Good Job	___	4. _____
___	5. Always doubles my work	___	5. _____
___	6. Discounts my sales; "Anybody Could have made that Sale	___	6. _____
___	7. _____	___	7. _____

	Example List		*Your List*
SLS		*SLS*	

_____	8. _____	_____	8. _____
_____	9. _____	_____	9. _____
_____	10. _____	_____	10. _____
_____	11. _____	_____	11. _____
_____	12. _____	_____	12. _____

Read the first item on your list. Close your eyes and visualize the person doing that behavior. Decide how stressed that makes you feel. Write the SLS in the left-hand column in front of the item number. Repeat for remaining behaviors.

2. *Build the Ladder.* In the box below, using the SLS as your guide, arrange in descending order the 10 behaviors that bug you the most.

How Much She/He Bugs Me

1. _____

2. _____

3. _____

4. _____

5. _____

6. _____

7. _____

8. _____

9. _____

10. _____

Using 3- by 5-inch lined note cards, write item 10 on the top line of the card. Use the rest of the card—one side only— to write a fairly detailed description of the last time the trigger person bugged you this way. For example:

Write one card for each item on your list. (We'll assume you have 10, but if you have only 4 or 5, that's fine, too.)

3. *Climb the Ladder.* Take that number 10 card, turn it face down on the table or desk, and write one or two coping statement on the back. For example:

```
┌─────────────────────────────────────────────────────────┐
│ 10. Interrupts me during meeting                         │
├─────────────────────────────────────────────────────────┤
│                                                           │
│  I was going over the Acme proposal with him, reading    │
│  it out loud, and asking questions about how he liked    │
│  it. Each time I began a sentence, he interrupted in     │
│  the middle to say something. This happened through-     │
│  out the entire presentation.                            │
│                        How RUDE!                          │
│                                                           │
└─────────────────────────────────────────────────────────┘
```

I can cope with this rudeness.
He doesn't mean to be disrespectful to me, he is just un-
    couth. I can handle that without losing control.

Now do this routine:

Close your eyes.
Deep breathe.
Take a favorite-place mind trip.

Read the coping statements to yourself.
Deep breathe.
Return to your favorite-place mind trip

When your SLS is at a comfortable level:

Turn the card face up.
Read it and visualize the scene.
If you feel your SLS level rising, turn the card face down
   again, and go through the previous routine.

Spend 5 to 10 minutes on this exercise or until you can read
card 10, visualize the scene, and *not* experience a sharp rise in
your SLS.

Once you've conquered card 10, go back to the list and write
a card for item number 9. Continue this process until you have
desensitized yourself to all 10 of the annoying habits—and until
you can "climb the ladder," or go through all of the cards at one
sitting, without becoming unduly stressed.

A good way to start each session is to go back to the last
card you were comfortable with, visualize it, and then begin
working on the next card. You will know you have succeeded
when you can read the entire deck of cards, or "climb the
ladder," at one sitting without becoming unduly stressed. When
you reach this point, tuck your cards away but don't throw them
in the trash. Keep them a month or so. If you find that the
trigger person is getting to you again, take out the cards and
climb the ladder.

4. *The nearness factor.* Sometimes, a particular person is
such a *noxious stimulus*—has become so offensive to you—that
just being near the person can be a stress trigger. That is, 'It
makes my skin crawl just being around that creep" or "I panic
when she comes into sight. She doesn't even have to *say* or *do*
anything." In this case, you will need to desensitize yourself to
being near the person.

First, *build a nearness ladder.* By now, you are the best
judge of the scenes to include on your ladder. The figure on
page 265 suggests the most to least stressful scenes you might
use when nearness is the problem.

List at least five nearness situations and rate them by SLS. Put them on 3- by 5-inch index cards.

From Highly Stressful to Least Stressful

1. Standing in front of the person looking at him looking at me.
2. Standing next to the person, each of us not looking at each other.
3. She is walking toward me, looking at me as she approaches.
4. He is standing down the hall. I'm walking in his direction. He doesn't see me.
5. I see her standing down the hallway.
6. I walk by his office, he is at his desk and doesn't see me.
7. I am at my desk. She is in the same building.
8. I walk by his office. He is out of the building.
9. I see her car in the parking lot.
10. I see his picture in the company paper.

Second, *take the danger out of being close.* At this point, you can do one of two things. You can combine your ladder of obnoxious behaviors with your nearness ladder cards. Or, you can practice the nearness ladder as a separate exercise. Whichever you choose, practice being near the trigger person, using the same routines as described for desensitizing yourself to obnoxious behavior.

Tips and Tricks for Making Your Ladder Climbing Easier

1. Relax for 10 to 15 minutes before beginning a practice session. Make sure you are calm and relaxed when you start your first visualization.
2. Start each session with a card that no longer stresses you—one you have already mastered.
3. If you find that a particular card still has some sting in it, go back one card.
4. Be sure you are relaxed between trials. That is, after each stressful visualization come back down to a comfortable SLS before visualizing the stress scene again.
5. If you find you aren't able to relax during a session, stop. Don't push yourself.

6. Move at a comfortable rate. Some people can work on three or four stress scenes in one session. Others are more comfortable with one or two. You decide what you can handle.

7. After you are able to climb the entire stress ladder without feeling anxious, expose yourself to the stress person again. (Sometimes you can't stay away completely while working on this exercise.) There will probably be occasions when the person will still get to you. Just keep your contacts with this person brief; don't jump in and expect to be able to wage stressless war right away. Ease into being near this person. Then move on to stage 2.

Stage 2: Belling the S.O.B.

Once you have completed the first stage, you should find your trigger person much easier to work with. However, there will still be times when he or she is in especially fine form and you begin to feel your SLS rise. This routine will help you keep your cool in the midst of a *confrontation* with your stress trigger person.

1. *Deep breathe.* With a little practice, you can deep breathe in front of anyone without his or her noticing. I'm deep breathing as I write this line. You didn't notice, did you?

2. *Distance.* Distancing is the process of mentally moving away from the person who triggers your stress response. First, develop a mental image of what this "confrontation" would look like were there no roof on the building and you were hovering over the scene like a bird.

Would it look as intense as when you were part of the scene? Would it look trivial?

Now move even farther above the scene. See yourself looking down from so high that you can see the whole building, all the people, the street, the parking lot, the whole neighborhood. From this vantage point,

How important does your confrontation appear?
How inconsequential does the trigger person appear from
   so far above?

Move farther away yet. When the room looks like a match-
box with tiny red ants in it, ask yourself:

Isn't this whole thing trivial?
Is there any real reason for this momentary confrontation
   to bother me?

Move so far above the building and the scene that you can
see the whole city, the state, now the whole country. Enjoy the
view as you rise above the situation. Slowly come back down
into the room and rejoin the person or people in it.

3. *Self-coaching.* Touch thumb and forefinger and repeat
at least *three* of the coping statements you have been developing
just for this situation.

4. *Mental imagery.* Take a favorite-place mind trip and
enjoy.

Final note: At first you may be reluctant to do all this "trip-
ping" and mental exercising when you are face-to-face with the
ogre. Believe it or not, the person won't even notice you are
gone, and you will still be able to keep track of what is going on
in the meeting. After all, we can listen three to four times faster
than others can speak. There is plenty of "space" to listen and
cope with the speaker at the same time.

Strategy Summary

Desensitization helps you unlearn stressful responses to unchangeable situations and irritating people. Use it when you
need to deal frequently and effectively with difficult people and
situations.

STRATEGY 6

REDUCING TYPE A BEHAVIOR: MOVING TOWARD TYPE C

Introduction

BY now, you are well acquainted with Type A characteristics. If Chapter 6 sounded as if we were picking on Type A's, it's because we were. But let's be perfectly clear about a couple of points. As a Type A, you are undoubtedly successful, at least in part, because of your Type A characteristics. So, our goal isn't to imply you're "doing it all wrong" and that you have to completely change your way of living. You wouldn't listen if it were. And we'd agree with you. The following exercise simply helps you learn to slide away from Type A behavior when you don't need it, to turn off the high energy level and hold it for when you want it.

The Reducing Type A strategy consists of seven exercises:

1. Do nothing—
2. Put it on hold—
3. Put off 'til tomorrow what you could do today—
4. Desensitization—
5. A letting-go mind trip—
6. Winning through losing—
7. Do something imperfect—

One more thing. These exercises work. If you are a real

Type A, you'll remain a doubter right up to the minute you become a full-fledged Type C. So trust us, follow the directions, and see for yourself what happens.

EXERCISE 23. Do Nothing

Overview

Doing nothing is tough for a Type A; most would rather cut a cord of firewood with a Swiss Army knife. So follow these steps.

Specific Steps

1. When you get to your desk in the morning, reach your car on the way to your first appointment, or complete your first call, sit down and do absolutely *nothing* for one minute.

2. If you feel yourself starting to stress up, deep breathe to maintain control, but do nothing else: no planning, no writing, and no thinking. Just sit and do nothing.

3. Repeat this procedure for about two weeks, increasing the time until you can go a full two minutes without doing anything.

EXERCISE 24. Putting It on Hold

Overview

Type A's sometimes have trouble shifting gears. Moving from one activity to another before the first is finished requires something that Type A's are bad at: stopping an activity before it is completed. The following steps will help you learn to interrupt an activity.

Specific Steps

1. *Start something.* Begin a job-related activity you like. Head for an appointment, start a report, read a proposal, or even rake your yard.

2. *Stop.* Set a timer or ask someone to interrupt you 10 minutes after you start the task.

3. *Take a nothing break.* Do nothing for two minutes. Deep breathe to keep your stress level in check but nothing else. Repeat this process twice a day for two weeks. Do it at home and at the office.

4. *Stretch it out.* For one week, give your spouse, a good friend, or fellow worker permission to interrupt you with a "stop" request at any time, up to three times a day. When that happens, your assignment is to do nothing for two minutes. If you are on the phone, finish the call quickly and hang up.

Stop dictating or whatever it is you are doing and do not resume for two minutes. Again, deep breathe if you need to, but no other activity is permitted.

EXERCISE 25. Putting Off 'til Tomorrow What You Could Do Today

Overview

Type A's have as much trouble waiting as they have doing nothing. But good things *do* often come to those who wait. Waiting, stalling, and putting things off is often an appropriate strategy. The following procedure can help you learn to tolerate waiting.

Specific Steps

1. *Make a list.* List at least 10 things you plan to do this week.

1. _____

2. _____

3. _____

4. _____

5. _____

6. _____

7. _____

8. _____

9. _____

10. _____

2. *Pick four items.* From your list of 10 things, pick the four *most important.*

1. _____

2. _____

3. _____

4. _____

3. *Don't do it.* That's right. Don't do at least one of the items on your list. Planned on buying a new lawnmower or new suit or dress or briefcase? Put it off one full week. If there's an important bill to be paid or if you have an appointment with the president or you have tickets for a play, do *those* things. But put off for one week as many important things from your "do list" as you can. Postponing an important client meeting is a blue-chip investment in your development of Type C behavior.

4. *Don't worry.* When you begin worrying and thinking about the things you're not doing, follow this routine:

Deep breathe
Thought-stop
Self-coach

EXERCISE 26. Desensitization

Type A's are notorious for butting their heads against brick walls. The cure for cursed persistence is desensitization. The desensitization procedure is described in Strategy 5. It's important that you learn to take the emotional tinge off unchangeable events.

EXERCISE 27. A Letting-Go Mind Trip

Overview

Type A's are notorious for butting their heads against brick walls. The cure for cursed persistence is desensitization. The desensitization procedure is described in Strategy 5. It's important that you learn to take the emotional tinge off unchangeable events.

Specific Steps

Trampoline

1. *Deep breathe.*
2. *Take a favorite-place mind trip.*
3. *Picture yourself standing on a trampoline.* Begin to jump up and down on the trampoline. Bounce higher—higher yet. Higher still. Bounce higher than ever before. At the top of your next bounce, do a spread eagle in the air. Land on your stomach on the trampoline. Bounce back high. Do a back flip and land on your back on the trampoline. You are slowing down, still

landing on your back. Now you are lying flat on your back on the trampoline. Relax. Feel yourself sinking comfortably into the trampoline. Feel your body relax, relax, feel your mind relax, relax, let go of worry, tension, troubles. Relax.

Come back. When you are ready, come back from the trampoline image.

4. *Do a postmortem on your trampoline trip.* Did your SLS change? Were you more tense? Less tense? Could you "go with" the fun? Did you feel inhibited? Free?

5. *Repeat when needed.* After practicing this mind trip a few times, you can use it to help you let go of worry thoughts, to interrupt tasks that you can't seem to let go of.

Skydiving

1. *Deep breathe.*

2. *Take a favorite-place mind trip.*

3. *Picture yourself poised at the door of a small airplane, ready to jump.* You jump. All is quiet except the sound of the air rushing past you. You hang suspended over the earth, moving but with no sensation of movement. You relax and float through the air, spread eagle. Slowly the ground moves toward you, you pull the ripcord, your chute opens, and you float toward the ground slowly. You feel like a dandelion seed floating through the air. When you are ready, land.

4. *Do a postmortem on the way the mind trip felt.*

EXERCISE 28. Winning Through Losing

Type A's can't take losing. It drives them crazy. Winning isn't everything, it's the *only* thing. So, practice losing. When you are engaged in a favorite sport or recreation, plan on not winning. If you jog, purposely run more slowly than your usual pace at least three times a week. Greet people as you pass, acknowledge other runners, look at the scenery. If you play tennis, racquet ball, golf, or squash, concentrate on form and style. If you find yourself tensing up and cursing lost points, call a time out. Then:

1. Bring your SLS under control.
2. Use a coping statement such as:
   I don't always have to win.
   I can enjoy without beating others.
   Doing can be as enjoyable as winning.
3. *When you are relaxed, begin competition again. Do not* be pressured into starting play again *until* you have your tensions back under control.

EXERCISE 29. Do Something Imperfect

Overview

The true Type-A needs perfection: to do it right; to be a paragon of form, fashion, and decorum, no hair out of place. Once you prove to yourself that being odd really can't kill you, you will free yourself of "perfection." Here are some pattern-breaking ideas that you'll hate, but that truly do work. The key is to control your tensions while doing something you consider odd or imperfect. This is the toughest assignment for the Type A, because it seems so pointless. So here's a promise: try it; you won't like it, but it will help you open up and relax a little.

Specific Steps

1. Go to work with two different colored shoes—or no makeup.
2. If suits are the mode of dress in your company, go to work wearing sports clothes.
3. Let a report, proposal, or idea you disagree with pass unchallenged.

Strategy Summary

Each of these exercises moves you into a Type-C position. Focus on those that represent your Achilles' heel (the ones that seem to be real stumbling blocks) to be moved out of the way.

STRATEGY 7

THE SALES CALL POSTMORTEM

Introduction

WHETHER people are learning stress-management techniques, new product information, or selling skills, new behavior comes into their repertoire slowly. We said earlier that learning a new skill requires time, incentive, and practice. Practice, however, is only useful if you know how you've done, if you have feedback. One of the most viable and valuable sources of feedback is yourself.

At one university, students learn public speaking by studying three speeches. What three speeches? Russell Conwell's "Acres of Diamonds"? William Jennings Bryan's "Cross of Gold"? Perhaps Lincoln's Gettysburg Address? No. Students examine the speeches they *gave*, compared and contrasted to the speech they *planned* on giving, and compared and contrasted to the speech they *would give* if they had a second chance. That's what a sales call postmortem is: a system for looking at the call you made, compared and contrasted with the call you intended to make and the call you would make if you could start over again.

The postmortem is a way of putting new behavior to work for you, of getting it into your repertoire by studying your progress. It is useful for making stress-management techniques part of your life.

There are four learning stages in the postmortem. First is

276

the standard sales-call autopsy. After the call, you review the sale, looking at both good and bad things that happened and speculate on how the bad could have gone differently. The second stage comes after a few autopsies. You will notice an increased sensitivity; that is, you will be more aware of what's happening *during* the call. You'll notice your stress level more clearly and the impact your behavior has on others. The third stage is the "check-that" point. Here you catch yourself just before making a mistake. You start to *avoid* mistakes. In the final stage, you are no longer conscious of the process. Managing your stress, anticipating your customers' stress, and the like have become part of your natural sales process.

By analogy, when you first learn to read, you make mistakes. You mispronounce a word, someone corrects you, you go back, and you pronounce it again. Eventually, you catch yourself making the error, correct yourself, and go on. Next, you see the word coming and quickly tell yourself the right pronunciation and do it flawlessly. Eventually, you just read the word as if you were born with it. But it all began by doing an autopsy of what you did wrong, a postmortem.

You can do a postmortem of either good or bad calls. Unfortunately, we tend to spend more time brooding about unsuccessful calls than successful ones. We are not as analytical and objective about calls that have good outcomes. We show you how to maximize that brooding time, but do consider *also* using this technique to learn from your successful calls. There are two parts to the postmortem: The Autopsy and The Drill.

EXERCISE 30. The Postmortem

The Sales-Call Autopsy

Answer the questions in the left-hand column, using the responses in the right-hand column as examples.

Examples

1. At what point did the sale seem to go wrong?

   a. I misquoted the price by $1,800.

b. I tried to close on the first call and irritated the prospect.

c. I explained and explained and explained and didn't do much listening because I was so uptight.

2. What led to the error? What did I think, do, say or *not* think, do, or say that brought about the mistake?

a. The day I wrote the proposal I had four others to do and I didn't bother to proof them. I just said, "Type it and send it."

b. I was told that the guy was a pushover. I was led to believe that he had a need and all I had to do was go in for the close.

c. I get jumpy with cold calls and slow talkers. The prospect was one of the slowest ever and this was a cold call. I lost control of my stress.

3. What do I know about myself and my tendencies that might have predicted this situation?

a. I am bad at pricing; I hate pricing. But there was no one in the office to help me with pricing.

b. I take other people's word for things too much. I just assumed that my information was right.

c. I get anxious when there isn't any talking going on or it's going too slowly. I always seem to jump in to fill the empty spaces.

4. What rule could I make—and follow—to keep this from happening again?

a. I won't price. Period! And I won't try to do two (or four) things I don't like at the same time.

b. I will make *no* assumptions about prospect needs. I'll always check it out.

c. I'll ask questions and listen. I won't be a "tell" person. I'll be aware of and orchestrate the tension.

5. Besides the rule(s), what else did I learn from this call?

a. I ended up learning something about the value of honesty. I didn't try to weasel on the bid. I admitted my mistake when the customer asked why the price was so low. Believe it or not, he accepted the real price. He said, "I've made some pricing mistakes myself."

b. I can't count on hearsay information being right. When I go against my training and try shortcuts, I get clobbered.

c. I can work with the quiet ones if I can handle my tensions. I've got to control myself first.

The Drill

When you are convinced that you have developed a good general rule—one that's worth making part of your standard sales behavior—drill it using the ten-finger exercise and then use it for decision making. Here's how that works:

1. Write your rule on a 3- by 5-inch card.
2. Beneath the rule, on the same card, write at least two coping statements. For example:
   Rule: I do not price alone.
   Others are better at pricing.
   I let the experts do the pricing.
3. Do a ten-finger exercise on the card.
4. When in a situation where the rule applies:
   - Stop.
   - If you are alone, repeat the rule aloud. If you are with a customer, repeat the rule silently.
   - Follow the rule.
   - If you need to give a customer an immediate answer, or make an immediate decision, use a variation of one of the coping statements.

Strategy Summary

The Sales Call Postmortem is a way of using your own experience to change and modify your sales performance. Using the postmortem technique to analyze calls—good ones and bad— you can eliminate bad habits, reinforce good habits, and build new habits.

STRATEGY 8

ASSERTING YOURSELF

Introduction

ASSERTIVENESS seems so simple. If you want something to happen or not happen, if you feel you are being taken advantage of or exploited, just say so! And once someone points out that there *are* word choices—ways of saying no or "knock it off" or "I'd rather not," that allow both the asker and the asked to feel OK about the exchange—that should be it. Shouldn't it?

Not according to two University of Indiana psychologists. R. Schwartz and J. Gottman studied high- and low-assertive people. They found that:

1. Both high- and low-assertive people know what an appropriately assertive response is.
2. In role-play situations, both high- and low-assertive people can successfully demonstrate appropriately assertive behavior.
3. High-assertive people have few *negative thoughts* about the way the other person will react to being told "no." Low-assertive people have an equal number of negative and positive self-thoughts when trying to decide whether or not to be assertive.[1]

In other words, the critical difference between high- and low-assertive people, according to these researchers, turned out to be neither knowledge nor skill but *attitude*. Low-assertive people worry about what others will think if they are told no. High-assertive people say positive things to themselves about being assertive.

Subsequent researchers have found that when people work on the self-statements or self-talk, as well as the practice of appropriately assertive behavior, the chances are greatly increased that they will be assertive when the chips are down and client, spouse, boss, peer, or children ask them to do or say something they don't want to do or say.

We won't demonstrate appropriately assertive statements for all occasions; there are books full of these suggestions and we recommend them. In particular, see the following for their appropriately assertive ways of handling many situations.

Title: *Stand Up, Speak Out, Talk Back! The Key to Self-Assertive Behavior*
Authors: Robert E. Alberti, Ph.D. and
            Michael L. Emmons, Ph.D.
Publisher: Pocket Books, 1975
Value: Alberti and Emmons wrote the original assertive-ness book, *Your Perfect Right!* This book is quite a bit better organized, has many examples of proper assertive statements, and is a good statement of the basic assertiveness philosophy.

Title: *I Can If I Want To*
Authors: Arnold Lazarus, Ph.D. and
            Allen Fay, M.D.
Publisher: William Morrow and Company, 1975
Value: This is a lot more than assertiveness. It is about becoming happier and more satisfied with yourself and the way you manage your life and work. We recommend it, because the authors' approach to assertiveness is compatible with ours and they have many interesting examples.

Title: *The Assertive Approach: Do You Lack the Killer Instinct?*
Author: Lawrence D. Schwimmer

Publisher: S&A Publications, 1978
Value: This deals almost exclusively with assertiveness in
             the workplace. The language is the least complex
             of the three and the content covers work areas not
             in other assertiveness books. The author is espe-
             cially sensitive to the problems women face in the
             working world. The author talks realistically to and
             about women as business professionals and their
             particular assertiveness needs.

There are two keys to proper assertiveness: understanding the situation you are in and having a behavior in your repertoire that is an appropriate match to your assessment of the situation. An assertive response that is appropriate in one context may *not* be appropriate in another situation.

EXERCISE 31. Assertive Response

Overview

The following sequence of steps is the process to follow when you are in a situation you believe requires an assertive response. When someone asks you to do something you don't feel is appropriate, or when someone tries to take unfair advantage or make unfair use of you and your professional or personal relationship, here is the way to respond.

Specific Steps

1. *Verify what you think you heard!*

- Don't jump right in. Hesitate and be quiet for a few seconds.
- Ask for clarification: "I don't understand," or "Excuse me, I didn't follow that."

2. *Assess the consequences of complying, even if you don't*

want to. Do a quick balancing of outcomes in your head. Something like this:

What going along might cost me	vs.	*What not going along might cost me*

3. *If noncompliance seems appropriate, construct alternatives.* Do a quick check on possible responses. Say to yourself:

• An aggressive response would be:

_____

• A passive or underassertive response would be:

_____

• An appropriately assertive response would be:

_____

4. *Try it out "in your head."* Do a quick visualization of the assertive behavior you are considering. Decide how well you can pull it off.

5. *Deliver your assertive response.* Keep the tone even, the emotion low, your body language under control. Delivering an assertive verbal response in a hostile, scowling way or nervous, with eyes lowered, defeats your goal.

6. *Stick to your guns.* People often will try to get you to change your mind when you assert yourself. Once you start, complete the stroke; to do otherwise trains the other person to whittle and cajole you at every turn.

7. *Control stress.* Use the Stress-Attack First-Aid Kit to help you keep cool so you can make a "no thank-you" that will stick.

EXERCISE 32. Assertiveness Preparation

The most important part of becoming assertive is being prepared when the occasion arises. Here's a practice routine that will get you started.

1. *Pick a situation.* For any of us, there are certain situations in which we are over- or underassertive. They could be encounters with specific customers, relatives, peers, boss, spouse, or even kids. Finish the following:

I tend to be (over/under) assertive when:

_____   _____
(person's name)   (situation description)

_____

_____

_____

2. *Construct an overassertive, an underassertive, and an appropriately assertive response to this situation.* Put an X next to the response you *usually* make.

An overassertive response would be:

_____

_____

_____

An underassertive response would be:

_____

_____

_____

An appropriately assertive response would be:

_____

_____

_____

My usual response is _____A _____B. The problem with this response is that:

_____

_____

_____

3. *Pick two positive self-talk statements.* From the following list of 10 self-talk statements, pick two that have special meaning for *you*, pick two that seem to support the assertive response you constructed, *or* make up two of your own.*

1. *What I think of me is more important than what they think of me.*
2. *It's important to my self-respect to turn down unreasonable requests.*
3. *I have a right to expect courtesy and respect.*
4. *Not telling the truth about how I feel and think is selfish.*
5. *"Giving in" teaches others to mistreat me.*
6. *Not telling others how I react to them cheats them of a chance to change.*
7. *Sacrificing my rights can destroy an effective relationship.*
8. *Standing up for my rights shows my respect for myself.*
9. *When I do what I think is right, I feel better about myself.*

---

* An aid to helping you write your own positive self-talk statements is "The Sales Professional's Bill of Rights" on page ii.

10. *I have a right to express myself as long as I don't hurt others.*

Others:

_____

_____

_____

_____

_____

_____

_____

4. *Put the assertive statement and the two positive self-talk statements on a 3- by 5-inch index card* like this:

ASSERTIVE STATEMENT
It is all right for me to say this because:
_____
(Self-talk statement 1)
_____
(Self-talk statement 2)

5. *Learn new self-talk.* The specific assertive statement you design for a specific recurring incident must be committed to memory and practiced in imagery or actual role-play. In addition, the positive self-talk statements must be programmed into your thinking so that you can draw on them to support your assertiveness in a given situation.

EXERCISE 33. Assertive Behavior Practice

1. Do a ten-finger exercise using the assertive card you wrote. During the practice, say the assertive phrase aloud and read the supporting positive self-talk statements to yourself.

2. Do the following:

Deep breathe.
Take a favorite-place mind trip.
Visualize the scene your assertive statement card was written to confront.
Stop the movie when you reach the point where asserting yourself is called for.
Say the assertive statement aloud.
Repeat the positive self-talk statements to yourself.
Continue the visualization, inserting yourself as delivering the statement you have been practicing.
Return to your favorite-place mind trip.

3. After you have practiced routine 2 two to four times, you can shorten the practice routine to these four steps.

Deep breathe.
Visualize the assertive scene, doing the appropriately assertive behavior.
Deep breathe.
Take a favorite-place mind trip.

Use this practice routine four or five times and, if possible, just before your first confrontation.

4. Not every assertive encounter has a positive sales outcome. Being appropriately assertive is something you do for yourself and the way you feel about yourself. Being appropriately assertive *can* help you get more sales—especially if you tend to be overassertive—but that's not the goal. Assertive communication should free you from bad self-feelings and help you develop a more direct and emotionally honest way of communicating with others.

Positive Assertive Communication in Action

Let's see how this strategy works by considering the example of Jim, a sales professional.

JIM is in a business that is known for side deals and lavish perks to good customers. This means that in Jim's business, salespeople have been known to kick part of their commission back to a key person in the buying organization. And Super Bowl Week is a homecoming for the high rollers and heavy hitters in the industry, customers and vendors alike. Jim hates the practice, as does his boss. In fact, there is a company rule against fee splitting and expensive perks. Jim has noticed that the practice is oozing down the hierarchy and even the lowest assistant purchasing agent expects to be wined and dined.

The worst case is Bill Owens. Bill is a new junior purchasing agent at Biltmore Glass. Jim has to deal with Bill for certain items of his product line with marginal profits. A good order from Bill can meet Jim's quota for these low-profit, low-commission items and get Jim's boss off his back about these nickel and dime goods.

Jim dreads calling on Bill because he knows that Owens is going to insist on lunch at the Purple Martin, the most expensive restaurant in the county. Jim decides to draw the line assertively. He follows the Assertiveness preparation exercise and comes up with this response:

> I tend to be underassertive when Bill Owens hints that we can do business "more properly" at the Purple Martin over lunch and a few drinks.

Jim constructs these optional responses:

Overassertive: "I don't buy business with expensive lunches, big shot. So stop pushing."

Underassertive: _Saying nothing or "Lunch sounds like a good idea" is my usual response. I'm just so boiling mad I'm afraid to start in on him._

Appropriately assertive: _I enjoy having lunch with my customers. It gives me a chance to get to know them better and we can talk shop away from interruptions. But I want to make sure, Bill, that you don't misunderstand my intent. I don't believe in trying to buy a man's business with expensive entertainment and the like. I think that is dishonest and in the long run it strains, rather than helps the buyer/seller relationship."_

The problem with my _usual_ response is that: _It leads Owen to believe I approve of this expensive and fancy lunch business. I'm sure he's going to expect more + more + more._

Jim decides that these two positive self-talk statements best represent his feelings and thoughts:

When I do what I feel is right, I feel better about myself. I have a right to express myself as long as I don't hurt others.

> "Having lunch with a customer can be pleasurable and productive. However, I don't believe in buying business through expensive entertainment. In the long run it hurts working relations between buyer and seller. I hope you can understand this position."
>
> It's all right for me to say this because:
> — When I do what is right I feel good about me.
>
> — I have a right to express myself appropriately.

He constructs the assertive communication card above to prepare himself for his next call on Bill Owens. Jim follows the practice procedures and notices that his tension level goes up when his visualization comes to the part where he asserts himself with Owens. Jim thinks about this for a while—he's surprised that the incident is as tension producing as it is—and ends up doing an exercise we call "What's the worst/best that could happen?" He decides that the best thing that could happen would be that Bill will stop asking for expensive lunches and hinting at other expensive perks. The worst thing would be that Bill will get upset and not do any more business with Jim.

Jim decides that either outcome would be OK with him. After thinking his way through the best and worst, Jim notices his tension level stays low during the visualization.

STRATEGY 9

INCREASING YOUR COMFORT ZONE

Introduction

REMEMBER the old joke about the tourist who stops the musician walking down the street carrying a violin case and asks, "Excuse me, how do you get to Carnegie Hall?" The musician smiles, looks the tourist in the eye, and says, "Practice, baby, practice." That's what stretching your comfort zone requires: practice—but a special kind of practice.

For example, when you first began selling, you probably didn't start with your company's most complex product or service, nor did you go up against the most sophisticated or hard-nosed buyers. You probably moved in gently, starting with the easiest cases you could find and proceeded slowly toward harder, more demanding ones. You gradually stretched your comfort zone. If that's *not* how you started, congratulations on being a survivor of the sink-or-swim approach to sales.

Here's how stretching the comfort zone works in another realm, public speaking. One of the most universally stressful activities is standing before a group and saying "a few words." The toughest of the tough have melted before the eyes of a roomful of expectant listeners. But a number of researchers have found that the stress of public speaking can be reduced through a step-by-step process involving visualization and real practice.

For instance, a would-be speechmaker begins by giving short talks to small groups of other people who are also learning to give public talks. Step by step, the length of the speech increases as does the size of the audience. And, of course, feedback from this "safe" audience is an important part of the exercise. At the same time, the speech trainee goes through a series of exercises wherein he or she visualizes speaking in front of progressively larger audiences and practices controlling the stress of these imagined speaking scenes. These visualizations are a mix of successful and not-so-successful experiences. This same mix of real and imagined practice also works for learning to deal with higher levels of stress.

EXERCISE 34. Stretching Your Comfort Zone

1. *List the most stressful and least stressful sales situations you normally face.* The most stressful situation should be one you feel overstressed by. (Refer to page 265 for some ideas, if necessary.)

Most stressful: _____

_____

Least stressful: _____

_____

2. *Imagine a sales situation with an SLS halfway between these two extremes.* Write it on line 4:

Most stressful:	7 _____
	6 _____
	5 _____
Moderately stressful:	4 _____
	3 _____
	2 _____
Least stressful:	1 _____

You now have a stress ladder you can climb to stretch your stress-tolerance level. You may rank-order the remaining items from number one.

3. Do the following in order:

Deep breathe.
Take a favorite-place mind trip.
Visualize the sales scene suggested by item 1 on your stress ladder.
Continue visualizations up the ladder until you reach a rung that you can't comfortably visualize, that is too stressful.
Move down the ladder one rung and visualize that situation again. Get comfortable with that rung.

4. *Practice in the real world.* On the line below, write down the item on the first rung of the stress ladder that you are uncomfortable visualizing.

On the following lines, write down a real-world plan for coming into contact with that situation at least twice in the next two days. (Your goal is to reach a little, risk a little, and become comfortable with a higher than usual tension level.)

For example, suppose the last rung you can comfortably handle is "Talking to a prospect on the telephone." The second step, then, is to make two phone calls to prospects in the next two days.

5. *Move up one rung on the ladder:*

Visualize the rung you just became comfortable with.
Deep breathe, take a favorite-place mind trip, and visualize the next rung up the ladder. If your SLS begins swinging upward, cease the visualization, deep breathe, and take a favorite-place mind trip.

Repeat the previous step until you are comfortable on the new rung of the stress ladder.

6. Repeat step 4, the actual confrontation with the stressful situation, for this next rung of your stress ladder. For example, suppose "Ask for an appointment" is just above "Talk to a prospect on the telephone" on your stress ladder. Begin the exercise by making sure that "Talk to a prospect on the telephone" is mastered in both imagery and practice and then move on to "Ask for an appointment." Practice "Ask for an appointment" in imagery until you are comfortable with the imagery.

Once you have mastered the imagery of asking for an appointment, you can move on to asking for an appointment in the real world. Continuing practicing in both imagery and real life until you are sure you have reached a new comfort level.

7. Continue to visualize and then put into practice each rung on the ladder until the ladder is fully mastered. By the end of the practice, you will notice your comfort zone has expanded in other areas as well.

Strategy Summary

You can stretch your comfort zone through steady practice. The principle is simple: when you stretch, you grow.

If you would prefer to stretch your comfort zone outside the selling context, if you prefer to practice somewhere else, pick an endeavor that has similarities to selling. Public speaking is similar to selling, for example, and can stretch your comfort zone.

Another way is to build a stress ladder of disconnected personal events and nonselling situations that are stressful. Start with a tolerable but noticeably arousing rung, do the imagery practice, and then try the real world. Each time you master a new rung on the ladder, go back to page 293 and estimate a new stress-tolerance level and calculate a new comfort zone. It is helpful to keep a log or make a graph of changes in your comfort zone.

STRATEGY 10

PHYSICAL EXERCISE

Introduction

EVIDENCE has been accumulating to prove that people who run, jump, and play a lot—people who are aerobically fit—have fewer heart attacks and tend not to be hypertensive. But ask us to point to a study that proves that connection and we can't. Physicians often prescribe exercise for tension relief, more out of faith than fact. As a group, doctors tend to be very active, and "Do as I do" is their prescription.

An exercise program is not the answer to everyone's stress problem but medical research does show it helps some people. Running or jogging has been promoted as a way to cope with anxiety and psychological stress. Many claim that running gives a person a sense of well-being, increased self-confidence, plus imaginative "powers" and creativity. Running can also help drain off tension and release negative emotions. Ron Zemke runs 6 to 10 miles a day—and has done it for years—but admits that he has yet to sprout a valve for draining off negative emotions and tension. Recent research in England suggests that vigorous exercise, like running, releases greater levels of the hormone epinephrine, a chemical purported to account for our "happy feelings."

Other people report that time away from others is an important asset of running. They use running as a time for thinking, problem solving, and getting organized. Meyer Friedman, however, suggests that the *last* thing a Type A person needs to be involved in is running. Dr. Friedman has suggested that Type

A people simply turn running into one more competitive effort and are likely to end up more tense after a run than before. Having others pass by on a track or running path is unacceptable and very upsetting to the Type A.[1]

We cannot make a blanket recommendation for or against exercise. There are too many factors—personal health, age, and temperament, for example—but here are some guidelines for making up your own mind about the value of exercise.

1. *If you are Type A:*

- If you are not already athletically active, think carefully about getting involved in an exercise program with the expectation that there will be a stress-reduction benefit.
- If you are already physically active, check your SLS before, during, and after exercise. If you do *not* see your SLS decreasing as you exercise, question the stress-relief value of exercise for you. If you see that your SLS increases as you play or exercise, *stop.*

FOR four years, Ron Zemke was an avid tennis player. But after finding that his SLS was higher *after* an hour of tennis than before playing, he quit. Now he engages in noncompetitive exercise and finds the stress relief he was hoping for.

---

2. *If you are a high A*—an individual who exhibits stress through behavioral activity—moderate physical activity and noncompetitive sport may be an effective antidote for a generally too-high SLS.

3. *If you are a high B*—and you tend to hold your stress in your muscle systems, exercise and sport may be for you. This is especially likely if you tend to have trouble with the physical relaxation exercises. The relaxed or relieved feeling you experience from exercise is very close to the feeling you should be able to achieve through the relaxation exercises and, eventually, through simple favorite-place mind trips.

Before undertaking any exercise program, you *must* consult your family physician. It is wise to have a physical stress test, an examination that can tell you what shape your heart is in.

There is good evidence that vigorous walking is as good for you and your cardiovascular system as are running and jogging. There are many mild exercises and physical activities that seem to lower SLS. Some are effective for people who can't, aren't interested, or shouldn't get involved in tennis, squash, racquet ball, running, jogging, skiing—the sweat and strain activities.

1. *Swinging.* A combination of a park swing two to four times a week and a series of pleasing mind trips has helped some people relax and gain control of their stress level. A caution: People look at you funny if you go "swinging" in a tie and business suit. Take off your coat and loosen your tie.

2. *Yardwork.* When done therapeutically, yardwork can reduce stress. Take raking, for example.

- Don't set a performance goal for yardwork. You might want to limit yourself to 30- to 60-minute bouts, but *do not* set a goal of bagging 10 bushels of leaves or four bags in the alley.
- Interrupt your raking whenever you start to tire. If you aren't the "tiring type," set yourself a time limit on the work and when the time is up,
  —Sit down.
  —Pick up a leaf.
  —Examine the structure, color, and feel of that leaf.
  —Don't draw any conclusions: just look at the leaf.
  —If your inspection suggests a mind trip down some memory lane, go with it.

3. *Walking.* When you walk, do two kinds of walking: fast pace and slow pace.

- Begin with a fast pace and continue for 10 to 12 minutes.
- Stop, sit down, and do nothing for 5 minutes.
- Slow walk for 10 minutes.
- Stop, sit down, and do a favorite-place or other mind trip.

• Fast walk and slowly wind down as you walk back to your starting point.

Walking is the most fun when you vary your route, time, and distance. Set aside about an hour for a decent walk. Anything less will pressure you to hurry.

4. Stretching, yoga, and flexibility exercises are good for body tone, are noncompetitive, and give you the time and space to do relaxing mind trips or nonthinking. An organized system of stretching and flexibility is the Chinese art of Ti-Chi. Most Y's and many community schools offer lessons.

5. Aerobic dancing is a more vigorous stretch and flex activity, one that looks strange from the "outside." Once you become involved in aerobic dancing, you will be surprised at how active it is and how relaxing and tiring it can be. Y's and community schools often offer aerobic dance classes.

6. "Camera hunting" is much more relaxing and stress lowering than hunting with a gun or rod and reel. It still offers walking, bending, and stooping in the great outdoors, but the tension of "seek and destroy" is absent.

We reiterate: Neither of us has anything against vigorous exercise. We do our share and then some. We simply can't endorse something like distance running, or morning swims, or tennis or racquetball, as a stress reliever. The data aren't sufficient at this point. At the same time, we have seen people change drastically in temperament as a result of diet and exercise programs. It is but one of several options you can try.

STRATEGY 11

GIVING AND GETTING FEEDBACK

Getting Feedback

FEEDBACK is information about performance that a person can use to confirm or modify the performance. In more human terms, feedback is the news about how you're doing at getting where you want to go. Your call-to-closing ratio is feedback about performance, and so is the remark, "I hate your guts!" But there are some obvious differences.

Numbers are fairly objective, and what you do determines what they are. When people tell you how they feel about you or how they view your performance, what they see and hear is filtered through their experiences, their emotions, their beliefs about you, what they know of your response to feedback from others, and what they think you want to hear. Feedback from people is much more subjective than feedback from a computer or your checkbook.

It would be less frustrating if we didn't need feedback from people, but we do. There are, however, some things we can do to ensure that we receive accurate feedback when we ask for it.

Rules for Soliciting Feedback

1. Ask for feedback only from people who have seen enough of your behavior that they can provide a balanced report, and who you trust and respect enough to accept feedback from.

2. Tell your feedback source exactly what behavior(s) or performance(s) you want feedback on, why you want feedback, and what you will do with the information. Asking someone who was on a call with you "What did you think of that?" is asking for almost nothing.

3. Ask for the feedback in a neutral fashion. Saying "Some people think I'm pretty abrasive. I want to know whether that is true or not," is neither neutral nor behavioral. It is similar to asking someone to tell you whether or not you are short.

4. Tell the person how you will respond to the feedback. Specifically, tell your resource that you won't take his or her head off for a clear, concise, honest report even if it contains negative elements.

5. When receiving feedback, ask clarifying questions but do *not* put your resource person on the spot. For example, ask:

"Could you say that another way?"
"Could you give me an example?"

6. Focus your attention on open-ended, future-oriented questions such as: "What could I do to keep that from happening next time?"

7. Tell resource people what the payoff is for them. Make the risk worth taking.

In essence, you are making a verbal contract with a resource person when you ask for feedback in this manner. And you should consider a breech of this contract as you would a signed legal document.

Giving Feedback

Giving feedback can be as stressful as getting it. We are all fragile, and poorly delivered feedback can elicit emotional reactions that block the message from getting through. The best feedback is:

- About behavior
- Nonjudgmental

- Unemotional
- Fair

Rules for Giving Feedback

1. Good feedback is solicited, not imposed, and it deals with a specific performance the "asker" wants feedback on.

2. Good feedback separates perceptions from *facts*:

> FACT: "I counted four interruptions while Jim was speaking."
>
> PERCEPTION: "The way I see this problem is. . . ."

3. Good feedback is a balance of positives and negatives. A useful rule of thumb is to give two positives for each negative. It helps you keep a balanced view. The receiver always retains the option of cutting the feedback off. Do not override that option.

4. Good feedback is specific and clear. For example, "The answer you gave to Jones' second price objection was very well worded. You said. . . ."

5. Good feedback deals with things that can be changed:

> APPROPRIATE: "The rabbit story may offend some listeners. Perhaps you could make it a little less sexist."
>
> INAPPROPRIATE: "You're pretty short and your voice is nasal."

6. Avoid emotion-laden, biased words. There is a world of difference between "You're cheap!" and "I feel that you are a very money-conscious person."

7. Feedback should be given at an appropriate time. Don't give feedback on the run.

8. When giving feedback, check the message received to be sure it coincides with the message sent. People sometimes miss the point because of emotional interference.

9. Good feedback lets the receiver determine how to change. Don't tell the other person what to do.

10. Leave out anything you are unsure of. If the point is too important to leave out, check with another person who knows the situation or was present.

When someone asks you for feedback, he or she is showing trust and confidence in you. Respect both. If you feel complimented by being offered this role, tell the other person. Open, honest feedback is hard to give and hard to ask for. Acknowledge the risk the performer took.

If you are contemplating asking people for feedback, let them read these guidelines. They will be grateful for the assistance.

Strategy Summary

Remember, feedback techniques usually work. It takes time to learn them and use them comfortably.

STRATEGY 12

BODY RELAXATION

Introduction

SOME people "hold" tensions and worries in their muscles. That is, when things go wrong they tense their muscles and can't let go. Surely you have seen people with their head, back, and shoulder muscles so tensed they look as if their muscles have turned to wood. The following relaxation exercise works best if you read the instructions into a tape recorder and then follow them. Read them at a slow pace and use as calm a voice as you can. After you have practiced a few times, you will be able to induce a state of relaxation simply by telling yourself to relax. Some people find that using a cue word like "Relax" or a cue activity such as touching thumb and forefinger together works to induce muscle relaxation. If you experience stress in your body, you will probably need to add relaxation to your Stress-Relief First-Aid Kit, right after the deep breathing exercise.

EXERCISE 35. Relaxation Sequence

Read the following instructions into a tape recorder. Pause for a count of three after each sentence. Where longer pauses are indicated, pause as directed:

Sit or lie in a comfortable position. Close your eyes. Raise your hands and make a fist. Tighten it. Feel the tightness across your knuckles. Tighten your wrists. Tense each forearm and now your elbow. Zero in on the tight feeling. Now tense each upper arm. Make each entire hand and arm tighter—and tighter until it trembles. Concentrate on feeling the muscles involved, sense them becoming as taut as wound-up springs. Hold it, hold it. Now just drop your arms. Go with the good feeling as the spring unwinds. Experience the feeling of relaxation that comes with it. You're feeling fine and good, calm and comfortable. Relaxed, just relaxed, and wonderfully, wonderfully well. [20 seconds]

Now make a face. Frown and tense the muscles around your mouth, around your eyes. Feel the muscles tighten across your cheeks and lips. Feel your jaw muscles tighten. Wrinkle your nose. Tighten the muscles in your chin. Now tighten your forehead. Hold it, hold it. Experience the tensions as the muscles all over your face become tighter, tighter. [7 seconds]

Now relax your face. Let all your facial muscles go. Experience the feeling as your mouth relaxes, your eyes relax, and your cheeks and jaw loosen up. Feel your lips and chin relax—and the muscles in your forehead. Go with the good, comfortable feeling. Feeling fine, good, and wonderfully, wonderfully well. Calm and relaxed. [20 seconds]

Arch your back and raise your chest. Hold it. Experience the pull as the muscles between your shoulder blades become taut, tighter, and hold it. [7 seconds] Now relax. Allow your back and chest to drop. Experience the wonderful, soothing feeling as you do so. Feeling comfortable and relaxed, relaxed and wonderfully well, calm and just relaxed. [20 seconds]

Now pull in your stomach and abdomen. Tighten your stomach and make it as hard as a rock. Harder, harder. Feel the tension in your stomach. Experience the muscles in your abdomen tighten. Now hold it. Hold it. [7 seconds] Just let go. Sink back and relax. Experience the wonderful feeling of relaxation throughout your stomach, feel the abdominal muscles go gentle. Relaxed and comfortable. Feeling fine, feeling good. Feeling comfortable and just great. How good it is to relax, just relax. Feeling fine, calm, and wonderfully, wonderfully well. [20 seconds]

Stretch out your legs. Tighten the muscles in your thighs.

Feel your thighs getting tighter and tighter, like a tightly wound rubber band. Now also tighten the muscles in your knees. Feel them tense up. Tighten the muscles in your calves. Turn your toes under and tighten each entire foot. Experience the tightness up and down each leg, in your ankle and your toes. Make each leg tighter, tighter. And hold it. [7 seconds]

Now let go. Just drop your legs and experience the wonderful sensation as the muscles in each leg relax. Feel your thighs, your knees, your calves, your ankles relax. Feel the restful feeling as even your toes go limp. How good it feels to unwind, from head to toe. Feeling fine, feeling good. Comfortable, relaxed, and wonderfully, wonderfully well. [20 seconds]

Now take a deep breath and concentrate on the air filling your lungs. Hold it, hold it. [7 seconds] Now let go. Let out your breath and feel the wonderful sensation as your tensions and worries slowly, slowly disappear, as they go out of you with your breath. Feeling relaxed, peaceful, and comfortable. Feeling wonderfully, wonderfully well. [20 seconds]

Now I will count from three to one. On the count of one, open your eyes feeling wonderfully well and relaxed. Now begin. Three, feeling good. Two, feeling just fine. One, open your eyes, feeling relaxed and great!

Do this relaxation sequence as many times as needed to feel deeply, comfortably relaxed.

Practice

You will need to practice this recorded relaxation exercise 8 to 10 times before you will be able to order your body to relax. Daily practice for two weeks should do it. Obviously, you will need to practice the relaxation instructions in a quiet, private place where you won't be interrupted. However, you can measure your progress by once a day closing your eyes, inhaling deeply, exhaling slowly through your mouth, and whispering the word "relax" slowly and quietly in your mind. Sit perfectly still for 30 to 60 seconds. As you become more skilled at relaxing to the recorded instructions, move your little trials into more active settings. If you make your first test in a quiet office with the door closed, make your second in the same room with the door open. Make your third trial in your car before turning on the ignition or perhaps sitting in front of the television set. Eventually, using this systematic approach, you will even be able to cue yourself to relax in a customer's office during a sales call.

STRATEGY 13

OVERCOMING CALL RELUCTANCE

Introduction

There seem to be two brands of call reluctance: a reluctance to pick up the telephone and call a prospect, and a reluctance to make or ask for an appointment. Just to keep things straight, let's call the first telephone reluctance and the second, appointment reluctance. Both have similar origins and solutions.

Both types of reluctance are the product of the "hot stove" syndrome. After a little child has touched a hot stove, he or she is doubly reluctant to touch another stove—hot or cold. After enough prospects have been rude, crude, and asinine over the phone, a salesperson can become pretty "phone-shy." The approach we show you here certainly isn't magic. It's simply the get-back-up-on-the-horse-that-threw-you advice with a little behavioral psychology and self-support thrown in to ease you back into the saddle.

EXERCISE 36. Getting Back on That Phone

Specific Steps

PREPARATION

Here are the "prep steps" you need to make those calls:

First, make a telephone-calling comfort ladder. Build a five-step comfort ladder, based on the SLS you experience making phone calls to different kinds of people. Visualize yourself making the following 10 phone calls. As you do, note the SLS you feel as a result of the imaginary calls and write it to the right of the description.

Visualize yourself calling:

	SLS
Your spouse from your office to say hello	____
Your boss	____
Your mother-in-law	____
An established customer	____
An auto-repair shop to check on repairs	____
A prospect you have never met	____
An advertisement in the newspaper's classified section	____
A friend from your office	____
A referred lead from a satisfied customer	____
Your banker	____
A prospect you met at a party	____
A close relative	____

When you have an SLS for each of these, put the six most stressful calls on the stress ladder below, in order of stressfulness. (1 is most stressful, 2 is second most stressful, and so on)

1. _____

2. _____

3. _____

4. _____

5. _____

6. _____

Second, go one rung at a time. Write your sixth most stressful call on this line:

_____

Now identify a person and a phone number that fits this situation:

_____   _____
(name)   (phone number)

Follow this routine:

1. Deep breathe.
2. Visualize making the call:
   - See yourself seated at the phone.
   - See yourself looking up the number.
   - See yourself writing down the things you want to accomplish with the call—do *not* make selling something or asking for an appointment one of the two.
   - See yourself dialing the call.
   - See yourself saying hello and identifying yourself by name.
   - See yourself making small talk.
   - See yourself saying, "Besides saying hello, the reason I called is to

     _____ ."

     (one of your two objectives)
   - See yourself relaxed and enjoying the call.
   - See yourself hanging up the phone.

3. Estimate your SLS (write it down).
4. Take a favorite-place mind trip.

Repeat this routine for each of the six situations on your comfort ladder. If, during a visualization of the situation, you feel your SLS rising, immediately stop the visualization, deep breathe, thought-stop, and take a favorite-place mind trip.

When you are back in control, return to visualizing the scene. Start with a part of the scene you have already mastered.

Option: You can work with the mental visualization of the six stressful calls until you master them all *or* you can alternate visualization of phone calls with real phone calls. Either will work, but we have a slight preference for visualization followed by real practice.

THE ACTUAL CALL

The following instructions are very detailed and you may not need them. Read through and have them near you when you start your first call.

First, write it down:

1. On a 3- by 5-inch index card, write down three or four sentences—things to say to the person you are calling— you can use to help you accomplish your objectives. (For sales situations, you will probably find good material in your basic sales-training manual.)
2. Practice saying those standard sentences aloud two, three, or four times before placing the call.
3. On the back of the same index card, write two, three, or four coping self-statements. These are those things to say to yourself when you start to feel edgy, like:
   - *Making phone calls is an important part of this business.*
   - *I can do this without panicking.*
   - *Hold on. A step at a time. You can do it.*
   - *One step at a time. Just think about the call.*

Second, face the phone:

1. Sit down in front of the telephone with:
   - The name of the person to call
   - The phone number of the person to call
   - A 3- by 5-inch card with standard statements and coping self-statements
   - A pad and a pencil

2. Deep breathe, thought-stop—if appropriate—and do a favorite-place mind trip.

Third, pick up the phone:

1. Use the Stress-Relief First-Aid Kit if any feelings of discomfort appear.
2. Do not draw back from the phone if you start to feel stressed. Leave your hand on the phone and work on bringing the tension down. Deep breathing and thought stopping are especially useful here.

Fourth, dial the number:

1. Control any tendency to feel stress with deep breathing and thought stopping.
2. When the dialing is completed—goes through or reaches a busy signal—stroke yourself with a positive self-thought: *You did good. Great job.*

Fifth, when the other party answers:

1. It is critical to "hang in tough."
   * Deep breathe.
   * Thought-stop.
   * Read your standard sentences.

Do not hang up. If the answerer has to wait while you do a stress-control activity, let him or her wait.
2. If the party you were calling answers, complete the call—your two objectives—using:

   * Your standard sentences
   * The first-aid kit

3. When the conversation terminates, you should be the one to terminate it.
   Sixth, when you hang up:

   1. Write a note to yourself stating:

      * Who you called
      * When you called

- Outcome—what you are to do and what they are to do

2. Deep breathe. Take a favorite-place mind trip.
3. Reward yourself for making the call. Do positive self-thought, have a drink of coffee, and so on.

Tips and Tricks for Getting Through

Some salespeople have found that phone calls become easier when they know what each call is worth. Here's how that works. Suppose it takes five phone calls to get one appointment, and five appointments to make a $1,000 commission sale. That means that each phone call to a prospect theoretically is worth $40. Simply by logging the number of phone calls you make, you can track your daily earnings. The rationale is simple: "If I am making $40 for every prospect call, whether an appointment results or not, a rejection doesn't hurt as much. I made $40 just for trying."

Some salespeople actually pay themselves for each call. We know one rep who keeps a stack of one-dollar bills in her desk. For each completed call, she puts a single bill in her wallet. She is essentially "earning" her coffee money through making phone calls. Another rep we know occasionally gives his boss's name when talking to a prospect. His logic? "If I'm feeling a little shell shocked, I start using my boss's name. Then they are rejecting him and not me. The S.O.B. could use a little rejection from time to time."

Don't evaluate your phone calls. The task is to call, not to be perfect. After you are back on your feet, you can start working on style. For now, concentrate on calling.

EXERCISE 37. Making Those Appointments

Overview

The hurt in asking for an appointment is the turndown. Everyone hits an occasional bad streak where nobody has a kind

word. The trick is to keep those inevitable bum times from becoming permanent.

Specific Steps

PREPARATION

Go through the following "prep steps":

1. Go through your sales manuals and any sales-skills books
you can get your hands on, and come up with half a dozen
approaches to asking for an appointment that suit you and the
way you like to do business.

2. Write each of these on the face of a 3- by 5-inch card.

3. On the back of each card, write at least two of these self-
statements.

> *I have a perfect right to offer my product or service to eligible
> prospects.*
> *I have a valuable product/service that many people need.*
> *People are sometimes hesitant to make appointments over
> the phone. That doesn't mean they are rejecting me.*
> *I have succeeded before and I will succeed again.*
> *I have the skill. I can do it.*

4. Do a ten-finger exercise with each card, front and back.

5. Do a mental rehearsal. Keep in mind that it should be
reality based. As you mentally rehearse, mix successes and failures. Make the mix three successes to one failure:

> Picture yourself on the phone.
> See and hear yourself talking to a prospect.
> Hear yourself using the phrases you researched and wrote
> down.
> Hear yourself overcoming an objection.
> Do 8 to 10 scenes every morning for about a week. If your
> reluctance is really heavy, consider twice-a-day practice
> sessions.

6. Rehearse with a friend. If you are unsure of your mental rehearsal, you can also rehearse or role-play with a friend. Ask your friend to read the section "Giving Feedback," on pages 301–302.

pages 301–302

ON THE JOB

We'll assume here that you are cured, or don't have "fear of phone" stress. You are able to call people, even cold-call prospects, but you are having trouble asking for an appointment.

1. Set a goal:

Write down your "normal" daily call rate.
Add two.
Divide that number in half.
Your day-one goal is the result.

2. Plan on going from this number to your "normal" telephone prospecting rate in five days. On a pad or piece of graph paper, write down your call goal for each day. Leave room to put a stroke count next to each day as you make your calls. For example:

	Goal	Actual
Monday	6	~~LHH~~ /
Tuesday	8	~~HHT~~ ///
Wednesday	10	~~HHT~~ ~~HHT~~
Thursday	11	~~HHt~~ ~~HHt~~ /
Friday	12	~~LHT~~ ~~HHt~~ //
Saturday		

3. Gather all the materials you will need for making your calls:

Names and numbers
Note pads and pens
Calendars and appointment books
Index cards with statements on them

4. Get ready:

Sit down.
Go through the Stress-Attack First-Aid Kit procedures.
Rehearse your first call in your mind.
Visualize a positive outcome.

5. Go:

While dialing and reaching your party, thought-stop any
    negative thoughts and replace them with one of your pos-
    itive self-statements.
When you reach your party, use one of the six standard
    sentences on your cards to present your proposition for
    an appointment.
If you are turned down, try another of your standard sen-
    tences.

6. If you succeed in making an appointment, celebrate:

Buy yourself a cup of coffee.
Do a positive for yourself.
Pay yourself a bonus.

7. If you fail to get an appointment:

Relieve tension by using the Stress-Attack First-Aid Kit.
Give yourself a pep talk. Use one or more of the following
    self-statements:

- *No single call can devastate me.*
- *I'll get one of the next ones.*
- *Not getting an appointment can't hurt me as a person.*
- *These things happen.*
- *One more down—to go.*

8. Get ready again:

When your stress is again in check, go back to step 4 and
    go at it again.

Check off the last call on your score card, and go after the next one.

Strategy Summary

This method has made it possible for sales pros like yourself to short-circuit the downward spiral. It's been a proven tension buster as well.

Appendix

EVERYTHING ELSE YOU WANTED TO KNOW ABOUT STRESS BUT DIDN'T HAVE A CHANCE TO ASK

I N the body of this book, we promised not to bore you with everything you never wanted to know about stress. This material is for those of you who want still more information about the mind-body effects of stress.

In stress-management workshops, we regularly encounter questions that go beyond the basics. We've included here answers to the ten most frequently asked questions. Since many of them are medical in nature, the answers reflect the time we've spent researching medical journals and talking to doctors, psychiatrists, and others concerned with the psycho-physiology of stress and stress management.*

* Much of the information here comes from a medical writers' seminar held as part of Cornell University Medical School's ambitious and highly successful educational program, "The Consequences of Stress: The Medical and Social Implications of Prescribing Tranquilizers." This program, developed under an educational grant from Roche Laboratories and sponsored by Cornell Medical

*1. There seems to be a growing concern about stress—
at least there is a lot being written and said about it.
Is there a stress epidemic in the United States?*

ANSWER: Believe it or not, the ancient Greeks complained about the pace of modern life. The difference between then and now—or even fifty years ago and now—may be a matter of awareness and labeling. Until relatively recently, people who didn't feel well, had trouble sleeping, were constantly tired, or suffered from vague aches and pains didn't connect those symptoms with anything as seemingly remote as job pressure, worry, or relationship problems.

Today, many people are aware of the connection among life events, stress, and physical discomfort. As a result, they are more likely to attribute emotional lows and physical maladies to these life pressures. People also are aware of medical research which has identified negative effects of pressure on health—psychological and mental—as well as on performance and productivity.

Those who are concerned that stress-related personal and organizational performance problems are on the rise—and for whom increased awareness isn't an adequate explanation—point to facts like these for support:

- In nine western European countries and the United States, 6 to 20 percent of all adults use anti-anxiety or sedative drugs.
- In the United States alone, over $1 billion worth of benzodiazepine tranquilizers (Valium, Librium, Tranxene, Ativan, Serax, and Verstran) are consumed each year.
- Americans filed a record number of stress-related worker's compensation claims in 1988.
- Stress among American workers costs the equivalent of $150 billion annually in health insurance and disability claims, lost productivity, and other expenses.

College, has generated a series of seminars and papers that greatly clarify information about stress, stress management, and especially the role of drugs in stress-relief programs. We acknowledge our debt to their work and thank them for openly and enthusiastically sharing it with us.

- Children as young as five and six have been found to be suffering from hypertension.
- Mental health experts estimate that as many as 15 percent of executives and managers suffer from depression and/or critical levels of stress that eventually affect job performance.
- The U.S. Government estimates that there are 3.3 million practicing alcoholics between the ages of 14 and 17.
- Physicians have estimated that 21 to 50 percent of their patients suffer from some psychosomatic problem—some form of stress-related problem. (Note, please, that this was a survey of physicians *excluding* psychiatrists.)
- Another study found that people who work and live in noisy environments tend to be more anxiety prone than others. Even the floor one lives or works on in a big-city high-rise can be a contributing factor; it is a potential stressor independent of occupation and profession.

The point is a simple one. Though some occupations seem to have a higher stress potential, closer examination reveals that the person, place, and situation match may be the most significant factor. Any job, life-style, or event *may* induce stress. It depends at least as much on the individual as on the occupation, craft, or trade pursued.

This stress interaction between the individual and his or her work is the focus of America's businesses. Company stress-management programs tend to take into account both job-related and personal life-style–induced stress. In the last five years, corporations have invested millions of dollars in a variety of wellness programs aimed at all levels of employees. For example:

- L.L. Bean keeps three fitness rooms open from 6 A.M. to 6 P.M. during the week. One reopens from 11 P.M. to 2 A.M. for second- and third-shift workers. L.L. Bean spends $200,000 a year on sponsorship of activities like running clubs, cross-country skiing, and formal stress-reduction courses.
- In 1983, AT&T began a Total Life Concept (TLC) program with an anti-stress target. Some 2,400 people took

part in the first program, and after one year, AT&T found substantial improvements in health and morale. In 1989, some 80,000 employees volunteered for the TLC program.

- Almost twelve years ago, Safeway tackled its tardiness and absenteeism rate, high accident rate, and low morale at one wholesale bakery plant with some personal well-being programs. In 1989, statistics indicated that lost days from accidents were near zero, tardiness and absenteeism decreased by 60 percent, and union grievances were down by 95 percent. The plant manager credited people in the plant who committed themselves to leading a healthy life.

2. Is it just sales people, high-powered executives, and air-traffic controllers who get sick from stress?

ANSWER: No way. Stress is very democratic. Among adults, doctors, nurses, dentists, waiters, and waitresses are highly likely to suffer from stress. Or consider the plight of a big-city police officer. Exposed constantly to the potential for physical harm, police officers, according to one study, develop symptoms of emotional exhaustion that include cynicism and detachment from others as well as the more typical physical responses to heavy stress, such as backache, ulcers, headache, and colds. In a sense, a police officer must erect an invisible protective shield between him or herself and others to avoid being hurt by the people he or she is trying to serve.

Also, consider your friendly family dentist. Dentists have a high incidence of alcohol abuse, divorce, and depression, not to mention high susceptibility to colds, flu, ulcers, and the like. All of these have been identified as stress-related or -induced problems.

A final note about who gets stressed. Dr. Lawrence Hinkle, Jr., Director of Human Ecology at New York Hospital, Cornell Medical Center, studied the careers of 260,000 Bell Systems employees for five years. He found that blue-collar workers and foremen had a much higher incidence of heart disease and disabling coronary events than did white-collar types and executives.[1]

Dr. Suzanne Ovellette Kobasa found that people's attitude toward life makes them prone toward health or sickness. Dr. Kobasa and her colleagues studied executives caught in the 1984 Illinois Bell Telephone divestiture squeeze. About half got sick (colds, chronic backaches, and headaches, for example) and half didn't, despite similar job situations and general life stresses. Her research led to a new stress word: "hardiness." Hardy people are involved and committed, feel general control over their lives, and see change as positive and challenging. It may be that these key ingredients can help people beat stress and stay healthy.[2]

Three unwarranted assumptions about stress crop up:

1. All unpleasant occurrences are stressful.
2. What is stressful for one person is inevitably stressful for another.
3. Stress automatically leads to disruptive or harmful consequences.

As we're beginning to discover, "it ain't necessarily so."

3. Aren't some people naturally more prone to be affected negatively by stress?

ANSWER: We all know people who seem to remain cool, calm, and collected—no matter what. And we've all met one or two who go into shock over a broken fingernail or come unglued because of a barking dog. What we've observed is that any two people can respond very differently to the same stressor and the same level or degree of stress.

Some individuals are by temperament more anxious than others. Some people seem to have an inborn susceptibility to anxiety under stressful circumstances, with a wide range of difference from one person to another. Individuals with a high tolerance for stressful situations might even have what may amount to a built-in tranquilizer system in the brain.

Psychologists and psychiatrists caution that the ability to handle stress is not all genetic or innate temperament. Far from it. How a person responds to stress or potential stressors is also tied in with early learning, cultural patterns, specific environmental expectations, and experience in dealing with or adapting to stress.

Individuals who learn to cope with and accept change early in life, and who are exposed to unusual or risky situations from time to time, seem better able to cope with large amounts of temporary stress and longer-lasting amounts of wear-and-tear stress. They seem, by learning and experience, to be inoculated against stress—in effect, able to raise their stress threshold.

But even this learned ability to handle stress has its limits. Much of this learning is tied to cultural milieus. Translating that into our world, we have all seen or heard instances of top-drawer, heavy-hitting salespeople who, when promoted to management, fold under the pressure like a flimsy lawn chair. The data on blue-collar background and white-collar ulcers say the same thing: we may be immune to stress and strain in one environment—love it even—and not be able to handle the same amount of pressure in a different, unfamiliar context. As a friend of ours so aptly put it, "A fern that flourishes in Florida may wither in Wisconsin."

Most authorities agree, however, that we can learn to tolerate and thrive under the pressures of a new environment if we are aware that new, unaccustomed stressors potentially exist, and if we understand that new learning may be necessary. By the way, when our current environment—family, job, city, friends, and the like—undergoes change, then it becomes something of a new environment and we sometimes need to learn new coping skills. If you've ever worked for a company that was acquired in a takeover or that brought in a new president from outside the system, you understand the problems and the stress-arousing potential of this suddenly "new" environment.

4. Aren't some personality types better able to handle stress than others?

ANSWER: Usually, when this question arises, the questioner has heard something about Type A and Type B behavior. Unless you've been living under a rock for the past fifteen or twenty years, you've heard mention of it, too. According to cardiology specialists Dr. Meyer Friedman and Dr. Roy Rosenman, authors of *Type-A Behavior and Your Heart*, people Friedman and Rosenman dub as exhibiting Type A behavior are three times more likely to experience heart attacks than those who exhibit Type B behavior. This conclusion is a result of a ten-year study of 3,500 healthy San Francisco businessmen between the ages of 31 and 59.[3]

The doctors intensively studied a number of facets in the lives of several hundred of these San Francisco executive guinea pigs and found that none of the three most commonly correlated heart-disease factors—cigarette smoking, high cholesterol level, and high blood pressure—proved to be as powerful a predictor† of coronary heart disease as temperament and personality.

And what is this doubly dangerous Type A behavior? You guessed it. Rosenman and Friedman describe the Type A as the hard-driving, aggressive, impatient, time-oriented, achieving individual who wants, needs, and tries to get ahead—to win—at all cost. And that, of course, is a near letter-perfect description of the stereotypical successful American way of living, loving, managing, and selling.

Discussion of Type A behavior can be scary, so we'll be careful to maintain a sane perspective. Type B's do not have heart attacks. And there are plenty of Type A's who do not, too. There's even that previously mentioned study of 260,000 Bell System employees, which showed heart disease to be more prevalent among blue-collar workers and foremen than among the aggressive fast-trackers—the normal Type A's.

Ten years ago, another wrinkle was added to the debate over what makes a stress-prone person. Going beyond the basic Type B questions, researchers began to look at the links between negative emotions, attitude toward life, and health. Following up on the earlier work of Friedman and Rosenman, recent researchers such as Dr. Redford Williams at Duke University Med-

---

† Note that we said *predictor*, not cause. The two are very different. Height is a good predictor of basketball success, but there are too many Ernie DeGregorios who make it in the round-ball world to say that short people always fail and tall people always succeed. There are Type A people who don't have heart disease or any other stress-related health problem. What Friedman and Rosenman are suggesting is that, in the long run, the odds are on the house's side if an individual is a Type A.

ical Center found that chronic hostility is dangerous to your health. He suggests that more cynical, antagonistic people die from heart disease than agreeable, good-natured folks.[4] So it may not be the Type A profile that's so lethal, but only one component—the "bitchiness" factor—that's the killer.

5. Isn't there a maximum amount of change people can take before the stress makes them sick?

ANSWER: Usually, when this sort of question comes up, someone has seen the very popular Holmes and Rahe schedule of life change events in a magazine article on stress. It is a list of forty-three life change events that have been found to be important precursors of illness. One simply marks an X next to each event that has occurred in the last twelve months of his or her life. There is a number representing units, which is assigned to each event. Once the subject has gone through all forty-three events, he or she adds up the units assigned to the events marked with an X.

The top five life events and their unit values are:

1. Death of spouse	100
2. Divorce	73
3. Marital separation	65
4. Jail term	63
5. Death of a close family member	63

The last five life events and their unit values are:

39. Change in number of family get-togethers	15
40. Change in eating habits	15
41. Vacation	13
42. Christmas	12
43. Minor violations of the law	11

According to this scale, one's total score predicts one's chances of suffering a serious illness within the next two years. If one's total score is less than 150, there is a 37 percent chance that individual will become ill within the next two years. For someone with a score between 150 and 300, the chances increase to 51 percent. And for those individuals scoring 300 or over, there is a 70 percent or more chance they will become ill within the next two years.

According to Holmes, if an individual's score is 300 or more, and that person gets sick, chances are good that the individual will suffer from a major illness, such as cancer, a heart attack, or manic-depressive psychosis.[5]

After twenty more years of data collecting by Dr. Stern and others, statistical analysis of the strength and direction of the relationship between stressors and illness shows it as fairly low. Some of the reasons include the following:

- People are complicated, and they vary in the way they react to life events. The way we think and subsequently feel acts as a mediator in stress. For example, if a late customer is viewed as a minor inconvenience rather than as a major frustration, the person is less likely to become stressed by the event.
- People are not passive. We act much more often than we just react. We have different and varied coping skills, support systems, and ways of working things out. Thus the different and individual responses to stressors need to be taken into account.
- Lack of change (understressors such as boredom) and the absence of illness in positive life events was not taken into account. Knowledge of the interaction of body chemicals and illness was in its infancy twenty years ago.

Holmes and Rahe's research has earned an important place in the mind-body stress connection; it's a beginning not an end to the story. Cautions of interpretation aside, it's important to realize that stress is cumulative. Change, challenge, and pressure do mount up, and we tend to reach a point wherein our stress cup *doth* runneth over. Forewarned—*aware*—is forearmed.

Life change is inevitable. Future shock is a present reality, and change is nothing to hide from. As Holmes wryly observes, there are worse things in life than illness. Change, adaptation, and growth are the seasonings that make life enjoyable and tasty. Yes, too much change in too short a time can frazzle nerves and, if Holmes and Rahe are correct, lower resistance and increase the chance of illness. But learning to plan ahead, to regulate the changes in your life, and to cope with the results are a small price for joyful living.[6]

6. What kinds of physical illnesses are caused by stress?

ANSWER: Let's get something straight. Stress is neither a disease nor a direct cause of disease. There's a distinct difference between true physical disease and ailments induced by stress that masquerade as physical illness.

With stress-related illness, the symptoms are usually diffuse. Unlike the symptoms of most organic disease, symptoms of anxiety tend to involve multiple body systems, sometimes *every* system of the body. If the patient has an organic (physical) disease, complaints tend to be clustered in one body system or to have a specific pattern. Stress, as we pointed out earlier, is a functional, not an organic, ailment.

Dr. Dorethea R. Johnson, former Medical Director of AT&T Long Lines (and current consultant to AT&T's Total Life Concept Stress Program), underscores the notion that at times stress symptoms can be rather specific. In a personal conversation with Dr. Stern, she related, "The average person doctors see coming into the office does complain of a variety of symptoms. However, there will often be a specific target organ in which stress manifests itself—one particular portion of the body or organ it centers on. That may be the individual's adaptive mechanism. After the organ is repaired, the problem may move on to another organ if the stress is not handled."

Part of understanding the role of stress in illness is recognizing that the physical and emotional effects of disease are inseparable. Human beings are an indivisible whole, not a collection of parts. Illness in general, and the stress connection in particular, must be looked at holistically. It is especially important to realize that illness can induce stress and that stress can exaggerate illness.

Besides coronary heart disease, stress is known to aggravate many other organic and functional disorders. Stress may be associated with all the following:

Bronchial asthma	Chronic hives
Peptic ulcer	Stuttering
Irritable colon	Learning disabilities
Obesity	Headaches
Menstrual problems	Chronic backache
Neurodermatitis	

Most recently, some researchers have linked stress with cancer (and other immune-system-suppression disorders). Dr. Carl Simonton, one of the authors of *Getting Well Again*, suggests that cancer patients have experienced critical stress six to eighteen months prior to the diagnosis of the disease.[7] Dr. Bernie Siegel, a well-known oncologist whose work is somewhat controversial, paints a clinical picture in which overwhelming stress triggers illness. He suggests that stress can set off a series of bodily processes that release chemicals that keep the immune system from doing its job, leaving the body susceptible to the development of a malignancy. He also suggests that this process can be reversed.[8]

7. Does stress cause heart problems?

ANSWER: The problem with the question—why it's a little tricky to answer—is the word "cause." Take an analogy: Tall people tend to weigh more than short people. Tall doesn't "cause" weight nor does weight "cause" tallness, but they may be linked.

Stress may be linked to heart disease, but the mechanisms of influence or complication aren't very well understood yet. There is no question that the link between stress and heart disease, the major killer of Americans, exists. But the process, or mechanism, of that influence is not completely understood. There appears to be an interaction effect.[9]

One of the clearest connections is how stress makes existing heart disease worse. Stress from anxiety or fear about the existing heart problem can bring about a disturbance of heart rhythms that can kill the person who has just had (and survived) a heart attack. Typical of these anxieties and fears are, "What's happening to me?" "Will I be debilitated?" "Is my love life over?" and "Who's going to pay for all this?"

Some of the more interesting correlational studies—the statistical-relationship studies between heart disease and stress—reported in the reputable medical journals and judged to be sound are these:

- For nine years, British researchers followed 4,486 widowers who were 55 years of age or older. The mortality rate during the first six months of bereavement was 40 percent above that for married men of the same age. The researchers reluctantly concluded that "died of a broken heart" was not a far-fetched explanation of the findings.

- Men of rural backgrounds who are in white-collar jobs have a two to three times higher incidence of coronary heart disease than do men of rural backgrounds who are in blue-collar jobs. One speculation is that pressure for upward mobility places people in life situations for which they are unprepared. (By the way, there's no evidence that country life is less stressful than city life. The stressors are just different.)

- Japanese-Americans who retain traditional Japanese cultural values and life-styles—including diet and exercise—have a coronary heart disease rate as low as in Japan. Japanese-Americans who hold values and life-styles normal to Western culture have five times the coronary heart disease. In addition, there seems to be no difference in the heart disease rate between Caucasian Americans and Japanese-Americans acculturized to Western values and styles.

8. *How dangerous is it to use drugs to cope with stress?*

ANSWER: Here's another of those issues that has been the subject of more purple prose than research reporting.

FACT: When an individual is overwhelmed by the emotional or physical consequences of stress, the most effective—and least dangerous—way to stop the stress cycle and bring the symptoms under control is through drug therapy. Once the patient's physical or emotional pain is brought under control by drug therapy, it may become possible to ferret out the real cause of the problem and do something about it.

The plight of the asthmatic is a good case in point. Asthma attacks frequently are precipitated as a stress response. When the attack occurs, the asthmatic can respond as if his or her immediate environment is short of oxygen. One response is to run about looking for oxygen, and the consequence is panic and an increase in the severity of the attack. In laboratory settings, experimental animals with artificially induced asthma attacks have commonly died during ensuing panic attacks. At the same time, animals treated with tranquilizers did not panic and survived the induced stress attack.

The point—one corroborated by medical experts—is that the stress response to a number of disorders can be more damaging than the disorder. The fear of drugs, of course, is the fear of drug abuse and dependence. The stereotype is the upper-middle class housewife suppressing the frustration and anxiety of suburban affluence in a Valium haze. That's the stereotype, but it is hardly supported by the data.

FACT: According to Dr. Theodore Cooper, one-third of adult Americans use some type of psychotherapeutic drug at least once a year. But that figure covers both prescription and nonprescription drugs. In any one year, less than half that number, or 15 percent of the U.S. adults, are treated with an anti-anxiety drug. Of that group, only 6 percent use the drug more frequently than once a month. To Dr. Cooper, this heavier usage of tranquilizers indicates a disability that goes beyond the stresses and strains of ordinary life.[10]

FACT: The United States is *not* the leading drug-taking society. We're midrange compared to European countries. Belgium, France, and Sweden report higher tranquilizer usage. Denmark and the United States are about equal.

FACT: The most common drug misuse is the combining of tranquilizers and alcohol. According to Stanford's Dr. Leo Hollister, consuming large quantities of both poisons the enzyme system and impairs the body's ability to rid itself of the drug.

The results can be fatal. However, such fatality is *not* a frequent occurrence.[11]

The "problem" with drugs is that when people are anxious, they tend to self-medicate with alcohol, tobacco, over-the-counter drugs, even prescription drugs borrowed from a friend. So there are actually two problems. First, self-medication isn't as effective as physician-diagnosed and -prescribed medication, and it's a deadly dangerous thing to do. Second, medication of stress-induced anxiety only relieves the symptoms, so the problem leading to the stress trigger can be dealt with. Self-medication fools the do-it-yourselfer into thinking the problem is solved.

9. *Don't things like diet and physical fitness have something to do with stress?*

ANSWER: The evidence on both points—nutrition and exercise or fitness—is unclear and inconclusive. Part of the controversy over nutrition, vitamins, diet, and stress has to do with the earlier mentioned confusion between organic and functional illness.

To translate, disease and illness—broken bones, infections, flu, measles, mumps, you name it—are stressful. When the body is sick, it works hard to regain homostasis, or get back on an even keel. Glands, organs, and body-repair systems work harder than normal, and this strain has noticeable effects on the whole person, mind and body. If you have a low-grade, undetected infection or are suffering from a vitamin deficiency, you can end up feeling fatigued, uneasy, low in sex drive, and psychologically "down." So being ill, malnourished, injured, or just generally unhealthy can lead to stress. It's at least logical to also believe that illness and disease will leave you more susceptible to the nonorganic sources of stress—the pressures of life, annoying situations, and carryings on we tend to think of when we talk about stress.

There is quite a bit of controversy over the hypothesis that functional, psychologically induced stress can be reduced or prevented through diet, nutrition, or any of the high-vitamin and protein additive routines.

A more important focus is on the role of inadequate and

low-nutritional diets. Modern processed foods are generally nutritionally substandard. B-complex vitamins, for example, need daily replacement but most of us eat foods that have had the B vitamins destroyed by processing. Because the sales professional's job makes him or her a regular consumer of restaurant food, vitamin supplements may be necessary for nutritional balance. The point here is that because of inadequate diets, many of us are more susceptible to disease in general than we would suspect. Diseases precipitated by stress are no exception.

There's one more note to this nutrition-healthfulness confusion. As detailed earlier, stress—the kind that comes from the ordinary and extraordinary pressures of life—may first have a psychological outcome that provokes a physiological arousal mechanism, triggering feelings of anxiety. Nervous system, immune system, glandular, and other reactions in the body are set in motion. These reactions show up in symptoms and mimic physical disease: chest pains, palpitations, hot and cold spells, shaking, chills, insomnia, headache, various muscle pains, diarrhea.

Though many of these symptoms are treatable as functional illness, it's equally true that stress is a major factor in predisposing, initiating, and sustaining such organic disease. The moral? Consult your family physician when in doubt about illness. Discriminating between organic and functional illness is what he or she is trained for.

Incidentally, there's pretty good evidence that eating is a strong anxiety reducer or suppressor, at least temporarily. So it appears that overeating is often a response to stress. Ironically, though, overeating also can cause subjectively related stress to increase—guilt, failure, and that sort of thing are at the root—thus setting up yet another of those vicious cycles: you eat to reduce stress but overeating stresses you so you overeat to reduce the stress—ad infinitum.

   10. How does job stress affect home and family relations?

ANSWER: Stress can take a heavy toll on relations at home. Stress can affect an entire family, and early recognition and control can prevent devastating consequences for both individuals and families.

Among the earliest signs of stress in a family is the clustering of symptoms. Specifically, when members of the same family show up in the doctor's office for a variety of physical and emotional complaints, stress may be the culprit. In one study, researchers found that one stressed family member can carry stress home and infect other family members. Whole families have been known to be engulfed with stress-related symptoms, infected by a single, highly stressed breadwinner, for example.

A study suggested that as many as 148 out of 200 hospitalized patients had illness linked to stressful family relations. In another reported study, two doctors asserted that 75 percent of their heart-failure patients had recently experienced either bitter arguments with a family member, illness or death in the family, business reversals, or other similar incidents.

Divorce doesn't seem to help, by the way. Hypertension is more common among the previously married and young widows. In the first year after divorce, "formerlies" have twelve times more illness than "marrieds," and as we saw earlier, widowers are extremely susceptible to coronary heart disease.

Family and individual stress even invade the bedroom. Sexual problems and stress are interconnected. Sexual interaction is part of the whole pattern of a person's everyday life.

In Dr. Stern's experience working with people, she has found sexual dysfunction, lack of libido, sexual unhappiness, and nonorgasmic response in someone who is ordinarily orgasmic are often manifestations of stress.

Particularly hard hit at home are doctors, dentists, and police. The latter two, dentists and police, have very high divorce rates. Both have a tendency to unwind with alcohol and an informal "bunch of the guys" support group. Both escapes take a toll on family time and interactions.

Stress is such an issue in police performance—on and off the job—that the International Law Enforcement Stress Association is dedicated to the problems of police officer burnout and impaired family relations. Both Boston and New York City police departments have ongoing stress-management programs and extensive help available to officers and their families.

Dual-career couples experience additional stress in trying to accomplish the home-work balancing act. When a man tries to be a top salesman and a top dad, he's in for a lot of tension. A *Newsweek* article called most fathers reluctant warriors in a social revolution. The result? According to a Boston University poll, 36 percent of fathers experience "a lot of stress" balancing home and work pressures.[12]

Women don't fare much better. According to a national business letter, more than one-third of women executives have sought counseling to deal with the stress of overwork and the conflicts between their office and home roles.[13] Dr. Stern has found that saleswomen are particularly vulnerable to anger and depression when they find it impossible to balance all their roles.

We have found that salespeople who must travel frequently, who work evening hours, or who spend three or more nights a week away from home and family tend to be more stressed than those who do not work under one of these three conditions. The families of these away-from-home salespeople often become stress victims as well.

There are also a number of studies showing, in effect, that the family or a familylike support group can be a buffer. One study has shown that even the most severe stressors—in Holmes and Rahe terms, the stressors with high LCUs—are modified when the stressed individual is a member of a supportive family group. Lastly, we have been finding—on a more informal basis—that salespeople who are members of long-running professional study groups or who have strong community social-service ties tend to be more resiliant to slow stress buildup.

NOTES

Introduction

1. "U.S. Training Census and Trends Report," *Training Magazine*, Lakewood Publications Research (1982).

Chapter 1

1. Wayne Dyer, *Pulling Your Own Strings* (New York: Thomas Y. Crowell Company, 1978).

Chapter 2

1. Alan McLean, *Work Stress* (Reading, Mass.: Addison-Wesley, 1979).
2. Diane E. Papalia and Sally W. Olds, *Psychology* (New York: McGraw-Hill, 1987).
3. Ibid.
4. Ibid.
5. Stewart Wolf and Harold G. Wolff, *Gastric Functions: An Experimental Study of a Man and His Stomach* (New York: Oxford University Press, 1943).
6. Hans Selye, "History and the Present Status of the Stress Concept," in *Handbook of Stress: Theoretical & Clinical Aspects,*

Leo Goldberger and Shlomo Breznitz, eds. (New York: Free Press, 1982).
7. Ibid.
8. Ibid.
9. Hans Selye, *The Stress of Life* (New York: McGraw-Hill, 1978).

Chapter 3

1. Roy R. Grinker and John P. Spiegel, *Men Under Stress* (Philadelphia: Blakiston, 1945).
2. Ibid.
3. Stanley Schachter and Jerome E. Singer, "Cognitive, Social, and Psychological Determinants of Emotional State," *Psychological Review*, No. 69 (1969), pp. 379–399.
4. Ibid.
5. R. S. Lazarus and E. Alfert, "The Short-Circuiting of Threat," *Journal of Abnormal and Social Psychology*, No. 69 (1964), pp. 195–205.
6. Ibid.
7. Joan Borysenko, *Minding the Body, Mending the Mind* (Reading, Mass.: Addison-Wesley, 1987).
8. Carl O. Simonton, Stephanie Matthews-Simonton, and James Creighton, *Getting Well Again* (New York: Bantam, 1980).
9. Sally Squires, "Visions to Boost Immunity," *American Health* (July 1987).

Chapter 4

1. Frances M. Stern, "A Workshop on Stress," *Dental Economics* (February 1979).

Chapter 5

1. N. E. Miller, "Learning of Visual and Glandular Responses," *Science* (1969), pp. 434–445.
2. J. B. Rotter, "Generalized Expectancies for Internal Versus External Control of Reinforcements," *Psychological Monographs* Vol. 81, No. 609.
3. Ibid.

Chapter 6

1. Meyer Friedman and Ray H. Rosenman, *Type-A Behavior and Your Heart* (New York: Knopf, 1974).
2. Redford Williams, *The Trusting Heart: Great News About Type-A Behavior* (New York: Random House, 1989).
3. Daniel Goleman, "Agreeableness vs. Anger," *New York Times Magazine, Good Health Supplement* (April 16, 1989).
4. Friedman and Roseman, *Type-A Behavior and Your Heart.*
5. Albert Ellis and Russell Gruger, *Handbook of Rational-Emotive Therapy* (New York: Springer Publishing Co., 1977).
6. Suzanne Kobasa, "The Hardy Personality: Toward a Social Psychology of Stress and Health," in J. Suls and G. Sanders (eds.), *Social Psychology of Health and Illness* (Hillsdale, N.J.: Erlbaum, 1982).
7. Friedman and Rosenman, *Type-A Behavior and Your Heart.*

Chapter 8

1. Leon Festinger, *A Theory of Cognitive Dissonance* (Stanford: Stanford University Press, 1957).
2. Ibid.
3. Michael J. Mahoney, *Cognition and Behavior Modification* (Cambridge Mass.: Ballinger Publishing Co., 1974).
4. Albert Ellis, *Reason and Emotion in Psychotherapy* (New York: Lyle Stuart, 1970).

Chapter 9

1. Norman Cousins, *Anatomy of an Illness as Perceived by the Patient: Reflections on Healing and Regeneration* (New York: Norton, 1979).

Chapter 10

1. Joseph Wolpe, *The Practice of Behavior Therapy* (New York: Pergamon Press, 1969).

Chapter 11

1. Leonard Pearlin, "Life Strains and Psychological Distress Among Adults," in Neil J. Smelser and Erik H. Erikson (eds.), *Themes of Work and Love in Adulthood* (Cambridge, Mass.: Harvard University Press, 1980).

Chapter 12

1. "Executive Stress May Not Be All That Bad," *Business Week* (April 30, 1979).
2. From the Wilson Learning Corporation, 7500 Flying Wand Dr., Eden Prairie, Minn., 55344-3795.

Strategy 8

1. R. Schwartz and J. Gottman, "A Task Analysis Approach to Clinical Problems: A Study of Assertive Behavior" (Unpublished manuscript, Indiana University, 1974).

Strategy 10

1. Friedman and Rosenman, *Type-A Behavior and Your Heart.*

Appendix

1. L. E. Hinkle, Jr., "The Concept of 'Stress' in the Biological and Social Sciences," *International Journal of Psychiatry in Medicine*, Vol. 5, No. 4, pp. 355–357.
2. Kobasa, "The Hardy Personality: Toward a Social Psychology of Stress and Health."
3. Friedman and Rosenman, *Type-A Behavior and Your Heart.*
4. Williams, *The Trusting Heart: Great News About Type-A Behavior.*
5. Thomas H. Holmes and R. H. Rahe, "The Social Readjustment Rating Scale," *Journal of Psychosomatic Research*, No. 11 (1967), p. 213.
6. Ibid.

7. Simonton, Matthews-Simonton, and Creighton, *Getting Well Again*.
8. Bernie Siegel, *Love, Medicine, and Miracles* (New York: Harper and Row, 1986).
9. Ibid.
10. Theodore Cooper, "The Consequences of Stress: The Medical and Social Implications of Prescribing Tranquilizers" (Medical Writers' Seminar, November 10, 1979).
11. Leo Hollister, "Management of Anxious Patient Proven to Drug Abuse," *Journal of Clinical Psychiatry*, Vol. 42 (November 1981), pp. 35–39.
12. "The Reluctant Father," *Newsweek* (December 19, 1988).
13. J. Warren, "Stress and the Working Woman," *Growth News*, Vol. 19, No. 1 (1989).

INDEX

345